Understanding
Archives & Manuscripts

ARCHIVAL
FUNDAMENTALS
SERIES II

Understanding
Archives & Manuscripts

James M. O'Toole & Richard J. Cox

SOCIETY OF
**American
Archivists**

CHICAGO

The Society of American Archivists
www.archivists.org

Library of Congress Cataloging-in-Publication Data
O'Toole, James M., 1950-
  Understanding archives & manuscripts / James M. O'Toole & Richard J. Cox.
    p. cm. — (Archival fundamentals series. II)
  Includes bibliographical references and index.
  ISBN 1-931666-20-2 (alk. paper)
  1. Archives—Administration. 2. Archives—History. 3. Archives—
Handbooks, manuals, etc. I. Cox, Richard J. II. Society of American
Archivists. III. Title. IV. Title: Understanding archives and manuscripts.
V. Series.

CD950.O57 2006
027—dc22
                            2006017311

Graphic design by Matt Dufek, dufekdesign@yahoo.com.
Fonts: Minion (text and footnotes); Meta (secondary text and captions).

TABLE *of* CONTENTS

Preface to the
ARCHIVAL FUNDAMENTALS SERIES II

There was a time when individuals entering the archival profession could read a few texts, peruse some journals, attend a workshop and institute or two, and walk away with a sense that they grasped the field's knowledge and discipline. This was an inadequate perception, of course, but it was true that the publications—basic or advanced, practical or theoretical—were modest in number.

The archival world has changed considerably since these more quiet times. A rich monographic research literature is developing. Scholars from far outside the field are examining the "archive" and the "record." Archives, archivists, records, and records managers are in the daily news as cases appear testing government and corporate accountability, organizational and societal memory, and the nature of documentary evidence—all challenging basic archival work and knowledge.

The new edition of the Archival Fundamentals Series (AFS II) is intended to provide the basic foundation for modern archival practice and theory. The original preface (written by Mary Jo Pugh in her capacity as the series editor) to the first editions, which were published in the early to mid-1990s by the Society of American Archivists (SAA), argued that the seven volumes "have been conceived and written to be a foundation for modern archival theory and practice" and aimed at "archivists, general practitioners and specialists alike, who are performing a wide range of archival duties in all types of archival and manuscript repositories." It is hard to state the purpose of the new AFS editions better.

There are some differences, both subtle and obvious, in the new volumes. The new editions are more open-ended than earlier versions, extending back to the Basic Manual Series published a quarter-of-a-century ago by SAA, reflecting evolving viewpoints about archival theory and practice. Even more important a difference is the broader and deeper context of archival publishing AFS volumes reside in. Mary Jo Pugh, in her introduction of just a decade ago, noted that the AFS titles are companions to "more specialized manuals also available from SAA." Now, SAA has four other series (some just underway), including Archival Classics (featuring reprints or new collections of older publications with pivotal importance to the profession), Archival Readers (both collections of new and previously published essays intended to supplement the descriptions of foundational theory and practice of the AFS II volumes), International Archival Studies Readers (both collections of new and previously published essays intended to provide glimpses of archival work and knowledge outside of North America), and Archival Cases and Case Studies (examining archival work in a variety of institutional types and with a variety of media). Added to SAA's own publications is a vast sea of new titles pouring from the presses of other professional associations and trade, professional, and university publishers.

Both the earlier Basic Manual Series and the Archival Fundamentals Series provide benchmarks in the development of archival knowledge and work. One can trace changing ideas and practices about archival reference services by reading the 1977, 1992, and 2004 volumes dedicated to this subject in the respective SAA manual series. One also expects to find in this volume current standards and consensus about this aspect of archival work. One also expects now, of course, that some may disagree with aspects of the current presentation, and may point to the growing research and case study literature being generated by the archival profession.

Many people participated in the production of the various volumes constituting the Archival Fundamentals Series II. The profession owes its gratitude not only to the authors, but to various chairs and members of the SAA Publications Board; Miriam Meislik, Photo

Editor for the series; the SAA Executive Directors, Susan Fox and Nancy P. Beaumont; and especially to Teresa Brinati, SAA Director of Publishing, whose good humor, organization, and steady commitment to a quality product helped keep the publishing of these and other SAA volumes on track.

RICHARD J. COX
Publications Editor
Society of American Archivists

Introduction

Recorded information is everywhere in modern society, as countless essays and books, media coverage, and popular discourse about the "Information Age" all attest. Individual, handwritten documents; texts produced on word processors and laser printers; published books and magazines; still photographs and moving images on film, videotape, and digital disks; sound recordings; automated data consisting of nothing more than invisible magnetic impulses on thin pieces of plastic; an ever-expanding World Wide Web full of things we can read, listen to, watch, copy, and transform for personal use—all these various forms of information surround us.

Many have lengthy histories, dating back thousands of years to the earliest writing systems and civilizations, leading some people to suggest that every age might be an "information age." Others are so recent that they will have emerged between the time we wrote this book and the time it was published. Now as in the past, many different people and organizations create records in the course of daily life and business, and many more seek to use them for a variety of purposes. Understanding those records—where they have come from, what they are made of, why they are made, what services they perform, how they can be organized and managed, and how they are used—is the purpose of this volume.

Several professions share the responsibility of caring for and managing recorded information. Archivists, librarians, curators, records managers, and automated data specialists are among those who preserve, organize, and make accessible records of one kind or another. In the past, these professions often emphasized their distinctions from one another, largely on the basis of the physical format of the information they held. Librarians worked with published books, while archivists cared for unpublished manuscripts. At the same time, those outside these disciplines usually failed to see the differences among them, perhaps because each group had appropriated as its own the rhetoric of the Information Age. Increasingly, the boundary lines have not seemed so rigid as previously supposed: there are at least as many commonalities as differences. The form in which records come is less important than the reasons why information has been recorded, kept, and used. At the same time, the goals of organizing information and making it available are shared by all these practitioners, regardless of the distinctions among the particular procedures they employ for achieving those goals.

The purpose here is to understand that portion of the world of recorded information encompassed by the phrase "archives and manuscripts." These words denote many things: the recorded information of the solitary individual participating in the ordinary events of everyday life; the small business maintaining records to satisfy financial and legal mandates; the voluntary organization keeping track of its programs and supporters; the large government or corporate bureaucracy churning out millions of documents. All these records are produced as the result of some activity, whether grand or mundane, and they are preserved because they have both an immediate and a long-term usefulness. They come in a variety of physical forms, but their intellectual significance is more critical than their format. Archives and manuscripts are not necessarily "old stuff"; they may also include valuable records of the very recent past—even yesterday. What makes these records "archives" is neither age nor appearance, but rather content, meaning, and enduring usefulness. While the original sense of "manuscript" (meaning something written by hand) may seem obsolete in a fully digital world, it is not. It remains a useful term to describe collections of personal records and documents. The term "archives," too, still has meaning, even as computer specialists transform it into a verb—"to archive," meaning to save something for as long (in their estimation) as six months. The word retains its original purpose of designating those records with an array of values that mandate their continuing maintenance.

The archivists who care for these records all share a common mission, even as they attend to the nuances of their individual institutions and clienteles. Archivists commit their time and their talents first to saving the permanently valuable records of individuals and groups, then to organizing those records in a systematic and coherent way, and finally (and most importantly) to making those records and the information they contain available to users. To carry out that mission, archivists must understand their holdings and the appropriate procedures for taking care of them. More generally, archivists make themselves students of the nature and varieties of recordkeeping itself, studying this human activity in the past and in their own times.

Understanding archives and manuscripts begins with understanding how and why records of all types are created. The wide diffusion of literacy throughout human culture has meant that an ever-widening circle of people creates records and continues into an indefinite future to make use of the information these contain. Originally, this was done through reliance on some basic and relatively stable technologies, particularly paper and the pen. As the means for making records evolved, particularly in the nineteenth and twentieth centuries, records became more abundant and more varied in their character. The records no longer consisted merely of hand-written words on paper, but also included those produced by mechanical and other means. Today, individuals can harness sophisticated electronic technologies to do everything from generating individual documents to publishing their own books, creating documentaries, and even (less nobly) pirating the works of others. Throughout, the fundamental reasons for the usefulness of records remain largely unchanged. Those who seek to know archives and manuscripts must understand why and how information gets recorded.

Understanding archives also depends on appreciating what makes those materials informative and useful, both in the short run and over a longer term. Archival records embody information born of some kind of human activity. A letter communicates over distance, for instance, and it fixes a message permanently. Often, records document one action so that others may follow. Architectural drawings direct the work of carpenters and plumbers, for example, and they mandate the purchase of supplies. Making a record also helps codify an initial event, and it serves as a kind of check that some related action will follow. The minutes of a meeting summarize the discussions and decisions made so that new work can be done. A contract between two parties specifies the terms of their agreement and sets a standard against which to measure performance. Many records appear in response to legal and other official regulations. Laws embody the individual and collective rights of people and help promote the cause of justice. The entries in a diary serve to establish in our memory important events and emotions that we do not want to lose through forgetfulness. Other personal recordkeeping, such as writing checks or taking receipts, is often dictated by the individual's need to be in conformity with regulations such as filing tax returns. In all these cases, the acts of recording and saving information serve immediate, practical purposes.

As time passes, however, new uses for recorded information emerge. Those meeting minutes can now provide a long overview of the organization's history, showing how it grew and prospered or how it withered and died. Architectural drawings continue to have a practical use as long as the building stands, but they also permit a study of changing aesthetics in the built environment. Contracts from the distant past convey information about social relationships when examined by someone asking historical rather than legal questions. Personal papers provide the stuff of biography and allow the readers of one century and locale to know people from altogether different times and places. They enhance public or collective memory just as they assist personal remembering. An understanding of archives and manuscripts includes an appreciation of this wide range of possible uses of records and of how the passage of time may increase rather than decrease their importance. Understanding archives and manuscripts also lets us see how they fit into society, from their use by scholars to their use by journalists or school children.

Archivists explore these questions—why and how records come into existence, why the information in them may be useful both now and in the future, how new uses may replace old ones—with the benefit of a particular perspective. When archivists look at records they see things that others who come into contact with those same records may not. The archivist's perspective derives initially from a broad knowledge, acquired and refined over the course of a professional career. There are several components to this knowledge. First, knowledge of the individuals, organizations, and institutions that create records allows the archivist to see how archival documents grow out of the many processes of life, establishing the critical context for records. Next, knowledge of the records that are created as a result— their nature, function, and significance—allows the archivist to understand what has been called the life cycle or continuum of records, long before the documents arrive in the archives, if indeed they ever do. Knowledge of how recorded information may be used follows, even if those uses go beyond those originally intended or foreseen, and this helps the archivist assist all users of the records, who will ask a range of unpredictable questions. Finally, knowledge of the archival principles and techniques best suited to managing those records (including an appreciation of the historical development of those principles) permits the archivist to control and make accessible the different portions of a collection.

These various kinds of knowledge serve as the foundation for the archivist's perspective, but equally important are the values that derive from them and that archivists apply to their labors. These characteristic beliefs guide decision making in professional settings, but even more importantly they allow archivists to see and state, for themselves and others, the underlying worth of what they do. Archivists believe that archival records ought to be preserved because they are useful, because they contain information that remains valuable over the long term. They believe that those records ought to be preserved and safeguarded, organized in such a way as to be understood and usable. Archivists also value the importance of dealing fairly with both their records and their users, protecting private and confidential information when necessary and treating all users equitably. These and other values contribute to the particular outlook of archivists.

The archivist's perspective is not detached, however; it is active, played out in the day-to-day work that the archivist does. An understanding of archives and manuscripts must therefore include consideration of the archivist's task, the responsibilities and duties in which professional knowledge and values are applied. For the archivist, this task includes three broad areas of activity, each with a number of specific duties. The first group includes all those actions that help archivists save and acquire archival records: identifying what the records are;

deciding which of them should be preserved and which may be discarded; formally transferring them to the archives; and preserving the physical integrity of the records. Given the particular challenges of the digital technologies now being used to create records, archivists have also had to expand their responsibilities to encompass helping to plan recordkeeping systems at the time of their creation so as to ensure that valuable records will be identified and maintained from the very beginning. Next come those activities connected with organizing the records: putting them into intellectual and physical order and describing what that order is in a format that can itself be understood and used. Finally, the archivist makes the records available to those who seek information—whether in person, by mail, by telephone, by electronic mail, or over the Internet. The archivist explains and enforces any restrictions on access to the records, while at the same time publicizing information about the archives itself and actively reaching out to a wide public audience through exhibits and other educational programs. The archivist's task is nothing if not varied, a circumstance that for most archivists only adds to the appeal of their profession.

This volume, a new edition of a shorter manual published in 1990, seeks to provide an introduction to these issues for the beginning archivist, for the administrator contemplating establishment of an archives, for the potential donor of archival material, for anyone interested in learning about archives. The structure and much of the original text from the first edition have been retained, but new discussions of professional research and debate have been added. Certain gaps in the original volume, which became painfully apparent with the passage of time—the Internet did not exist in its pages, for example, a measure of just how long ago 1990 was—have been filled. Understanding archives and manuscripts is never a static matter, but rather a dynamic one. While expanded versions of the earlier chapters remain the core of the book, a new chapter, addressing several contemporary challenges, has also been added to convey some sense of the changes that continue to affect the archival world. A bibliographic essay has been retained and updated, though we are acutely conscious that it excludes as much important recent work as it includes.

Any book about archives is a book about fundamental aspects of human life and society. Because of their intimate connection with the processes of life that produce them, archives and manuscripts are alive with human nature in all its diversity. Understanding archives and manuscripts opens the door to understanding ourselves, and that remains one of the enduring challenges and enduring joys of archives work.

CHAPTER 1

Recording, Keeping, and Using Information

Recording information and finding ways to keep and use it for long periods of time are very old problems for human culture. In its more or less insatiable desire to gather, comprehend, and utilize data, humanity has sought various means to fix knowledge in such a way that it can be called back to mind when necessary or desirable. The ability to do this, some contend, is what separates humans from other creatures, allowing information to "be held in the mind as in a store" and producing languages that are like "sponges," possessing a "wonderful creativity," "adaptability," and "vitality."[1] The need to remember and to learn from past experience demands that we consolidate what we know in reliable ways. Over the course of human experience, the species has accomplished these tasks in a number of ways, with an ingeniously broad range of solutions, including both the development of record systems and the formation of archives with their manifold utilitarian and symbolic uses. Understanding the nature and characteristics of recorded information is essential for anyone who records, keeps, or uses it—that is to say, for everyone.

The Oral World

Humans are natural speakers. Physiology has endowed us with the ability to form complex sounds, and the world in which we live is first and foremost an oral one. We emerge from the womb making noise, and the habit endures. We gather data, acquire knowledge, and achieve understanding through speaking and listening. In the same way, we pass that information on to others, whether in our own time and place or to those more remote, through word of mouth, a phrase that suggests a marvelously succinct image. The ultimate storage facility for all information is the human mind itself, and it is in the collective mind of all its members that society preserves what it knows. Continuing research about language shows that all humans form into groups and learn to communicate (whether through informal means like gossip or more formal means like writing), suggesting that the current popularity of technical achievements such as electronic mail, the World Wide Web, and cell phones may rest simply on our basic impulse to talk to each other, about anything and for any purpose.[2] Written letters, diaries, scrapbooks, and marginalia often mirror this interest in oral conversation.

The ways of storing and transmitting information in an oral world have many advantages. Those tasks are unavoidably social, depending for their success on individuals talking face to face with one another. People analyze data progressively, drawing out meaning and conclusions in the mutual process of thinking out loud. They question each other until full understanding is achieved. Unfortunately, several problems accompany these benefits. Oral communication is necessarily transient: it exists only as it is going out of existence. When we say the word "information," the "infor-" is and must be gone by the time we get to "-mation"—and then it is gone too. More serious is the inescapable fallibility of human memory: no matter how we learn something or how well we know it, we are liable to forget it altogether or to remember it imperfectly. Thus, before the invention of writing, humans had to find ways to enhance their ability to remember and thus retain information they might want or need at some later time.

The memories of preliterate people were not really better than ours, as overwhelmingly literate moderns sometimes assume. Cultures without writing did, however, have to devise ways to improve their ability to retain what they knew. They wrapped important information in poetic and formulaic language, for example, language whose very meter and pacing assisted the memory and thus increased the chances that the information would survive. They used religious and secular ritual in the same way. Combining oral and visual techniques, they associated ceremonial objects with significant events in the lives of individuals or of entire communities. Recent scholarship in Mesoamerican and North American precolonial societies has demonstrated that their pictorial and abstract writing systems were quite efficient in communication and fixing memory through images.[3] These oral and visual devices helped preserve information and forestall forgetting.[4]

Techniques to save and transmit information orally are not confined to remote times. They are equally evident in the present, and even survive in cultures that are otherwise fully literate. Nursery rhymes and ditties that children chant while skipping rope demonstrate the power of rhythm in preserving what has been learned and in passing it on to others. In old age, we can still recite the ritual prayers of youth, even if we cease to be religiously active and thus lose the practice of repeating them. The custom of wearing wedding rings shows that objects still serve as reminders of important events. When the mind is the primary storage medium for all information, significant or trivial, anything that improves the mind's capacity to retain what it knows is welcome. It is even possible to speak of archives in traditionally oral societies, grounded in social constructions of reality, methods other than texts, and imaginative devices for social and organizational memory.[5] Linguists, for example, often compare language itself to archives. In the end, understanding orality is not unlike trying to understand literacy.[6]

The Rise and Spread of Literacy

Writing was a relatively late development for the human species. Unlike speech, it is external and technological, having no basis in physiology or nature. Still, its advantages over purely oral means of saving information were apparent from the outset. Written language can accommodate more than a million words, while oral speech usually has only a few thousand: the dictionary knows more words than any of us does. Because literacy makes it possible for us to write information down using a system of conventional symbols that themselves have no intrinsic meaning—why should the symbol that we write as "T" be associated with the sound we automatically assign to it?—we have a more flexible and a more reliable way to preserve data of all kinds. If we forget something, a written memory of it survives. In fact, we can forget certain information deliberately, or never learn it in the first place, confident in the knowledge that a written memory will be available when necessary. Once introduced, writing everywhere proved popular. People of all classes and occupations scribbled whenever and wherever they could.[7] Even in societies where literacy was modest, people used it to communicate, understand their surroundings, and move through society. Scribes or other intermediaries (sometimes mistaken by modern records professionals as their antecedents) might be needed to do the reading and writing, but the benefits of literacy were many.

What is more, with writing humans can store information in a more precisely fixed form. We can be more definite about things: in an oral world, a story or analysis is accurate if it conforms to the general thrust and meaning of the original. In a world of writing, accuracy means something more precise, the conformity and continuity of a text, word for word. Just as important, we can preserve written information over a longer term, and we can more easily send it across great distances without having to rely on direct, personal transmission: individuals widely separated, whether by time or space, can speak to each other through writing in a way they never could orally. Written records proved to be the best kind of *aide memoire,* more efficient than remembered cadences or ceremonial objects.[8] Even the word "record" itself underlines this connection. Combining the Latin word for "heart" *(cor)* with the verb "to give" *(dare),* "to record" *(re-cordare)* something is to find a way to give it back to the heart and the mind after the passage of time. By offering so many advantages, literacy challenged orality as a more efficient and effective means for information storage, transfer, and use.[9]

These characteristics of writing have led some scholars to speak of the "power" of writing and to argue that literacy preempts orality. An anthropologist, for instance, has compared the power associated with

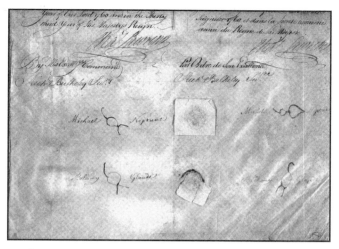

Two forms of writing—pictographs and alphabetic writing—on a treaty between English colonists and Penobscot Indians signed at Falmouth, Casco Bay, Maine, on July 6, 1754. Courtesy Archives, Commonwealth of Massachusetts.

those cultures that know and practice writing with those that do not.[10] Nevertheless, even in societies, such as our own, where writing is fully established, orality continues to play an essential role. Indeed, many written records (documents of practical transactions) and other texts (literary and philosophical works) retain characteristics that suggest they were once meant to be read out loud, even after they were written down. They can be, another scholar points out, "by all modern standards, bombastic, pretentious, disorganized, repetitious, even scattered, filled with digressions and incidentals."[11] Read them silently, they are confusing and stiff; read them aloud and they come to life.[12]

Even so, a mental world with writing is very different from a purely oral world. After the advent of writing, knowledge can be objective rather than subjective, acquiring an existence of its own, apart from the knower. We can compile and store information in significantly greater quantities: a single written volume can hold more data, both facts and the particular manner of expressing them, than even the best of human memories. Whereas knowledge in an oral world tends to be conservative and slow to develop—we must remember things in fixed, unchanging ways or crucial details may be lost—written information is more dynamic, subject to greater analysis and elaboration, if only because the mind is freed up for other business. Technology also works its magic, and all records, from the beginning, have been the products of some form of technology (paint, clay, stone, papyrus, vellum, paper, and silicon). We can benefit from the development of evermore efficient means of making records, though there may be corresponding dangers: the physical deterioration of writing materials presents the possibility of a loss of memory just as surely as does human forgetfulness.[13] Above all, recording and keeping information in written form make that information less evanescent and fragile, more durable and usable. An adage of Horace states the case succinctly: *verba volent, littera scripta manet*—"words are fleeting, written letters remain." It is precisely because they remain that written records are so versatile and effective.

These advantages of writing as a medium for storing and transmitting information guaranteed the spread of literacy. Successive technical revolutions in storage media and formats—from clay tablets to papyrus scrolls to the parchment and paper codex, from hand literacy to movable type printing and mass production—made writing easier and more widely available. The critical cultural shift came not, however, with the mere fact of literacy itself—that is, who could read and write and who could not. Rather, the key turning point for any society undergoing a transition to literacy was the point at which it came to rely on writing and written records in its everyday operations. Managing the far-flung Roman Empire would have been impossible without written communication, for example, even though the level of general literacy remained low by almost any standard. More telling is the example of thirteenth-century England. During the reign of Edward I (1272–1307), a nobleman was asked by what warrant he held a certain parcel of land. Brandishing the rusty sword with which a forebear had seized it in the Norman Conquest, he declared, "This is my warrant!" A generation later, that combination of venerated relic and oral tradition would be unacceptable as legal proof, and a written charter would be required instead.[14] The change was as much psychological as practical. Even those who could not read and write themselves agreed that written records would be acceptable proof—indeed, the only acceptable proof. Reliability, legality, and proof now depended on writing. Recording rather than remembering became essential to society, even as orality and literacy existed side by side: written systems superseded oral traditions, and oral traditions were adapted in new recorded forms.[15]

Though literacy came to different cultures at different times, the effect on the production and use of written records was always the same: the amount of recorded information grew at a steady pace as literacy advanced. For the most part, this happened in what seems at first a counterintuitive way. We might expect that people would first learn to read and write—those are distinct, if related, skills—and only then would documents proliferate. In fact, most cultures experience the transition in precisely the opposite way. Small groups of individuals, especially those with political and economic power, began to produce and rely on written records. Only then does the rest of society recognize the need to acquire literacy themselves, if they hope not to be left behind. In recent years, we have witnessed this same phenomenon at work with electronic technologies. Computers emerged first as crucial tools in certain segments of society (business, science, government) and only after that did "computer literacy" seem important, as it spread to the rest of the population through the personal computer.

Once literacy began to spread in society, an ever-increasing number of people could and would create records, whether for formal or purely personal reasons. Farmers could keep track of the weather or the production of crops and livestock; artisans could monitor supplies and sales; lovers could exchange expressions of devotion to be read over and over again; individuals could keep diaries intended for no one's eyes but their own. On a broader scale, official bureaucracies developed, consisting of departments that did what they did in large measure by making records and by using them to communicate with similar departments. Whatever business they were in, offices whose daily tasks were to produce, manage, and exchange formal records multiplied. Personal records, too, became common. More than two thousand letters and documents, for example, have been found at the site of a Roman fort on the frontier from the first century CE. These, one scholar says, attest, "to writing's pervasiveness in ancient Roman society, even in this farthest reach of the Empire. . . . The fact that such a trove, in such an isolated locale, exists at all testifies to the great amount of correspondence that must have been taking place among Romans throughout the Empire."[16] Once the practice of making records began, the tendency would always be toward making more of them, never less, toward complexity rather than away from it. In recent times, governments have taken periodically to passing "paperwork reduction acts," which seem to do everything except reduce paperwork. Whether in the first, the twelfth, or the twenty-first century, governments, institutions, and individuals created more and more records.[17]

The irony of this expanding rate of production of records was that as the quantity went up, the quality generally went down. The total volume of records increased, but the significance of any single item tended to decrease. The complaint of one fourteenth-century Italian merchant that "we spend half our time reading letters or answering them" sounds familiar to anyone who worries today about how to control too much information.[18] When writing materials were scarce and expensive, when the act of recording information was itself rare, whatever was recorded and kept had to be of sufficient importance to justify the cost and effort. With complex bureaucratic agencies regularly producing large files of correspondence, reports, and financial information, however, records were meaningful principally in context and in the aggregate. The individual letter explaining inner motivation or fundamental belief became less common, replaced by the voluminous records of a corporate body in which critical information was scattered. Meaning emerged from the whole rather than from any one part. The key single document that would answer every question was less important (and less likely to exist) than the totality of recorded information and the processes that had produced it.

Archivists have the responsibility to care for the recorded information of society and its organizations, a task that would not exist (or would at least be very different) in an oral world. Successful understanding of that task rests on understanding several fundamental things: the reasons for recording information in the first place; the reasons for saving it for long, possibly indefinite, periods; the reasons for *not* saving it; the technology that supports records creation; and the characteristics and uses of recorded information. These matters represent the core of archival knowledge.

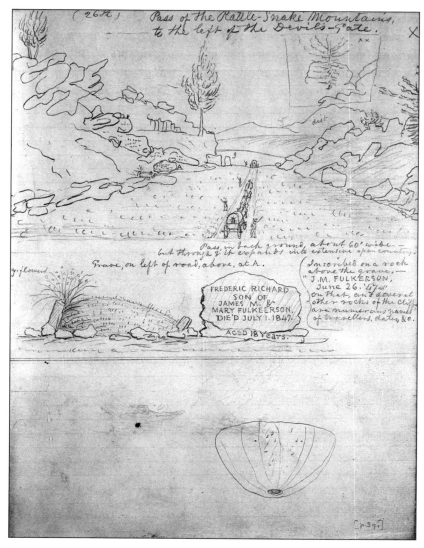

Sample page from the 1849 diary of a western pioneer. PHOTOGRAPH COURTESY JOSEPH GOLDSBOROUGH BRUFF DIARIES, JOURNALS, AND NOTEBOOKS. WESTERN AMERICANA COLLECTION, BEINECKE RARE BOOK AND MANUSCRIPT LIBRARY, YALE UNIVERSITY LIBRARY.

Reasons for Recording Information

What are the human activities or motivations that lead to the making of records? What kinds of information are important enough to be written down and saved? What kinds of records are made in the process? Answering these questions requires that archivists study records and recordkeeping systems. Archivists are not merely the passive receivers and describers of records judged by someone else to have value. Nor are they mere assistants to researchers wishing to use such records for their own purposes. Several broad categories of motivation for record making are familiar to archivists, although all records exist for a particular reason. These motivations all derive from some sort of warrant: laws, regulations, standards, professional practices, and even cultural or traditional notions that mandate what records are created and what they look like. Behind each reason for recording, there is an explicit warrant.[19]

Most common are the *personal* reasons for creating records. Personal records relate to particular people in their private, individual, and family capacities. These may include records of significant life events, such as birth, marriage, and death, and they come in a variety of forms: the written entries in the family Bible, the videotape of the wedding, the shoeboxes full of vacation snapshots. Scrapbooks and commonplace books are similarly personal, reflecting an individual's peculiar interests and temperament. Life-history narratives, whether composed contemporaneously (such as diaries) or retrospectively (such as memoirs or autobiographies) are likewise personal, as are some direct communications, especially in the form of correspondence. Even the tendency to write annotations into the margins of books reflects a basic human impulse to create documents that we can consult again when we want them. These may take a variety of forms, including most recently the records created by "bloggers" who generate journals for the World Wide Web. In many of these instances, we readily share these personal records with others—this is very apparent with the Web—but that intention can also be secondary: we make the record in the first place to promote personal memory and meaning.

Beyond the personal, other records are clearly *social* in character. These deal not with individuals alone, but with individuals acting together in groups. Social organizations (those based on common vocational interests, for example) produce records of the activities themselves and of individual and collective participation in them: membership rosters, minutes of meetings, and records of special programs and other efforts all document social activities. While the nature of these records may seem routine and uninteresting, the process of their creation is often imbued with an almost religious sensibility, giving meaning and status to those involved in such organizations. Cookbooks, for example, both manuscript and printed (many with the annotations of their owners), have served as critical documents for women in various eras and cultures, especially as they were often the expression of the shared values of a group rather than the work of a solitary author.[20] Religious affiliation likewise produces records, including evidence of formal church membership and of participation in rituals and sacraments. Political activity, including work on behalf of candidates or causes, produces recorded information: records of voting, financial contributions, speeches, and campaigning add to the overall body of documentation. Records can be powerful agents in creating and sustaining communities, both real and imagined.[21]

Economic motives are a third source of records. The acts of acquiring, managing, and spending money produce large quantities of recorded data which is useful in providing a picture of economic health, whether personal or collective. Historically, these motivations are the source of some of the earliest records in the ancient world, including lists of barter and sales, as well as accounting records. One historian examining the records of ancient Mesopotamia estimates that "approximately four-fifths of the almost half a million records are 'business documents' which betray an extraordinary passion both for formalism . . . and for accounting that deals in the most meticulous way with the circulation of goods: stock inventories; accounts of property and of people and of issues; contracts of selling and of buying of landed property and of people, of loans, of marriages, of dowries, of adoptions, of wet-nursing, of service; wills; litigations and court protocols."[22] Still today, there are voluminous economic records. In most government archives, more than half the records produced are fiscal in origin or maintained for fiscal purposes. Personal record-keeping may be similarly weighted toward those records that are necessary in accounting for one's own funds as well as for money held in trust for others. Hiring, firing, paying, and evaluating workers create records that are important to employer and employee alike, both in normal times and whenever problems arise. Perhaps because of the importance people usually assign to economic activity, there is a great deal of duplication in economic recordkeeping: the bank keeps a record of the balance in your account, for instance, but so do you. Duplication permits more extensive cross checking and thus seems to increase the likelihood of accuracy. All we need to do to remind ourselves of the origins of such economic records is to look at our own wallet or purse, noting the array of credit, bank, and other cards that we use daily to generate documentation.

Much recorded information deals specifically with *legal* matters. Governments have always been systematic recorders of information for purposes both benign and sinister. Records may be used to protect citizens (constitutionally expressed rights, for example) or to harm them (such as secret police files in totalitarian states). The development of writing, the particular genres of documents, and the ultimate formation of archival repositories are all most closely associated with legal factors, partly because they are efforts to impose control and order, reflected in hierarchies of governance and power.[23] More broadly, ownership of property, contracts of various kinds, and the performance of the responsibilities of citizens all produce written information that may be significant both immediately and over the long term. Deeds to real property, agreements to perform certain tasks or services, proofs of nationality and citizenship, and public service records (voter registrations, jury lists, and military service records, for example) constitute documentation of the social relations that take place within the specific context of a society's legal system. Likewise, records produced or gathered in court proceedings—civil, criminal, or those dealing with property or estates—form a major portion of the recorded information that deals with legal matters. Such records, maintained at first for the court's own purposes, have later been used by social and cultural historians to explore hitherto underdocumented groups.

Some recorded information must be characterized as purely functional or *instrumental* in nature. All records have some function, but

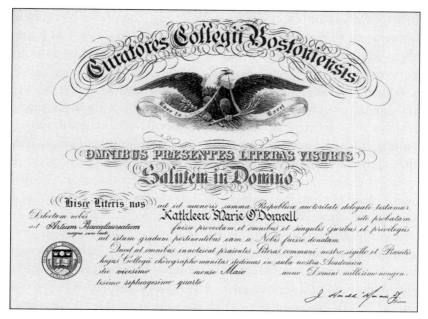

Diplomas are records with largely symbolic significance.
COURTESY KATHLEEN M. O'DONNELL.

many of them are designed especially to accomplish a specified task, either because they are used in a particular way or simply because they exist. Architectural drawings and blueprints, for example, are created with a practical, instrumental purpose in mind: to build buildings that serve certain needs, that represent a particular aesthetic, and that do not fall down. Though these records may later be put to other purposes as well—restoring deteriorated buildings, studying the architectural styles of different periods, or even studying the drawings themselves as works of art—their original purpose is instrumental: creating these records helps you do something else. Maps and navigational records serve the pragmatic ends of permitting safe and efficient travel from one place to another and of acting as a reminder of a route once discovered. Scientific and observational data permit analysis that may lead to further experimentation or perhaps to prediction. Even a record as mundane as the written combination to a lock assures the continuing ability to open it. The technology of these instrumental records may change significantly. The Global Positioning Systems (GPS) in automobiles are computerized in a way that paper maps were not, but they are no less instrumental in getting us from here to there.

Finally, some records are not really practical at all, but rather are intended for *symbolic* purposes or, at least, they are gradually transformed into artifacts imbued with symbolic and cultural values. Family Bible records, for example, may have some practical use, though the information they contain is also recorded (perhaps more reliably) elsewhere, usually by civil or religious authorities. The real significance of recording names and dates in the family Bible or on a family tree scroll is the way it symbolically reconstructs the family across the generations and in spite of physical, temporal, and geographic separations. Photographs circulated with Christmas cards may do the same. Diplomas awarded at school graduations symbolize the attainment of a desired goal, offering an artistic presentation of the facts. Still, the diploma itself, which is almost always highly prized, serves virtually no practical function. Employers rarely ask actually to see it and, since these particular records are often written in a foreign, allegedly dead language (Latin), both the recipient and anyone else would be hard pressed to put it to a practical purpose even if they were so inclined. In these instances, the records still stand for something; they are important and effective means to *record,* to call the memory of an event back to the heart and to hold it there. The records themselves, however, serve a symbolic rather than an instrumental purpose.[24]

These six categories—others could be enumerated—highlight the motivations for the making of records in the first instance. They illustrate the goals, both short and long term, that record making is intended to achieve. In all cases, the question of who is doing the recording is noteworthy, and a variety of permutations is possible. The recorders may be individuals making records about themselves or about their relations with others: diaries and letters would fall into this category. The recorders may also be corporate entities such as governments, organizations, or institutions, recording information about their own affairs (the minutes of meetings, for instance, or internal communications relating to policy) or about individuals in relation to the whole (church membership records, for instance, or employee personnel files). What is more, the purposes are not mutually exclusive and may overlap. Some economic records have a clearly defined legal purpose, and some personal records may be heavy with symbolic meaning. As in most things, human motivation remains complex, and this complexity is what makes archival work challenging and worthwhile.

The Impulse to Save

Information is usually recorded with some direct, intended usefulness in mind, and thus keeping the records (or copies of them) as soon as they are made has an obvious benefit. Most records are probably not needed for more than a few months, however, and the question of what records to keep longer has always challenged archivists. The public's perception of archives is that they save everything forever, and this often produces amazement or even protest when it is discovered that they are in fact selective.[25] Each motive for creating a record may have its parallel reason for keeping it temporarily. But what is the source of the impulse to save them for a longer, perhaps even indefinite, period after that original usefulness has ceased?

Though records may not always be created exclusively for practical reasons, the impulse to save them frequently has a resolutely practical basis. We save records because we think we will need them again in the future, even if that specific time or particular use cannot now be foreseen precisely. Archivists acknowledge that these future uses are difficult to assess and can impede the careful appraisal of records; it is easy to fall into the trap of saving everything "just in case." Still, the information recorded today may be needed again, its potency or effectiveness undiminished by the passage of time. Especially when the record is made for legal, economic, or instrumental purposes, there may be an ongoing need to recall that information, and saving it thus has a pragmatic value.

Just as the origins of writing suggest utilitarian purposes with lists of property, commercial transactions, and public decrees, so the most obvious reasons for saving records suggest very practical uses. Proving ownership of a piece of land may be necessary, for instance, for both the original owner and any successor. Perhaps more likely, determining exactly where one's property ends and another's begins may be critical. Records may also set the terms and conditions for the performance of specified duties (as in contracts), and saving them will therefore provide the basis for judging whether those obligations have been fulfilled. Such practical reasons for saving records always exist within the given legal and economic structures of different societies, and the usefulness of saved records will thus vary with place and time. Understanding those legal and economic requirements is critical for any saver of records long term. Moreover, it is important to document why records are saved, thereby allowing archivists and researchers alike to comprehend the full documentary universe from which they came.

Though certain uses of records may be foreseen at the time of their creation, in most cases it is the unpredictability of future use that reinforces the impulse to save them. When we record information, we cannot always anticipate the uses to which it might be put in the future. We are reasonably certain that the financial data recorded today will be needed at the end of the fiscal year to balance the books. It may also be needed next year, however, in an outside audit, and perhaps even required again five or six years hence in connection with a government tax investigation. It may be useful in charting long-term trends: are we making money or going broke? Perhaps none of these specific needs will arise, but they are all at least possible, and the record is kept against that possibility. The unpredictability of future uses of records demands the security that saving them provides.

At the same time, however, there are also nonpractical reasons for saving records, reasons that are personal, social, and even symbolic. Records are saved because they are a form of individual or collective memory. People will often hang onto even the most innocuous stuff—scraps of paper, old receipts, ticket stubs, canceled checks—because the document helps them remember something that is special to them. What did we do, why and how did we do it, and what were our thoughts and feelings as we did it? Letters, diaries, and photographs can provide that information, and so we save them in the interest of remembering what we once knew but have since forgotten, or of remembering it more vividly. We want to relive happy experiences of the past or, perhaps, recall the lessons of unpleasant experiences, and so we save the records that will help us do so. For individuals, preserved love letters call good times to mind; for whole societies, records such as those of the Salem witch trials or the Holocaust remind us of a past we might want to forget but know we should not. It may also be that we save records even when it would be in our best interests not to. One of the enduring mysteries of the Watergate scandal of the 1970s is why President Nixon did not simply destroy the tape recordings that eventually helped destroy his political career.[26] Like various kinds of physical objects, records can be prized as relics, things in themselves with both physical and intellectual meaning, and we save them in the hope of calling back the presence of persons, events, or emotions with immediacy. We reread letters we wrote and received in college, for instance, or we look again at drawings made in childhood and proudly preserved by parents. These feelings too may be somewhat unpredictable, but the desire to recollect our individual and social past is common enough that we preserve the records that will make recollection possible. Such impulses may well be unexplainable in a coolly rational way; they may place us, together with book collectors, "among the gently mad."[27] But can everything be saved? Archivists and curators know that it cannot; otherwise, the shelves would be full tomorrow and all further collecting would have to stop. How archivists decide what to save is therefore critical, but before making those decisions they must understand the impulse to destroy no less than the impulse to save.

The Impulse to Destroy

The mirror image of the impulse to save records is the impulse to destroy them. This is done most directly by the literal physical destruction of documents through such means as burning or shredding—or, in the case of electronic records, deleting—but there are other forms of destruction as well, both real and metaphorical. It may be done by neglecting them, deliberately or through more "benign" methods, so that the normal processes of deterioration can do their damage unimpeded. Finally, it may be done by falsifying or misrepresenting them, causing records to seem to say things that they do not

Ancient statues of Buddha in this village of Afghanistan were destoyed in 2002, a product of the impulse to destroy records and other cultural artifacts.
Photograph courtesy Morten Hvaal/World Picture News.

actually say. The motives for destruction are manifold, and every literate society has examples of them, although such efforts have been especially prevalent in the twentieth century. Germany, France, Japan, South Africa, Yugoslavia, Bosnia, and the United States all have engaged in efforts to eliminate or seal documentation concerning genocide, social injustice, and mere political high jinks. "Truth commissions" in many countries have tried to undo this damage, and their work has led to the creation of archives and to greater access to records of past injustices.[28]

Records, archival or otherwise, are powerful factors in society, and, as a result, they are often the targets for destruction. Book burning has occurred everywhere there are books, and the destruction of libraries usually includes the elimination of archival documents as well. Some scholars argue that the legendary ancient library at Alexandria was destroyed by subsequent struggles between Christians and Muslims, each eager to purge texts that were either sacred or diabolical, depending on which side one was on. During the Reformation, each denomination enthusiastically burned the heretical books of the others. Crowds in the French Revolution sometimes directed their fury against repositories of documents that embodied aristocratic privilege, destroying records of debt and service obligations while plundering the finery of manor houses and noble coats of arms.[29] Nor should we think of such actions as confined to a remote past, perpetrated by those who did not have the sensibility we moderns claim for ourselves. The smashing of Confucian texts during the Cultural Revolution in China in the 1960s and 1970s is a reminder that no society, however advanced or sophisticated, can entirely avoid the temptation to destroy records.

The impulse to destroy may come first from the creators of records themselves. Some leaders seek to destroy the records of their predecessors, eager in effect to begin the world and history over again with themselves. Hitler and his lieutenants destroyed the evidence of those peoples they tried to eradicate, all the while documenting their own activities to create a supposedly purer version of history.[30] More common is the desire to destroy records so as to remove evidence of wrongdoing, illegality, moral turpitude, or simple incompetence. Once again, the Watergate scandal offers a good example, in which possession of the tape recordings of White House conversations became critical. Archivists, historians, and public interest groups joined in a lawsuit to establish the principle that presidential materials were public records, not the personal property of the president, precisely because they feared that the incriminating recordings would be destroyed if President Nixon retained control over them.[31] In the corporate accounting scandals of the early twenty-first century, the destruction of damaging records by company officers was added to charges of insider trading and mismanagement of funds.[32] Any record creator with something to hide could readily see the advantages of destroying records to keep the secrets secret.

The impulse of others to destroy records after the fact is no less common, and the destruction is often justified in the name of larger ideological or cultural causes. In the early 1990s, libraries and archives in Bosnia were burned as part of a concerted effort by Serbian nationalists to eradicate evidence of Muslim and Croation peoples. "Throughout Bosnia," one reporter noted, "libraries, archives, museums and cultural institutions have been targeted for destruction, in an attempt to eliminate the material evidence, books, documents and works of art that could remind future generations that people of different ethnic and religious traditions once shared a common heritage in Bosnia. . . .While the destruction of a community's institutions and records is, in the first instance, part of a strategy of intimidation aimed at driving out members of the targeted group, it also serves a long-term goal. These records were proof that non-Serbs once resided and owned property in that place, that they had historical roots there. By burning the documents, by razing mosques and Catholic churches and bulldozing the graveyards, the nationalist forces who have now taken over these towns and villages are trying to insure themselves against any future claims by the people they have driven out and dispossessed."[33]

After-the-fact destruction of records may also derive from less sinister, more personal, and perhaps even understandable motives. The son of a World War II veteran tells a story which, though heartbreaking to historians and archivists, offers an enlightening window into the intense emotional meaning records may have and how that may lead to their destruction. The American serviceman in question, the son of immigrants, wrote regular letters home throughout his service in the European theater of the war, and the letters were lovingly passed around to members of the extended family as a way of assuring everyone that he was safe. On the day he returned home, discharged at the war's end, his father ordered one of the soldier's sisters to shred the letters into confetti. They now offered only painful reminders of the danger their loved one had experienced, the persistent anxiety the whole family had felt for his return, and these troubles were to have no part of the brighter future they all looked to.[34] Better to enforce forgetfulness of those dark days by destroying the records of them.

Falsifying or consciously misrepresenting records may also be seen as a form of destruction—if not of the records themselves, then at least of the trust we normally place in them. Together with outright plagiarism, the fabrication of documentary evidence is rightly condemned, but examples of it persist nonetheless. Those writers who have made a sinister cottage industry of denying the historical reality of the Holocaust have refined this technique to a fine art, but the practice is not unknown even among more apparently reputable scholars.[35] Michael A. Bellesile's *Arming America: The Origins of a National Gun Culture* was published in 2000 to wide acclaim: it won Columbia University's Bancroft Prize for the best book in American history. The work quickly sank into a sea of controversy, however, as charges were first made and then proved that the author had misquoted, miscited, and miscalculated documentary evidence from public and private archives, all (it appeared) in a conscious effort to support his predetermined conclusions. There were even suggestions that he cited records that did not exist: when asked to produce the research notes for some of his more controversial assertions, he could not. Other historians tried without success to find records he claimed to have seen, while still others followed his documentary footsteps and found very different evidence. He was eventually placed on leave from his university, his career ruined, and the prestigious prize was taken away, to the embarrassment of him and of the original judges.[36] While this did not involve the actual physical destruction of records, the effect was the same: it undercut the reliability of records and skewed the documentary basis for understanding the past no less than flames or the shredder would have done.

The Technology of Record Making

All records, whether made, kept, or destroyed, possess certain characteristics, determined by the ways in which they are created. Because writing has no foundation in nature, humans must rely on external means—tools, in the anthropological sense—to record their information. Records thus depend on the technology available to produce materials that support the recording process. Originally confined to a limited number of types, which remained more or less stable for centuries, these technological means of making records have expanded rapidly in the last few hundred years. The advent of modern digital means for the creation of records has also reminded us that all records and recordkeeping systems are intimately connected with technology.

Paper. Ancient societies relied on a variety of media for recording information. Depending on circumstances, these might be abundant (baked clay for tablets), cumbersome (carving on stone), or difficult to prepare (papyrus sheets or animal skins), but they served the purpose and often retained a certain aura. Even in the present, for example, parchment and vellum are used because they seem to add gravity to laws and diplomas. It was the perfection of paper by the Chinese in the early second century CE, however, that provided the best, most versatile surface on which to write. Coming to Europe by way of Islamic civilization, paper-making technology was common by the fourteenth century and remained essentially unchanged for the next five hundred years. Some rulers forbade the use of paper out of concern that it was not durable enough or did not have the feel and texture of animal skins. For centuries, many of the most important records—public decrees, for instance—were still written on parchment or vellum. Paper, however, was more common. Organic fibers, generally derived from cotton or linen rags, were broken apart, suspended in water, and matted together to form sheets that, once dried and smoothed, were lightweight and flexible. Paper was originally made only by hand (thereby limiting the size of a sheet that could be made at any one time), but by the time of the French Revolution a growing demand led to the introduction of machinery. Increased production outstripped the availability of rags, and in the nineteenth century, manufacturers experimented with other materials, quickly settling on wood pulp, a decision that was to affect the preservation of documents and books for generations. Chemical means for preparing and treating paper were also developed. This "progress" brought an increased availability of paper and an eventual reduction in its cost, but at the same time it contributed to a decline of paper quality. More paper meant that more information could be recorded, but the declining physical constituents of record material posed the ironic prospect that writing would lose some of its advantage over oral information storage: written letters could no longer remain if the paper on which they were written did not. The technological advantage of readily available paper was now balanced by the sobering disadvantages of deterioration.[37]

Paper has been a great success for recordkeeping, but its proliferation has also had a downside. Common speech uses "paperwork" as a symbol of bureaucratic sloth and ineptitude. The filling out of paper forms is characterized as the repetitive exercise of organizations, especially governments, which mindlessly do what they do. The high-tech industry consistently suggests that the elimination of paper will make organizations more efficient and competitive. Predictions about the so-called paperless office, the emergence of the e-book, and the supposed demise of the printed book, together with acclaim for the increasingly ubiquitous mobile technologies of laptops, personal data computers, and other wireless devices, all seem to signal that the era of paper is over. These predictions, like so many, are vastly overstated. There are now more paper documents than ever before, though their relationship to digital records is complex.[38] Paper is unlikely to disappear anytime soon.

Writing Materials and Implements. Traditionally, information was recorded on paper by hand, using ink and some instrument for applying it to the paper. Ink consists of particles suspended in a solution, and the devices for writing with it have taken several forms. The sharpened quill of bird feathers offered a greater degree of control than earlier brushes or tubes, and quills therefore remained the most common writing tool from the sixth century BCE until the refinement of the steel-pointed pen about 1830. Since then, a number of cheaper and more practical alternatives have been developed, including the fountain pen (containing a reservoir of ink, thus eliminating the need to dip the pen repeatedly into a supply), the ballpoint pen (using a metal roller to apply the ink evenly), and the soft-tip pen (employing an inexpensive, porous synthetic).[39]

Pencils, too, mixing graphite powder with clay, became common means for records creation. A seemingly mundane device, the pencil is actually the product of extended experimentation to find the right woods, the best substance for the graphite lead, and even the best mechanical means for sharpening.[40] There probably have been more records created by use of the pencil than by any other technology, and the pencil's persistence demonstrates the continuing reliance on old technologies even as new ones appear.

Even today, with the ease of composing and sending electronic mail messages, many people still use fountain pens to compose formal handwritten messages, since they seem to carry more symbolic or empathetic meaning.[41] Moreover, there is a steady market in pens and other writing implements as collectibles, suggesting that the tactile attractions of working with traditional materials have survived the

Early papermaking as depicted in a woodcut by Jost Amman from Piazza Universale by Tomaso Garzoni, 1641. PHOTOGRAPH COURTESY HARRY RANSOM HUMANITIES RESEARCH CENTER, THE UNIVERSITY OF TEXAS AT AUSTIN.

transition to personal computers, laptops, and hand-held devices.

Printing. The perfection of movable type printing in the middle of the fifteenth century provided a means for disseminating information more widely than ever before. Writings of a single page or of thousands of pages could be produced, copied, and distributed around the world. Common texts (such as the Bible and other sacred literature) and important documents (such as law codes or statements of rights) could be readily available. Records formerly made only by handwriting were now mass produced, and many early printers made substantial profits by printing forms used by governments, religious organizations, and universities. With printing, recorded information expanded to include more than just the often unconscious byproducts of an activity. It now more easily accommodated conscious literary productions (novels, poetry, essays), created deliberately for a wide audience to educate, uplift, and entertain. The greater availability of such materials had a self-reinforcing effect on literacy: books and other printed items were created to meet a growing demand from literate people, but the increase of printed matter itself produced pressures toward greater literacy.[42]

The increase of texts for reading helped make societies more aware of the role of documents in their lives. Unique original documents could be replicated and made more widely available than ever before. Consider the differing characteristics of two famous documents: the Magna Carta of 1215 and the United States Constitution of 1787. The Magna Carta was "simply a document, not to be read as such, but to be produced as legal evidence if ever transgressed against." The Constitution, by contrast, was printed and distributed in thousands of copies because, as Benjamin Franklin insisted, citizens had both the right and the responsibility to read it. "Certainly no gesture could signal reading's social advance over the intervening centuries more poignantly."[43] By the mid-nineteenth century, people everywhere were immersed in written texts, all of them the descendants of print's innovations.

Mechanical Record Making. Printing could produce and multiply texts in large numbers, but individual record makers sought other mechanical means to speed their writing, to make it consistently legible, and even to make more than one copy simultaneously. The long search for an efficient device that could do all this finally paid off in the nineteenth century with the perfection of the typewriter. Early versions of this contraption were slow and clumsy, but by the 1870s a machine that could write rapidly and uniformly was perfected with all the recognizable modern characteristics: type-blocks containing both uppercase and lowercase letters, keys with trigger mechanisms, an inked ribbon, and a roller to hold and advance the paper evenly. The later development of electric and portable versions of this basic machine led to the widespread availability of the typewriter as a means for creating records. Especially in institutional, bureaucratic settings, the typewriter became the usual agent by which records were created, and the very ease with which it could do so increased geometrically the number and variety of records produced. A kind of technological imperative took over in record making: it was possible to generate a greater body of records with ease, and so a greater body of records was in fact created.[44]

Other devices such as the adding machine, the telegraph, the telephone, and the phonograph (adapted for stenographic work), joined the typewriter in the first wave of automation of the office. It was not always a smooth transition, but the introduction of these machines transformed the social and administrative structure of the office. For a while, the word "typewriter" referred both to the device itself and its user, and it was also used as a verb to describe the act of employing it. "These lingering, linguistic confusions between the device and its function, between the typist, typing, and the typewriting machine," says one historian, "indicate the lengthy negotiation of typing as a modern activity and typists as a labor cohort."[45] Typewriters led to the reorganization and redesign of offices, encompassing new divisions of labor, changes in career trajectories, and, perhaps most notably the feminization of the office.[46] The role of records in human affairs also changed. These devices streamlined the production of records, but they also relegated records work to lower-level, often marginal, clerical positions.

Copying Machines. The ability of the typewriter to make neat and uniform documents underscored the need for some efficient means for producing multiple copies. In combination with carbon paper, the typewriter could produce one or more copies at the same time as the original, but only if one had decided in advance to do so. This was a distinct improvement over hand copying or earlier machines, including an eighteenth-century "polygraph"—literally, "multiple writing"—developed by that incorrigible tinkerer, Thomas Jefferson.[47] For much of the following century, use of the often messy press copy, in which the ink of an original document was blotted into a thin copying paper using water and pressure, was widespread. Turn-of-the-century duplicating machines that ran off large numbers of copies from a single master were also helpful, but in all cases copies still had to be made at more or less the same time as the original. Anyone who wanted to make a copy later on, whether for wider distribution or even for simple portability, was out of luck. Photographic processes were some help, but the real advance did not come until the 1950s with the invention of xerography ("dry writing"), which produced copies using electrical charges and reflected light. Now copies could be made at any time, long after the original. Once introduced, these photocopying machines steadily shrank in both size and price—they eventually became available in hand-held models that produced a copy after being swept across a page—while at the same time becoming more widely used. By the 1980s, copiers had been linked to telephone lines in the "fax" (shorthand for telefacsimile) machine, making it possible to send documents anywhere. Copies could now be transmitted over great distances in a matter of seconds. By the 1990s, the same basic technology was being used to convert hard-copy documents into electronic ones through the use of scanners. All these developments had a significant impact not only on the volume of records created (which increased phenomenally), but also on the nature of the records themselves. In a world in which thousands of copies of a record might exist, all looking more or less alike, which one was the original? Did it even matter any more?[48]

Such questions and challenges continued into the twenty-first century. The growing dependence of the modern office on the Internet, word processing, spreadsheets, and databases added tremendously to the quantity of records generated. The increased connectivity of individuals, made possible through portable devices such as personal data assistants (PDAs), complicated the problem of copying by increasing access to information sources. An ongoing study has concluded that the "amount of new information stored on paper, film, magnetic, and optical media" doubled in just three years (1999–2002). The "amount of information printed on paper is still increasing, but the vast majority of original information on paper is produced by individuals in office documents and postal mail, not in formally published titles such as books, newspapers and journals."[49] As organizations and individuals come to rely even more on these digital recordkeeping systems, notions of authenticity and originality become more difficult to understand.

Filing Systems. The growing quantities of paper records created the need for improved methods for keeping track of them all. Individuals could file papers however they liked in their own, entirely personal systems, which never had to be rationalized or explained to

The desk of Jonathan Edwards expanded to increase its storage capacity.
PHOTOGRAPH COURTESY THE JONATHAN EDWARDS CENTER AT YALE UNIVERSITY.

anybody else. This was often done with the help of desks full of little compartments. The great eighteenth-century divine, Jonathan Edwards, was a strenuous keeper of all documents and, for this purpose, he designed a truly amazing desk, with added space and compartments to hold his notebooks and papers. Starting from a simple writing surface with a few pigeonholes, Edwards and his cabinet-maker kept adding onto it over the years. First came drawers of different sizes to hold papers of various dimensions; next came two cupboards on either side; finally, more compartments were added on top, detachable for use as packing boxes when the minister moved from one town to another.[50] Edwards's contraption was a harbinger of desks developed a century and a half later by William S. Wooton, a pioneer of modern office furniture and technology. Wooton opened a desk company in 1870 and four years later patented a "cabinet office secretary," featuring numerous compartments that stored both records and office supplies conveniently in one location. These desks, which usually featured doors that opened on either side, interior pigeonholes, and a drop-down surface for writing, were produced until 1897. The motto for these desks was "a place for everything and everything in its place," a sentiment of which both Edwards and twentieth-century office workers would have approved.

In organizational, governmental, and business settings, however, the problem was more serious than it was for individuals. In those offices, too many people were creating and compiling too many records. From early modern times, governments had often relied on registry systems, in which individual documents were controlled by means of elaborate numbering, sometimes including greater or lesser indexing or notation of the contents. The late nineteenth century brought experimentation with different sorts of flat files, in which documents could be stored loose in boxes (often designed to look like books, interestingly enough) or small drawers. These systems were flexible because they permitted all the documents on a particular topic or from a single correspondent to be grouped together and rearranged as necessary. Vertical files—the ancestor of the contemporary filing cabinet—swept flat filing aside in the 1890s. These vertical files made more efficient use of available floor space, and they permitted filing of incoming and outgoing letters together, according to categories that could change over time.[51] The filing cabinets eventually became metal, fireproof, and utilitarian rather than oak and ornamental; sometimes they are lateral, sleek, and modernistic in design or hidden behind modular cubicles. Whatever their design, in most offices they are still there.[52]

Photographic Records. Beyond their increasing quantity, records experienced a qualitative change in the middle of the nineteenth century, when technology made it possible to record information in formats other than written words or numbers on paper. Foremost among these was photography, which recorded not written information about people, events, and things, but direct and clear images of them. A written record describing an event might be valuable enough, but how much more informative was a photograph that showed what the participants themselves actually saw and did. Now we could have these seemingly more accurate visual representations of events to accompany and expand text. Governments, corporations, and other entities hired photographers to create visual evidence about everything from public works projects to publicity shots. If writing could freeze time by describing what had happened, a photograph could freeze time even better by showing what recognizable individuals looked like and how they behaved. The visceral appeal of looking at people from the recent or remote past was powerful, and photographic records seemed more immediate—more "true" somehow—than secondary descriptions. When, by the early twentieth century, it became possible to record not only still, fixed photographic images but also moving images (to which coordinated sound was eventually added), the sense of reality was enhanced even further. If a picture was indeed worth a thousand words, photographic records expanded the possibilities for capturing, storing, and presenting information.[53] How to "read" photographs remains a tricky business: a single image may be "about" many different things, depending on the viewer. The very analogy to reading written words, however, suggests the connection between photography and other kinds of record making.[54]

Altered Record Formats. Photography not only presented the opportunity to record information in a new way, but it also offered the possibility that information already recorded in one format could be changed and stored in another. Just as one could photograph a person, so one could make a photograph of a written document and keep that photograph either in addition to or instead of the original. The development of microphotography, available technically by the 1870s but not widely employed until fifty years later, presented new options. By making very small images of documents that could be enlarged to full legibility when necessary, microphotography made possible the storage of a great quantity of information in a small amount of space.[55] Optical disk technology, perfected in the 1980s, offered the same advantage, followed by a vast array of other digital technologies that permitted the copying of records and their easy dissemination via the Internet/World Wide Web. As a result, the original format in which information was recorded no longer needed to be immutable: if the usefulness or efficient management of the record required it, the physical form could be readily altered. Such a possibility, however, as helpful as it may be, created other problems. The information in an altered format may itself be altered while making the switch, perhaps without detection. What happens to the integrity, authenticity, and reliability of the record in the process? Beyond that, many records could no longer be read with the naked eye, requiring instead some machinery or device. These devices themselves become obsolete, creating an open-ended need for new technology to address the problems of older technology. These difficulties notwithstanding, the new options available for recording and storing information in altered formats mean that both record creators and record keepers have greater flexibility than they once did.[56]

Recording Sound. If light could be captured in various ways in photographic images, late nineteenth-century technology also found a way to capture sound and thus to open the way for aural records. Whether produced on grooved phonograph (the word means "sound writing") disks that reproduced sound electrically, on magnetic tapes, or on digital disks, the possibilities for reliable recordkeeping in this format were impressive. Indeed, the sounds themselves were even called "recordings." A photograph could present a visual image of what historical figures looked like, but aural recordings could offer direct evidence of what they sounded like. The record-making process moved from the written text of George Washington's inaugural address to a still photograph of Abraham Lincoln, and then to a sound and moving picture of Franklin Roosevelt, with his own distinctive cadences and tone. The user of such records could actually hear the record creators speak, taking note both of what they said and how they said it. Summaries of the actions taken at a meeting, for example, could be supplemented with a recording of the proceedings, a fuller and more complex form of evidence that approached the historian's long-sought goal of knowing "what actually happened." At the same time, sound recordings could be created deliberately as a means of capturing the thoughts and recollections of participants in particular events after the fact. This practice, dubbed "oral history," represented an important development since it was a planned and purposeful creation of records that would not otherwise have existed. The availability of inexpensive and generally reliable sound recording technology made this expansion of the world of recorded information possible.[57]

Computerized Information. Machines that could perform simple arithmetic functions trace their origins to the ancient abacus and to work by Pascal and Leibniz in the seventeenth century. In more recent times, successive generations of machines evolved that could do more than "compute" (that is, perform mathematical computations). These were devices that could store data and manipulate it in increasingly sophisticated ways. After World War II, the capacity and abilities of these machines expanded exponentially while their size and cost decreased equally dramatically. The perfection of the integrated circuit and the silicon chip in the 1970s made possible increasingly flexible computer networks, linking various sources and users of information together. At the same time, computer technology became cheap enough to be affordable on a wide scale. Once available only as large, powerful mainframes, small personal or home computers became available in the 1980s, quickly followed by an array of even smaller, portable digital devices that could sit comfortably on one's lap, be held in one's hand, or even be worn as clothing. Marvels such as these became commonplace in a stunningly short time.

The speed of technological change is apparent, too, in noting how the Internet was formed and became the World Wide Web. Electronic mail first emerged in the early 1970s as an ARPANET (Advanced Research Projects Agency Network) application developed by the U.S. Department of Defense.[58] A connection of local networks was brought together as the Internet a decade later, and that in turn produced the Web, a system of Internet servers supporting specifically formatted documents, in the early 1990s. The most impressive and perhaps most common aspect of this has been the growth in the use of e-mail and the scale of the Web. Today there are nearly two hundred million Web hosts, fifty million Web servers, and billions of Web pages. Billions of e-mail messages are exchanged worldwide annually. Some are important; others (derisively called "spam") are almost deliberately worthless. Today's networked society has given rise to concepts such as e-commerce and e-government, all promising to place the power of the Internet into every household in practical ways.

As a result of all these developments, records could be created and manipulated in computer format, a change from the days of hand-written records that was as much qualitative as quantitative. Information was now recorded, used, and even destroyed without ever passing through a stage at which it was printed out and read with the naked eye. In bureaucratic settings, the change was swift and the impact remarkable. One writer estimated that in 1970 only 7 percent of the information held by the United States government was in com-puterized format, while in 1985, a scant fifteen years later, more than 80 percent of it was.[59] Today, the percentage is higher still, restrained perhaps only by recent national security concerns. In personal set-tings, the shift was no less dramatic. Form letters that looked like personalized originals could be readily produced. Physical letters themselves became increasingly rare, as e-mail and "IM" (instant mes-saging) became normal methods of interpersonal communication. The notion of drafts of literary manuscripts rapidly lost meaning, since constantly evolving texts might never be in fixed form long enough to be written out separately or differentiated from one another. Periodically, casual events symbolized the change that had taken place. A speaker at the Society of American Archivists' annual meeting in 1988 surprised his audience by bringing to the podium not a written text but his laptop computer, from which he read his remarks, arguing that last-minute elaborations made this the most efficient means of presentation. His action, which seemed remarkable and amusing at the time, is now too unexceptional to notice, as speak-ers commonly use PowerPoint (a means of connecting computer information to photomechanical projection onto a screen), connect to websites for demonstrations, and combine video, audio, text, visual, and live presentations. So common have these become that the most serious challenge seems to be how to survive yet another PowerPoint presentation.[60]

Unrecorded Information. The development of modern tech-nologies made easier the creation of many new kinds of records, but sometimes progress moved backwards. By the early twentieth century, certain records that might have been created in the past were no longer being made. The perfection and use of the telephone, for example, meant that individuals and corporate entities no longer

The Electronic Numerical Integrator and Calculator, more commonly known as ENIAC, contained 19,000 vacuum tubes, weighed 30 tons, and could perform 5,000 calculations per second. PHOTOGRAPH COURTESY U.S. ARMY.

communicated exclusively in written form. Rather, they could revert to the fleeting communication of the oral world in a way that, under normal circumstances, left no traces. To be sure, telephone conversations could be recorded on tape, whether knowingly or not. In some official settings, the practice of writing out a "memo of record" following a telephone conversation developed, but in most instances this was rare; in personal situations, it was virtually never done. Private and intimate matters that were once put into letters, sent physically over great distances and eventually preserved for sentimental or other reasons, were now lost in the electronic ether of the telephone line or the satellite relay. Subsequent developments in telecommunications—the wireless cell phone and the personal data assistant (PDA), both of which appeared in the 1990s—proliferated rapidly in both personal and business affairs.[61] Such devices may or may not, as their advertisers liked to claim, make us smarter, but they certainly make us poorer in recorded information. If technology could assist in the creation of records, it could also aid and abet the process by which records were *not* created. Like Sherlock Holmes's dog that did not bark in the night, the records that did not come into existence likewise became a fact of modern life.[62]

If a century ago people marked their life's journey by what they recorded in diaries, wrote in letters, and gathered in reports and memoranda filed in offices, today their counterparts must navigate through a world with voicemail, electronic mail, websites, and other digital means.[63] The difference is that now much of their trail is less clear and, of its very nature, fading rapidly. Despite the overwhelming sense of the fragility of digital records, one of the characteristics of the modern era is a buoyant hope that the new technologies will enable us to save more in an innovative way that makes every person their own archives.[64] Perhaps terming our modern era *the* Information Age is as much wishful thinking as an effort to describe some of its chief characteristics with the constantly transforming digital technologies.

Characteristics of Recorded Information in the Modern Age

Taken together, these developments affected the way records were made, how they were used, and ultimately what they meant. The nature of recorded information, therefore, has evolved substantially since mankind first began to write things down, even as the impulse to capture a transaction or the desire to remember something has remained constant. Some four thousand years ago an Egyptian scribe brushed in ink, "A man has perished and his body has become earth. All his relatives have crumbled to dust. It is writing that makes him remembered."[65] Today, people may keep diaries, but they also create Web pages for the same purpose. The amount of recorded information in the present is vast and growing inexorably more so. To keep this quantity in perspective, however, archivists generalize beyond particular documentary items and consider the broad characteristics of the records they encounter. A number of characteristics are worthy of attention.

Most obvious, perhaps, is the overwhelming fact of *abundance* rather than scarcity. In modern, fully literate cultures, records exist not as rare single items but in large aggregations. Record making is so easy and relatively inexpensive—and, as the society becomes more complex, so apparently necessary—that large quantities of records are produced and compiled. One almost never encounters a single document on a particular subject or from a particular source; rather, one encounters lots of them, sometimes measured in hundreds or even thousands of cubic feet or by the gigabyte. Just as the number of books in libraries has grown exponentially, so the quantity of records has mushroomed. Duplicates, differing versions of similar items, documents that result from long processes of development, a large number of narrowly focused documents that all treat different aspects of complex phenomena, collections of files produced by individuals or entities over long periods—these are now the rule. The archivist is typically responsible not for a single letter but for boxes of them, not for one set of blueprints but for thousands of them, not for one personnel or case file but for rooms full of them, not for one physical repository but for multiple virtual repositories in the new digital environment. The consequence of this abundance is necessarily a shift in perspective: the archivist must focus on the forest rather than the trees. Recordkeepers must develop methods and techniques suitable to the administration and control of records in collective groups. Similarly, they shift their attention from records as unique artifacts and pay greater attention to the policies and procedures that lead to the creation and management of records systems. No archivist will live long enough to lavish detailed attention on individual documents, not to mention records created for the first time as digital operations. Archivists must therefore decide what level of activity is appropriate in acquiring, organizing, and making available whole bodies of records.[66]

Connected to the inescapable fact of the abundance of recorded information is another characteristic: the significance and meaning of records is *collective* rather than individual. In many ways, this has always been true, but the collective import of information is more apparent as records increase in quantity. Many researchers still look for the one key document that will magically explain every mystery and answer every question, but this hope is usually illusory. While some records are plainly more informative than others, record makers rarely commit their innermost thoughts, intentions, or motivations to paper in so concise and self-consciously transparent a form. Instead, patterns and conclusions emerge in the aggregate, depending on the context of the records. The nature of public attitudes and policy toward orphaned children, for example, is revealed not by the single letter of an orphanage director, a social worker, or even an orphan. Rather, it is discerned by studying the administrative and case files of various institutions, photographs, the recollections of former orphanage residents, the legal and political climate of the time, and other factors.[67] Indeed, major breakthroughs in historical research usually involve the imaginative uses of aggregates of records. Describing the research by Ulrich B. Philips on slavery nearly a century ago, one more recent scholar writes, "Although many American historians had turned their attention to slavery, no one had as yet immersed himself in archival materials and manuscripts in the same way as had Philips. He drew on plantation records, census data, letters, travelers' accounts, tax records, and other sources to construct his analysis of slavery."[68] Examining a variety of sources in this way became all the more essential as more and more information was recorded and available.

 One of the principal reasons that records exist in such abundance and need to be treated in the aggregate is that the making of records has become steadily more *decentralized* and *democratic.* Literacy is no longer a privilege reserved to an elite segment of society; instead, modern society expects that virtually everyone will be able to read and write—indeed, that everyone should be able to do so. This means that every individual can and may create records for any purpose, constrained only by time and inclination. Thus, there are now a vastly greater number of sources for the creation of records than ever before and, at the same time, less definable grounds for making choices about whose records are "worthy" of preservation and whose are not. Personal computers, laptops, and portable devices provide templates for creating every imaginable kind of record: programs are readily available to file a tax return or write a will. There are still legitimate concerns about the so-called digital divide—not everyone has access to computers, and there are significant disadvantages for those who

Palestine

do not—but the embedding of computers in schools probably means that these concerns will diminish rapidly. Other concerns have been expressed about the interruption of both work and private life by the phenomenon of electronic mail, but most people are nonetheless generating greater amounts of letters, notes, memos, and reports and at a faster rate than ever before. Even a small organization of a dozen people might be generating and receiving thousands of messages a month. As a result, selection is obviously necessary, for even in a world of democratic record making not everything can be saved. How the archivist chooses, how representative the choice is, and whether that choice is deliberate or accidental all become critical concerns.[69]

In a world in which abundant records originate not with a small number of sources but with a great many of them, the *interrelatedness* of records becomes both more apparent and more real. Just as modern institutions—government, business, the nonprofit sector, groups of private citizens—are all interrelated, so are the records of those institutions overlapping and connected. Archivists must therefore regularly look beyond their own collections to those in other repositories if they hope to understand either. Similarly, interrelatedness also demands a vision that is not limited by record formats. In the past there may have been justification for different professionals keeping separate from one another. Librarians could pay attention to published books and records managers to ongoing, current records, leaving to archivists only those unique manuscript sources that were prized precisely because they had lost their immediate usefulness. Such divisions are now difficult to sustain, for the distinctions on which they were based are no longer clear. "Near-print" and Web-based materials blur the line between published and unpublished information, while computer-generated, multiple-copy "originals" cast doubt on the difference between unique, archival records and duplicates. Though they each remain responsible for portions of the totality of recorded information, all records and information professionals have learned to be less restrictive in defining their work solely in terms of the physical form of material. If nothing else, they must do this to assist their researchers, who have also come to disregard the barriers between different kinds of sources. Users are often more interested in information than in the forms of that information.

The abundance of records, the widening circle of those who produce and use them, and the interconnections among institutions and records all point inescapably to the *social nature* of recorded information. Records are means of communication among people; they are intentional substitutes for speech. Records are ways of addressing other people in different times and places, even the other people we ourselves become with the passage of time. Archival records are preserved, therefore, not for their own sake or to satisfy some mystical need to save evidences of earlier times. Rather, records are preserved to be used, and their useful life does not end as they enter the archives. The particular uses may change, but individual and social usefulness of some kind always remains. The ways in which archivists organize and administer their collections must therefore always be done with this usefulness in mind. Exchanging information is a means of building and sustaining community, and even the most mundane records support complex social and symbolic interactions.[70] They even sustain imagined communities, constructed through rituals and functions, including writing.[71]

Their *shifting usefulness* is a final characteristic of records. All records are made in the first instance with some purpose in mind: personal, social, economic, legal, instrumental, or symbolic. From the beginning, however, archivists have recognized that those original purposes could be supplanted by others and that, in the process, the records would become more valuable rather than less. T. R. Schellenberg, one of the leading American archival thinkers, even maintained that records properly acquired archival value only when they were preserved for reasons other than those for which they were originally created.[72] Records did not become archives, in other words, until their usefulness had shifted. Archivists sometimes designate this as a transition from "primary" values (those purposes originally intended) to "secondary" values (important for their information concerning persons, things, or events that may be of research or broad cultural interest). The democratization of the production of records and the multiplication of kinds of records only opens the possibility that the purposes to which records can be put will expand still more widely. The consequence is a serious one, for it complicates the problem of selecting certain records for preservation while permitting others to be destroyed. With a steadily enlarging range of secondary purposes, might not all records acquire some value someday? If that is so, however, how could we possibly save all of them, even if we wanted to? Archivists must address these questions in a way that makes the continuing usefulness of records possible.

The Usefulness of Archives

Society at large uses archives and the information they contain in an impressive variety of ways. Anyone who looks on the care of archival records as esoteric, isolated, and irrelevant to any but a small group of specialists misses an important part of the story. Especially in recent years, archivists have come to recognize that their clientele is diverse and extensive, perhaps partly because archivists themselves have become diverse. At one time the typical archivist was a historian, by training and inclination, but now archivists come from academic backgrounds across the humanities, social sciences, and natural sciences. Public contact and personal interchange are the regular, everyday reality of the archives. Large numbers of people with a great range of interests seek information from archival records. That breadth of usefulness is the ultimate justification for the establishment and maintenance of archival programs. It is also the principal source of the joys and satisfactions that come from working with archives, that come from working with the people who use archives.

Many archival records are useful because they are a source of personal, individual identity. On a practical level, county and state birth records or church baptismal and membership records are used to demonstrate citizenship or eligibility for Social Security and Medicare benefits.[73] Beyond that, however, countless family historians and genealogists use those same archival records. This is not just a frivolous hobby. Rather, such users of archives are engaged in the important psychological task of anchoring themselves and their family in time, setting a fixed and reliable context for themselves in an increasingly fluid, changeable world. Any archivist who has seen users of these records cry on locating the marriage record of immigrant parents or grandparents—many have had this experience—knows the powerful, positive, and intensely personal meaning such records can hold. Commentators often criticize Americans for their lack of sense of the past, but the intense interest many have in collecting and arranging family mementos, visiting historical sites, and other activities suggests a deeper sense of the past and a quest for roots in a transitory culture. The extensive scholarship on public memory acknowledges the importance of activities such as genealogical research and even combing through flea markets. More than that, writings about the Information Age and cyberspace suggest that people still long for identity and stability amid the immateriality and speed of the Internet.[74]

Using archives also brings larger societal benefits. Medical researchers, for example, use archival records to trace the symptoms and patterns of disease in their search for treatment and cure. Public health officials use archives to locate toxic waste sites in the interests both of cleaning them up and of protecting the public. Scientific researchers use climatic records in weather prediction. A number of public and private archives in the recent past have made their records available in settling Native American land claims. One state archives has seen its records used to establish the rights to offshore oil reserves, and the resulting revenue helped keep tax rates low while maintaining state services. In all these cases, the public at large reaps genuine benefits from supporting public and private archival programs. The return on the investment in archives is substantial. More generally, records are used to hold public officials and agencies accountable to the citizens. Increasingly, the newspapers are full of stories in which records are used to expose wrongdoing in foreign and domestic affairs.[75]

Corporate bodies, too, derive benefits from the usefulness of their archives, though they may be relative latecomers in establishing archives.[76] Legal requirements and sound administration demand control over such critical documentation as contracts and financial data. Scandals involving corporate accounting practices only serve to underline the importance of maintaining records accurately and fairly.[77] Nonfinancial records are equally useful. The physical plant department of a company or a university relies on the blueprints and construction records of the buildings for which it is responsible. Some of these buildings may be quite old, perhaps even historic, with their records, together with those of more modern structures, stored in the archives. When the roof leaks, however, or the windows need replacement, even very old records may have an immediate, practical usefulness. The cost of reconstructing the information in those records (by remeasuring and redrawing the blueprints, for example) is so high that, while technically possible, it is prohibitive. A good archives program makes such costs unnecessary. Many businesses also use archival records in advertising and promotional efforts, relying on images and associations from the past to show their tradition and to draw on customer goodwill and loyalty. Think of reproductions of turn-of-the-century glassware and trays in advertising Coca-Cola, for example, or copies of historic photographs of the surrounding community now displayed on the walls of your neighborhood McDonald's. In those and in similar cases, companies draw on archives for support in the all-important area of public image and marketing, without which the businesses shrivel and die.

Archives support traditional forms of research, of course, and this usefulness cannot be overlooked. Those who search the past to understand the present find in archives the raw materials with which to construct their narratives and analyses. Indeed, most such researchers are guided by a slogan they learn early in their training: no archives, no history. These archival users are not confined to scholarly academics, however, interested only in narrow and arcane topics. Rather, a broad range of researchers visits archives every day for relevant information from the past: faculty members; students at all levels, from elementary school through graduate school; local historians; biographers; documentary filmmakers; and writers of all kinds. For these and others, archives are useful because they inform, entertain, enlighten, and educate. Books, television programs, and motion pictures draw on archives both for broad, important stories and for telling, authentic detail. Alex Haley's fabulously successful book and television miniseries, *Roots*, would have been impossible without extensive use of the records of a large number of archives. The immensely successful documentaries of Ken Burns also relied heavily on archival images, even as they provoked discussions about how these documents were used.[78] The powerful authority of archival records may also be seen in reverse. Oliver Stone used the authentic Zapruder film in his 1991 movie *JFK*, thereby lending credibility to the wildly conspiratorial view of the Kennedy assassination that the film advanced.[79]

What is more, many archives actively plan and implement educational programs using the records in their care. Archival records help senior citizens relive their own experiences and tell the stories of their lives to others. Those same records help young school students reach back beyond the extent of their own personal memory and give them a sense of place in their larger communities. Anniversary celebrations of churches, social clubs, schools, neighborhoods, and towns are all enriched by drawing on archival sources: original letters, photographs, reminiscences, and other records. When individuals make contact with such archival sources—not only the information they contain, but also the real things, written or created by real people— they transcend the bounds of time and realize in a personal way that they are part of a larger whole. That is a crucial, if somewhat intangible, benefit of archives, one that is no less important for human society even if it cannot be precisely measured in dollars and cents.[80]

Conclusion

Recorded information, therefore, derives from a variety of sources and is created and saved for a complex of reasons. In the modern age, that information possesses a number of distinctive characteristics, and it is used for an impressive array of purposes, some of them expected, some not. But where and how is that information kept, organized, and made available? Those are the responsibilities of archives and archivists. A history of archival institutions and the people who have been archivists will offer an understanding of the origins of this profession, as well as a deeper sense of its nature and purpose.

CHAPTER 2

The History of Archives and the Archives Profession

The archival profession in the United States is both extensive and diverse. Even a cursory review of archival repositories and activities highlights the availability of a wide range of documentation on all facets of life. Archival repositories, large and small, of all types, are evident in every community of the nation.[1] Government archives at every level—national, state, and local—maintain the records of the public and of the officials and agencies that conduct the public's business. Historical societies, emerging at the end of the eighteenth century, set the direction of archives as acquirers of historical materials. Research libraries, founded in the nineteenth and twentieth centuries, assembled archival collections of broad historical and cultural significance. More recently, universities, maintaining their own institutional archives and gathering manuscripts, rare books, and other special collections for the use of students and faculty, have become a principal employer of archivists.[2] A steadily growing number of private institutions and organizations are also devoting attention to their records. Substantial archival efforts can be seen among business firms, religious bodies, hospitals, schools, labor unions, museums and other cultural institutions, and voluntary organizations and other agencies. The growth of these archives, together with the popularity of genealogy and history-related tourism and volunteering, shows a spreading awareness of the importance of archives.[3]

The pace of growth in the profession during the last half of the twentieth century was especially impressive. In the late 1950s, Philip

Hamer and staff from the National Archives sought to identify the agencies and institutions that held archival records, and they eventually described some thirteen hundred of them. A little more than fifteen years later, Hamer's successors updated this work, and they found more than twice as many repositories, the result of both better reporting and the expansion of absolute numbers. Another decade after that, in 1988, the number of archives had almost doubled again, with some forty-two hundred archival repositories reporting their holdings. By the opening of the new century, there were more than five thousand archives maintaining websites, suggesting that the total number of archives is actually larger than that and continues to grow. The number of people pursuing careers as archivists similarly expanded to meet this growing demand. The Society of American Archivists, the principal national organization for the profession, was organized in 1936 with only 125 members, but by the time of Hamer's work it counted more than a thousand; it has more than quadrupled since then. Regional, state, and local archival organizations have also proliferated. More recently there has been a growth in the creation of online archival listservs, focused on specific types of repositories, archival functions, recording media, and professional standards.[4]

How have these changes come about? How and why have American archives and the American archival profession assumed such a diversified character? What were both the opportunities and the difficulties that this diversity presented? What does the archival profession's past imply for its present and future? If "what's past is prologue"—this line from *The Tempest* is inscribed in stone at the entrance to the National Archives building in Washington, D.C.—an understanding of the history of archives and archivists will provide the context for understanding what they are and where they are going.[5]

Old World Antecedents

The habit of preserving records appears almost immediately with literacy. From the fourth millennium BCE, when the inhabitants of the ancient Near East were writing by making wedge-shaped ("cuneiform") markings on clay tablets, archival records have been accumulated, and the continuity from that age to our own is more or less unbroken. In general, the word *archives* was used in the ancient world to designate any collection of written records, including materials we now would consider the domain of libraries, and not just those of enduring value, as modern usage implies. Still, despite changes in the form of the materials used to create them—from Babylonian tablets to Egyptian papyri to Greek and Roman wood blocks and stone inscriptions—archival records were produced by governments and other official bodies, and they were preserved because of their lasting official and administrative usefulness. In ancient Greece and Rome, leading families had archives as well, sometimes housing them in official repositories but just as often maintaining them in their own homes. These records are decidedly rare today, only a few having survived the intervening centuries, but they are nonetheless evidence of the world in which they originated. They are the prototypical examples of the connection between records and the processes of life that produce them.[6] While we know that the ancient world was the cradle of writing and hence of recordkeeping, scholars still debate the meaning of these classical archives. Some think that the archives of the ancient world had many of the same elements we now associate with their modern counterparts, while others doubt that interpretation.[7] What is certain is that the quantity, importance, and use of recorded transactions were all increasing throughout antiquity, leading to the growth of archives.

In medieval and early modern Europe, literacy spread more widely, though it was still far from universal. First parchment and then paper became the most common media on which to record information in the hope of preserving and making use of it. Records became numerous and necessary, a part of the systems by which society held itself together. Many societal functions increasingly relied on documentary records, and even people who could not read and write themselves accepted the idea that written records would serve as the guarantors of legal and other rights: a parchment charter proved land ownership, for example, even if the owner could not read it. The language itself came to underline the connection between records and life: *acts* and *deeds* denoted not only the things that people had done, but also the written records that affirmed that those things had been

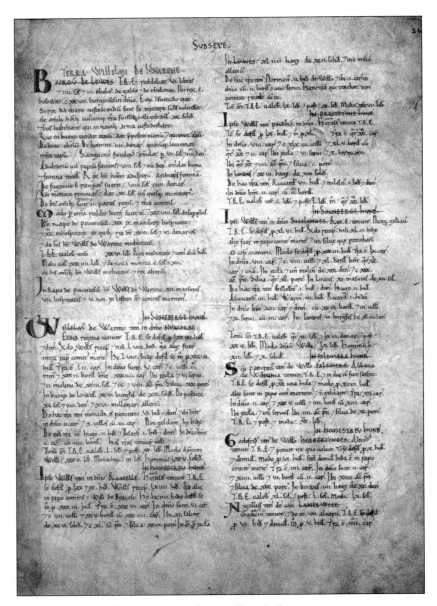

A page from Great Domesday describes a village in Sussex.

done.[8] Despite the increasing complexity and quantity of records, however, the motivations for creating them remained largely unchanged. Records were a more objective means for preserving critical information, a means more reliable than human memory, which remained fallible.[9]

"will to conquer"

Nowhere was the fundamental nature of records more apparent than in the case of what is perhaps the single most famous written record of all times: the Domesday Book. Motivated by a desire to legitimate and consolidate control over his newly acquired kingdom in England, William the Conqueror ordered a survey of the entire territory in 1085 in the interest, he said, of compiling as much information as possible "about this country—how it was occupied and with what sort of people." Compiling such a comprehensive record was designed to achieve those practical goals. At least in some measure, however, the record was also weighted with symbolic significance, underlining the psychological point that the country had been conquered and was now subservient to the new king's will in all things.

The result was a detailed social, economic, and political record bound together into two massive volumes (known as Great Domesday and Little Domesday) that compiled information on land ownership and use, the social status of inhabitants, tax obligations, and feudal as well as religious rights and duties. So all-encompassing was this survey and so crucial to the continuing regulation and governance of William's domain that it was compared with the great metaphoric book of judgment that medieval Christians believed would be opened on the last day ("Doomsday"), its decisions forever fixed and unalterable. The record was used for such practical purposes as assessing land values, proving claims of ownership, asserting various rights and privileges, and settling disputes. As time went on, it also acquired the patina of a venerated relic from an earlier and somehow purer era, a standard against which more recent times could be measured. Valued today for its usefulness in historical research, Domesday is still significant for the way it fixed in writing information that served the practical needs of its society.[10] The Domesday Book has remained a symbolic record of permanence in our present digital information age as well. In the 1980s, all the data from it was computerized, marking the nine-hundredth anniversary of the document. Unfortunately, in less than a decade the computer disks had become unreadable, a circumstance that highlights the challenges of digital preservation and the need for techniques to emulate older computer hardware and software. One of those involved in trying to salvage the electronic Domesday said that the project had "become a classic example of the dangers facing our digital heritage. . . . We must not make the mistake of thinking that recording on a long-lived medium gives us meaningful preservation."[11] In this way, the similarities between medieval recordkeeping and its modern counterparts attest to the nearly universal aspects of human record making.

The proliferation of medieval documents solved many societal problems, but it also created some new ones, including the problem of forgery. As many societies made the transition from orality to literacy, some documents were fabricated to create new authority for legitimate ownership or rights, and we have the curious spectacle of the making of fake documents to support genuine claims. Records were also revised and the documentary record shaped to create a usable past. One scholar describes how scribes and others used the records with "great freedom, destroying, revising, recopying, and especially reorganizing. The result was a winnowing and restructuring process that provided the parameters within which subsequent generations could hope to understand the past."[12] As governments grew in size and importance, along with commercial enterprises, the veracity of records became a critical issue. In 1381, during an uprising in England, peasants demanded of the abbot at the monastery of St. Albans "a certain ancient charter confirming the liberties of the villeins, with capital letters, one of gold and the other of azure; and without that, they asserted they would not be satisfied with promises."[13]

The rise of modern sensibilities inevitably broadened the creation and use of records, and as in so many other things the French Revolution proved a watershed event. Fired by the desire to democratize all aspects of society—even those instruments of aristocratic privilege that land, feudal, and other records had frequently been—the revolution nonetheless sought to preserve systematically the evidences of the past. Many records were destroyed, but many were saved, and for a variety of reasons. Some of these were new: to assist historical understanding, to redefine the notion of posterity, and to glorify the new Republic. Even more important, the revolution established the principle that records were critical because they helped protect the rights of the people. Thus, care of the nation's records was a national responsibility. Equally important was the corollary principle that the public at large had the right to inspect and examine the records made and kept by its government. This example was followed in most other Western countries in the decades following the French Revolution. By the beginning of the twentieth century, the notion that all citizens had a right to the protection records offered was well established.[14]

American Origins: The Two Traditions

European explorers and settlers brought their recordkeeping practices with them to the New World. Spanish missionaries made careful records of the baptisms and marriages they performed among both colonizers and native converts in the West and Southwest. French businesses kept economic records of the activities of fur trappers and traders ranging the wilderness of Canada. The formation of entirely new societies required the making of records that could provide fixed points of reference in a world that had little in the way of precedent. Recent scholarship shows how the records created as part of this colonial impulse often reflected the dynamics of cultural interaction, including different means of communication. New England Indian deeds reveal different ways of conceiving the universe, with natives combining oral tradition and site names and the English settlers using written descriptions mimicking names from their homeland.[15] Personal correspondence flowed between the American colonies and Europe despite a number of obstacles: slow and uncertain travel, high costs of writing materials, and a high level of illiteracy. That so many of these early letters were preserved is not only an indication that personal recordkeeping was thought important, but it also suggests that the documents were treated with extra care to ensure their survival.[16]

Among the English colonies crowded along the eastern seaboard of North America, writing and recordkeeping were seen as perfectly natural and normal activities, deriving from patterns already well established in the world the settlers had left behind. Several colonial leaders kept diaries or wrote memoirs, partly to demonstrate the superintendence of divine providence over the colonizing effort, partly to serve as promotional tools back home that would help bring new settlers to America. In most cases, these descriptions were not scrupulously accurate. The journal of Massachusetts Governor John Winthrop, for instance, was a combination of entries written very close in time to the events described and entries written much later as part of self-conscious literary endeavor and interpretation. Winthrop moved back and forth between journalism and history, and his diary is thus a very complicated documentary form.[17] In the same way a century later, William Byrd II of Virginia used his diary as a mirror for self-evaluation of his life, status, and progress, shaping the reality of his world around his perceptions of what he had done and what it meant.[18]

More important for practical purposes, some systematic means for recording land titles by civil authorities was essential, since the equitable division and efficient use of land were central to the success or failure of the colonies. Many colonists, of course, were functionally illiterate, and they had to depend on government authorities and educated elites to maintain records on their behalf.[19] As early as 1626, Virginia had a detailed procedure for recording all land sales in a commonly held set of books kept at Jamestown. Contemporaneously in New England the public responsibility to keep records was rapidly expanding to include so-called vital records (that is, information about births, marriages, and deaths) and of matters pertaining to wills and estates. The American colonists came early to the conclusion that making and securing such records was a community responsibility rather than a private one. In a frontier society such as theirs, a single, privately held document could easily be lost or destroyed; if civil authorities maintained such records the chances of loss (not to mention the possibility of deliberate falsification) would be minimized.[20] Records—instructions sent from home, for example, and reports sent back to financial backers—were as much an integral part of the colonization of the New World and other parts of the globe as military power, supplies, and shelter.[21] One surveyor wrote in 1607 of the value of *cadastral* (that is, "property") maps: "A plot rightly drawne by true information, describeth so the lively image of a mannor, and every branch and member of the same, as the lord sitting in his chayre, may

The Declaration of Independence is one of the most recognizable documents of all time. PHOTOGRAPH COURTESY NATIONAL ARCHIVES AND RECORDS ADMINISTRATION.

see what he hath, and where and how he lyeth, and in whole use and occupation of every particular is upon suddaine view."[22]

From its earliest settlement, then, America developed two approaches to records. One was a *public archives tradition.* It was assumed that government authorities at both the local and the colony-wide levels, as representatives of the whole community, would be creators and maintainers of records. In those colonies with established churches, even local vestries or other congregational officers provided a form of local government, with a heavy emphasis on maintaining detailed records: church records could sometimes be public records.[23] It was taken for granted that those records provided guarantees for all citizens, ensuring legal rights and preventing infringement of those rights either by their fellow citizens or by the government itself. Belief in the importance of keeping records and of making them accessible even took on political and ideological dimensions. Most colonies saw disputes over the physical control of records, together with efforts to inspect the condition of records and to provide for their copying as one means of ensuring their survival and usability. Controversies such as boundary disputes often had colonial officials and their agents drawing on records both here and abroad, conducting a form of research to demonstrate the validity of their claims. In a few colonies, we can even find evidence that they built public records repositories—one can still see such a structure at restored Colonial Williamsburg in Virginia—intended to be more stable and, importantly, fireproof. As the revolutionary crisis deepened in the middle of the eighteenth century, many colonial legislatures adopted the practice of keeping and publishing journals of their proceedings, in large measure to document their resistance to what they took to be unwarranted royal and parliamentary encroachments. Printing was only a more expeditious manner of copying, then and later the primary means of preserving and making accessible American records, until the advent of microfilming and digitizing.

So critical a role did Americans ascribe to impartial, publicly held, and openly available records that they even emphasized them in their most fundamental political testaments. The long indictment of King George III in the Declaration of Independence contained the charge that he had maliciously "called together legislative bodies at places unusual, uncomfortable, and distant from the depository of their public records." Without their records to refer to, the implication ran, the colonists would be unable to defend their rights. The charge related to a temporary transfer of the Massachusetts legislature from Boston to Cambridge—a distance of all of four miles, as the Tory governor Thomas Hutchinson acidly pointed out—but the point had been made nonetheless. The Constitution drafted a decade later included the explicit requirement that the House and Senate keep journals (article I, section 5, paragraph 3), and it gave to Congress the power to determine both the form and the legal force of "acts, records and proceedings" (article IV, section 1). The Fourth Amendment later ensured "the right of the people to be secure in their persons, houses, papers, and effects, against unreasonable searches and seizures." State constitutions and local government charters echoed the importance of records, and various secretaries of state and other officers were given the responsibility to maintain government records. Public authorities did not, of course, always maintain public records as carefully as they should have, any more than roads and bridges were always in good repair. The expectation that governments would keep records on behalf of the citizenry, however, was evident in the United States from the outset and was sanctioned by its highest authorities. We should not overstate the attitudes of the nation's founders and early leaders in a way that conflates republican rhetoric with modern ideas of open access to government records. The idea of an informed citizenry and of the kinds of information citizens should be able to access evolved slowly and sometimes painfully.[24] Still, a tradition of maintaining public records was part of the American experience from the beginning.

Another American approach to records has been called a *historical manuscripts tradition.* Motivated perhaps by a sense that they had just made history, members of the American revolutionary generation turned in their later years to establishing historical societies that would, in the words of one of them, "preserve the manuscripts of the present day to the remotest ages of posterity."[25] The first of these was the Massachusetts Historical Society, formed in 1791, and it was followed eventually by hundreds of state, local, and even national organizations, all devoted to collecting records and documents that were useful for studying and understanding the past.[26] Though many societies collected public records, their main focus was on the private papers of individuals, an impulse encouraged by the steady growth of personal correspondence. Between 1840 and 1860, the number of personal letters per capita increased fivefold, spurred on by improved transportation and lower paper costs.[27] This was also the era of the first craze in autograph collecting, supported by improvements in the postal service, which further encouraged people to write one another asking for autographs.[28] Early historical organizations also collected items other than manuscripts and documents—including objects, artifacts, and scien-

A stylized bust of Jared Sparks, a pioneer editor of historical documents.
COURTESY HARVARD UNIVERSITY PORTRAIT COLLECTION, GIFT OF STUDENTS UNDER
THE PRESIDENCY OF JARED SPARKS TO HARVARD COLLEGE, 1857, S5.

tific specimens—but their principal goal was to preserve documents that supported the growing interest in historical study. Collections of papers that were no longer useful for current, practical purposes became valuable precisely for that reason: even though they no longer affected the present, were important for their insights into the past. Not surprisingly, these societies often reinforced the position of political and social elites who founded them, though with time they broadened their focus to other strata of society as well.[29]

These early efforts to preserve American historical manuscripts applied a twofold approach to the task. The first was simply to gather together whatever papers could be found. The American Antiquarian Society, organized in Worcester, Massachusetts, in 1812, saw its mission as providing "a fixed and permanent place of deposit" for historically valuable materials. A smaller society in Ohio a few years later thought it had made quite an accomplishment by developing a system for keeping its manuscripts in "air-tight metallic cases, regularly numbered and indexed, so that it may be known what is in each case without opening it." American historians learned early to rely on such collections for the original documents they needed in their investigations. The young George Bancroft had returned from Europe in 1822 with an understanding of how to use manuscript sources as evidence in his studies of American history and the American character, and his example was quickly followed by the other scholars of his era, many of whom were prolific collectors of their own source materials. By the 1880s, Herbert Baxter Adams of Johns Hopkins University was training a new generation of "scientific" historians who viewed historical scholarship as valid only to the extent that it was solidly grounded in the critical use of original documentary sources.[30] His students first met in the rooms of the Maryland Historical Society, surrounded by manuscript collections and other primary sources, and then in a specially designed seminar room, described as a "laboratory," with additional historical documents close at hand for research and experimentation.

The second approach to records preservation in the historical manuscripts tradition embraced the editing and publication of the texts of these records. Gathering documents into repositories where they would be secure and well cared for was certainly essential, but fears lingered nonetheless that accident or natural disaster might still result in their loss. Against that possibility, publication was the most effective remedy, as it had been for centuries: at least the information that was in the records would be saved, even if the originals themselves were somehow destroyed. "There is no sure way of preserving historical records and materials, but by *multiplying the copies*," declared the Massachusetts Historical Society, embarking on a program to publish its collections in 1806. The printing press was an effective preservation tool, and considerable effort went into compiling, editing, and publishing historical manuscripts. Ebenezer Hazard of Philadelphia issued two volumes of *Historical Collections* in the 1790s, and in the next generation Peter Force oversaw production of multivolume sets of *Tracts* and *American Archives.* Jared Sparks, a future president of Harvard College, likewise contributed to this movement in the 1830s by producing the first published edition of the letters of George Washington, a collection of Benjamin Franklin papers, and a compilation of Revolutionary War diplomatic correspondence. Many other scholars have followed suit, and the tradition of producing carefully edited texts of historical documents endures to this day, emerging by the mid-twentieth century as a distinct branch of historical scholarship with its own meticulous standards.[31]

Throughout most of the nineteenth century, these two activities of collecting and publishing historical manuscripts were generally more successful than the parallel efforts to preserve and manage public records. In government settings, the people responsible for keeping and managing records were public officials, including town and county clerks, clerks of courts at various levels, and secretaries of state or other government bodies. Except for instances where private and public historical societies acquired government records—the Maryland Historical Society, for instance, held many colonial- and revolutionary-era government records from its founding in 1844 until the creation of a state archives in 1934—government archives were often neglected and difficult to use.[32] These officials collected and maintained records as a part of doing their jobs, but recordkeeping was only one of their many duties. As a result, attention to older, retrospective, and less frequently used records generally took a back seat to more immediate demands, including the proper management of records needed in current business. The general expectation certainly was that public records would be retained into the indefinite future, but the energy and resources devoted specifically to records problems were too often minimal. Nor was specialized records-training for personnel very systematic. As one reads through legislative acts and executive orders regarding public records, it is easy to see that these records were loosely administered; legislative proceedings often commented on the problems caused by local officials who maintained official files in their homes or places of business rather than at the courthouse or other public building. Most public "archivists"—it is misleading even to use the word in this context—came to their archival duties through the channels of public administration rather than through any preexisting association with records.[33]

In the historical manuscripts tradition, by contrast, the custodians of records came to their task with an interest in historical

research, and thus a concern for the raw materials supporting research, already fully formed. Many of the nation's leading amateur
historians, along with those interested in the past for its help in the
cause of economic "boosterism," were among the founders of historical societies and similar organizations. What is more, they found
themselves working in historical societies and research institutions in
which the value of caring for archival materials was already taken for
granted: indeed, it was at the very core of their mission. In these institutions, the manuscripts room and the research library with its rare
collections were the heart of the organization. The distinction they
made between historical research generally and archival work in particular was neither sharp nor significant, since both the preservation
of documentary materials and their use in writing history were
viewed as parts of the same whole. Curators in those settings knew
that they acquired, preserved, and published historical records precisely so they could be used, as often as not by the curators themselves.
The best preparation for archivists—again the word is not entirely
appropriate—in historical manuscripts settings was therefore training
in historical research and writing. The treatment of historical records
was more like that given to precious physical artifacts, and, in many
instances, there was little distinction made between organizational
records, personal papers, decorative arts, material culture, and even the
often odd mementos that reflected the antiquarian bent of these institutions.[34] While the private historical societies often served the interests of
social class and filiopietism, they also at times seemed to be as much
about entertainment and amusement (similar to the dime museums
and circuses of the period) or the educational functions of public lectures by scientists and inventors demonstrating their knowledge.[35]

Emergence of the Archival Profession

The rapid expansion of the historical profession at the end of the
nineteenth century led first to a greater concern for taking care of the
sources of history; ultimately, it brought about formation of a distinct
archival profession in the United States. History was a lively discipline
in the Gilded Age, and signs of its vigor and growth were readily

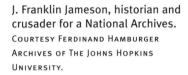

J. Franklin Jameson, historian and crusader for a National Archives.
COURTESY FERDINAND HAMBURGER ARCHIVES OF THE JOHNS HOPKINS UNIVERSITY.

apparent. American historians drank deeply at the well of European historical method, introducing into this country the rigorous continental approach to graduate education and scholarship that demanded close, critical reliance on primary sources to determine (in the words of their German slogan) *wie es eigentlich gewesen ist*—"what actually happened" in history. History, like many other disciplines, was seen as a science, a search for universal laws and principles, with its raw data the evidence and information contained in documents. It is no wonder, then, that so many historians supported the establishment of archives and the publication of documentary sources.[36] The American Historical Association (AHA), formed in 1884, committed itself to the promotion of these goals, and just before the turn of the century, it undertook an effort that would focus attention specifically on archival and records problems.

Under the leadership of J. Franklin Jameson, the longtime director of the historical research bureau of the Carnegie Institution and later the leader in the movement to establish the National Archives, the AHA established an Historical Manuscripts Commission in 1895, charged initially with the responsibility to find out what original sources were available for study. Almost immediately, the effort proved more complicated than first envisioned. Eliciting usable responses to a mail survey of historical societies and private collectors of manuscripts was difficult, and the commission was chagrined to discover that "some of the societies evince a desire to keep their documents from public knowledge." The commission's members also emphasized documentary publication over the more basic problem of collecting, arguing that nothing would "win the confidence of collectors and possessors [of manuscripts] so well as the sight of a volume of good historical material, well edited." Commission members were easily sidetracked by their own research interests, focusing on the production of documentary editions (among them an early publication of the John C. Calhoun Papers) before they had laid an adequate general groundwork for understanding the problems of historical manuscripts as a whole. Concurrent effort by the Library of Congress to begin organizing its holdings of original documents was a positive step, but the care of private manuscripts remained a scattered, uncoordinated affair.[37]

Despite this not very promising start, the work of the Historical Manuscripts Commission had an impact in large measure because it helped spawn another, more specialized body within the AHA: the Public Archives Commission, established in 1899. Devoted by design to the special problems of government records, this group was much more active than its parent, seeking not only to identify what public records existed but also, through a network of historians and interested citizens in almost every state, to encourage better care of those records. The effort coincided with a larger interest in scientific management and efficiency throughout the Progressive Era, concerns that were applied to the administration (usually defined to mean crisp, effective organization and retrieval) of records within repositories.[38] Government committees were busy studying big business for clues to improving control over burgeoning paperwork, on the assumption that the sound administration of records was a key to sound administration in general. The Public Archives Commission eventually surveyed and reported on the archives of thirty states, as well as those of New York City and Philadelphia, and it also turned into an effective lobbying organization for the passage of archival legislation. It began work on what it hoped would become a standard textbook for records work, a "manual of archival economy," but the volume was never completed. Most important of all, in 1909 the commission helped call into being within the AHA a Conference of Archivists, a group that would become the locus of professional archival activity.[39]

The commission also helped encourage emerging archival activity in the states, and many state archives programs came into being at the same time. Led by states in the Deep South (partly from a desire to preserve the history of "the lost cause"), public authorities began to take seriously their responsibility to care for their records. Alabama was first in 1901, founding a state department of archives and history, a move that was imitated by Mississippi a year later and by other states elsewhere in the South and Midwest in the remainder of that decade. In 1906, the territory of Hawaii, which would not achieve statehood until fifty years later, became the first American political jurisdiction to construct a building specifically designed as an archives facility. The movement to establish state archives would not be complete until 1978, when New York became the last state to do so.[40] The movement to care for public records helped produce a growing body of technical publications on how archives should be organized and managed. In particular, these state archives found it necessary to abandon quirky, in-house classification schemes based on subject analysis and to rely instead on state administrative structure as the most flexible and appropriate system for managing state records.[41]

The AHA Conference of Archivists continued its work amid these encouraging developments, and it became increasingly interested in the promotion of archival programs where they did not already exist. The most obvious deficiency was the absence of any national archives to care for the voluminous records of the government of the United States. Since at least the 1880s, historians had recognized the need for such an agency and had worked to fill the gap. Two scholars, C. H. Van Tyne and Waldo G. Leland, had compiled a *Guide to the Archives of the Government of the United States* in 1904, a work that only highlighted how dispersed and disorganized federal records were. The cause of establishing a national archives worthy of the name was soon taken up by the tireless Jameson, who lobbied successive presidents and Congresses to commit the funds necessary for the task. In the period between the two world wars, these efforts finally paid off.[42] At the same time, the American Library Association saw its interest in archival matters wane (although these interests were never great or sustained in comparison to those of historians), and it would not be until some decades later that the association's archival interests would reemerge, mostly in preservation management and conservation.[43] The development of archives would thereafter be principally the work of archivists themselves.

The Crucial Decade: The 1930s

As frequently happens, legislators found it easier to visualize a national archives as a building than as a program, a problem that persists and is not confined to government officials. Accordingly, the first encouraging step came with a congressional appropriation in 1926, after nearly forty years of lobbying, to acquire a site and begin construction of a building to house federal records. Construction proceeded slowly; the cornerstone was not laid until 1933. By that time, however, concern over the services and materials to put into the building was getting attention, and in 1934, amid the rush of New Deal legislation, Congress passed a bill establishing the National Archives as an independent federal agency reporting directly to the president. Later that year, President Franklin Roosevelt, an avid reader of history who had been eager to see the archives established, appointed Robert D. W. Connor of North Carolina as the first Archivist of the United States. The nation at last had a pinnacle to its archival system, an institution to provide national leadership for the development of archival theory and practice.[44]

Concurrently, another crucial movement—this one to form a distinct professional organization for American archivists—was coming to fruition. The Conference of Archivists had continued to meet annually at the convention of the American Historical Association, but many conference participants perceived the need for a separate society. Not only was the number of practicing archivists approaching a "critical mass," but also the more precise, technical concerns of archivists were demanding increased attention. Historians continued to focus necessarily on the use and interpretation of archival records, whereas archivists were concerned with more fundamental questions: what were the best ways to identify, gather, and organize those records? Professional interests were diverging as each side felt a need for specialization.

Meeting in Providence, Rhode Island, in December 1936, the conference transformed itself into the Society of American Archivists (SAA). Rejecting earlier proposals that only the directors of large archival institutions be eligible for membership, the society adopted a more democratic view of itself, welcoming all "who are or have been engaged in the custody or administration of archives or historical manuscripts." SAA began the practice of holding an annual convention of its own in 1937, a gathering that would remain the single most important meeting of archivists each year. From the beginning, the rate of participation in these meetings was always high (often more than half the total membership) in comparison with that of other professional organizations, giving the profession a lively sense of solidarity. In 1938, the society took the next important step toward the development and promotion of professional identity by beginning publication of a quarterly (later, semiannual) journal, *The American Archivist*. Reflecting on the Rhode Island genesis of the organization, more than one SAA president would later attribute its success to the "blessings of Providence."[45]

Yet a third development in the 1930s marked that decade as the critical one for the development of the archival profession: the Historical Records Survey (HRS) of the Works Progress Administration (WPA). As a part of the New Deal's efforts to combat unemployment, the WPA provided public works jobs, some involving scholarly work. These included a program to survey the historical records of state and local governments as well as those in private repositories. First organized in late 1933, the HRS sent teams of archival field workers to repositories of all kinds to identify their holdings and sometimes to prepare both general guides and finding aids for particular collections.

On the whole, public records repositories received most of the attention—more than 90 percent of the counties across the nation got at least some survey work—but other archives were included as well. In some states, church records were a high priority, while in others the microfilming of records that were physically deteriorating was the focus of activity. The survey began with ambitious plans to publish the results of its work, though by the time the program wound to a con-

Archives pioneers, Margaret Cross Norton and Theodore Roosevelt (T.R.) Schellenberg. PHOTOGRAPHS COURTESY SOCIETY OF AMERICAN ARCHIVISTS.

clusion at the end of the decade, the published results were not nearly so extensive as first intended. Still, the original survey forms survived in many states to serve as a guide for future archival work, providing a "snapshot" of what records had been in existence at that time. The principal goal of the HRS, of course, had always been to put people to work, rather than to promote the care of archival records as such. Even so, the latter goal had also been accomplished, together with the unanticipated result of providing a new generation of budding archivists with practical experience and an entrance into the profession.[46]

Meanwhile, both within the National Archives and elsewhere, what would later be recognized as the founding generation of American archivists was beginning to articulate a body of archival theory and the application of that theory to the particular problems of modern records. The National Archives staff began to publish a series of *Circulars* and *Bulletins* on technical matters, many of which remain in use today.[47] Throughout the 1930s, because they were building the national archival collection from scratch, these archivists had to find a way to acquire and organize large quantities of records efficiently. There were only a few European theorists to rely on, and

American archivists faced the question of whether those writings were applicable to the American scene. They took as their standard the principles that had been laid down by Sir Hilary Jenkinson, the premier British archivist of the early twentieth century, and by three Dutch archivists (Samuel Muller, J. A. Feith, and Robert Fruin) in their 1898 textbook, *Manual for the Arrangement and Description of Archives*; a staff member of the National Archives helpfully translated the Dutch manual into English.[48] Those principles demanded strict attention to the administrative structure that produced the records as the surest guide to organizing them.

With these broad theories in hand, American archivists set out to apply them. Margaret Cross Norton, archivist of the State of Illinois for more than thirty-five years, argued eloquently for the administrative importance of archives, and she almost single-handedly convinced her colleagues that there was more to their profession than esoteric historical scholarship.[49] Administrative usefulness demanded an administrative approach. Led by Theodore Roosevelt Schellenberg (a historian from Kansas and an alumnus of the National Park Service) and Oliver Wendell Holmes (another historian, who was no relation to his poetic and judicial namesakes), the staff of the National Archives evolved the modern notions of record groups and record series, a set of concepts that became influential and useful far beyond Washington.[50] By developing this way of arranging records, these early archivists helped to define a structural way of looking at archives, regardless of the particular administrative organization that had produced them. This structural approach to modern records became characteristic of all archivists. It proved to be very flexible: even though it had originally been put to use to organize government archives, it was equally applicable to the archives of other institutions, including schools, religious organizations, businesses, and voluntary associations. Schellenberg's paper applying these European principles to America was first distributed within the National Archives as a staff circular in 1939, but its influence was broad and long lasting.[51] Jenkinson, Norton, and Schellenberg all helped codify early archival practice, and the influence of their writings has been immense. Though sometimes challenged in subsequent years, they nonetheless set the parameters of debate about archival knowledge and practice.[52]

Diversification and Development

The period following the Second World War was one of diversification for American archives. The number of repositories grew at a steady rate and eventually included archives in organizations and settings that were previously thought unlikely hosts for them. At the same time, fortified by a growing body of archival theory and a number of "flagship" archives, the profession expanded its intellectual boundaries. Greater specialization was both possible and necessary, as archivists confronted the increasing complexity and importance of their task.

Specialization was nowhere more evident than in a growing differentiation between archives and current records management during the 1950s and 1960s. The growth in quantity and variety of records that came with the expansion of government activity and the demands of wartime had affected private as well as public records. It was increasingly necessary to confront the problem of bulk by gaining some measure of control over active records, long before they found their way to the archives—if indeed they ever did. At the same time, an increasing volume of records demanded that archivists become more selective in what they added to their collections, since it was plainly becoming impossible to save everything. Not only would total preservation exhaust storage space and financial resources overnight; it would also multiply the intellectual problems of understanding and organizing what had been saved. If every single record were preserved—routine correspondence, invoices, overlapping financial reports, duplicate copies, cancelled checks—how would the wheat be distinguished from the chaff? What is more, the development of a distinct archival profession demanded that choices about records retention be made deliberately and that consistent standards be applied in making those choices. Survival of valuable records could not be left to chance, and the standards for deciding what would survive had to be the same this week as last. Whether they were creating the National Archives or a new organizational archives, archivists had to make do with whatever records fortune had left them, but they sought to reduce the role of chance, so that their successors would not face the same problem. Many federal government agencies hired records managers for the first time, and they often looked to the staff of the National Archives or to individuals who had gained experience with administering records in the military during the war. Private corporations, too, established records management programs.

The result was the emergence of records management as a distinct profession. SAA had established a Committee on the Reduction of Archival Material in its early years, and that group worked to define the principles and procedures for reducing the quantity of records while retaining the quality of information. Government commissions on paperwork reduction became a recurring part of the political and administrative landscape, while business firms and other private entities devoted attention to legal and financial needs, as well as the general efficiency that a carefully planned records program could promote. Originally at home within the SAA, this formative group of records managers began to perceive their interests as diverging from some of the more scholarly interests of archivists, especially those associated with the historical manuscripts and research tradition. Accordingly, a separate organization, the American Records Management Association (ARMA: the acronym now stands for the Association of Records Managers and Administrators), was organized in 1956. The division of the two groups of professionals has not been without problems, not least the loss of symmetry in understanding the concept of records life cycle or continuum. Many organizations have archives but no records management or vice versa. Moreover, organizational leaders often have a hard time discerning the difference between archivists and records managers, creating problems in getting such programs started and in knowing whom to hire.[53]

Even after this split, however, the growing interest in records management as a subset of archival work offered archivists many opportunities. To begin with, by systematizing the means by which records were identified for eventual archival preservation, it offered the prospect of more complete and better archival collections. Archivists had always been interested in preserving "good stuff" (that is, important and useful information), sweeping the "bad stuff" out of the way, both intellectually and physically. Records management offered a more efficient way of doing just that. At the same time, when records management and archival concerns could be combined in a single program, archivists acquired an additional argument to present to administrators about the value and usefulness of their work. In tandem with records management, archives could be seen not merely as scholarly research institutions—fine in themselves, of course, but not really relevant to practical concerns and thus susceptible to elimination during budget cutting time. Archivists found they could strengthen the case for their programs by adding the benefits of administrative efficiency through records management to the historical and cultural benefits of archives. Sometimes, they made this argument too well: in 1949, a government reorganization commission placed the National Archives within the General Services Administration (the federal housekeeping agency), an unhappy marriage from which the archives did not reemerge as an independent agency until 1985. Still, many archivists in and out of government came to appreciate the benefits of combining concern for current records with concern for older records.

About the same time as records management established itself as a distinct field, the discipline of information science was also beginning to take shape. Information science, the systematic study of collecting, controlling, classifying, storing, and retrieving recorded information, has been variously connected to library science, computer science, informatics, statistics, and other social sciences. Computer scientists, spurred on by the need to improve code breaking, military weaponry, and various logistical support activities and by the arms race and intelligence gathering during the Cold War, gradually joined with others to support the new field. These developments created still greater differentiation of professions involved in records generation control. In the 1950s and 1960s, the impact of information science on archival work was modest, but the foundation was laid for influences ranging from educational preparation of records personnel to the organization and classification of the information found in records.

By the 1950s, virtually every state had a records program of some kind. Support for such programs was uneven, as Ernst Posner, the foremost archival educator of his generation, concluded in a survey of state archives published in 1964. Still, the legal foundations for archival development in state government were generally strong. At the same time, with the broad expansion of higher education in the postwar period, many colleges and universities established formal archival programs to care for their own administrative records, as well as their collections of manuscripts, rare books, and other "special" items. Major national research collections that focused on particular subject areas—women's history, immigration and ethnicity, and international affairs, to name but a few—also flourished, buttressed by a new emphasis of scholars on social history.[54] By the 1970s, religious archives, which had previously been confined largely to the mainline Protestant denominations, were expanding rapidly. New archives were established at a sometimes dizzying pace, especially among Roman Catholic dioceses and orders of nuns, as well as among evangelical Protestant, Jewish, and other groups. Concurrently, interest in the archives of business organizations increased. Spreading beyond a few large firms, business archives were founded throughout the for-profit sector, both to support company operations and to assist in public relations and advertising.[55]

The effect of this diversification was to bring under archival control a far greater variety of recorded information than would otherwise have been available. Each type of archives could define its collecting interests more precisely, focusing on a narrower portion of the possible documentary universe and thus concentrating its attention and resources. In an earlier era, with only a few collecting agencies—such as state archives or large research-oriented historical societies—the collecting scope of American archival institutions was necessarily limited, guided by a traditional definition of history. In that kind of archival world, only the members of small, elite groups were considered important historical characters; relatively few people were thought to be worthy subjects of historical study and, therefore, worthy candidates for having their papers preserved and organized. In studying the American Revolution, for example, one wanted to know what George Washington and John Adams thought and did, not what ordinary soldiers or their wives back home thought and did. What is more, since history was a deliberately literary effort, relying on literary sources, only the leading classes (that is, the most literate) left the records that were thought necessary for successful history. Accordingly, archives collected and organized the papers of figures such as Washington and Adams while overlooking, whether deliberately or tacitly, the records of ordinary people.

Criticism of this approach to history coincided with the widening variety of archives to broaden the scope of records preservation. In the late 1960s and early 1970s, American historians embraced what was called a new social history, an approach that studied large numbers of ordinary people, not just their leaders. Drawing increasingly on rapidly developing computer technologies to manipulate large quantities of primary source data, researchers turned to archives with entirely new questions and needs. They wanted to look at history not from the top down, they said, but from the bottom up. As one of the leading proponents of this view pointed out, it was no longer sufficient to lavish attention on "the papers of great white men," or even on "the papers of a few great black men and a few great white women." Rather, a more encompassing historical vision was needed, one that required a broader base of archival collections. Fortunately, the diversification of archives addressed this need. As long as elite, private historical societies were the dominant collectors of archival records, the archives of certain groups of people would always be overlooked. With a variety of new religious, ethnic, and social history archives coming into existence, a fuller range of sources was available for use.[56] While this diversification expanded considerably the poten- tial for what archives would collect, it also necessarily placed greater importance on the question of how archives decided what records they would keep. This heightened interest in the appraisal theories and techniques archives used. By the 1980s, lively discussions ensued about the meaning and methods of archival appraisal and acquisition.[57]

More than the intensifying demand for new information encouraged the development of American archives. It was also aided materially by a sudden infusion of grant money to support a wide range of archival projects. The National Endowment for the Humanities, created in 1965 as part of President Lyndon Johnson's Great Society, became a regular supporter of archival endeavors, in addition to its other scholarly interests. It offered "challenge grants" to help broaden the financial base of libraries and archives, and it encouraged applications to prepare descriptions and published guides to collections. It supported multirepository surveys of archival holdings pertaining to specific topics, the most notable of which was probably the two-volume *Women's History Sources,* which appeared in 1979. The endowment also took an active interest in the identification and preservation through microfilming of historic newspapers, investing millions of dollars over the years in such efforts based in the individual states. Endowment funds were obviously welcomed by archives and libraries, the more so because of the way federal funds could be used to draw matching money out of private foundations and sources, together with increased internal support from an archives' own parent organization.[58]

Of even greater impact for archivists were the programs of the National Historical Publications and Records Commission (NHPRC). First organized to provide support for the preparation of scholarly editions of the papers of the founding fathers, the commission's scope was expanded in 1975 to permit it to assist a wider variety of archival projects. Though it received only limited funding that was constantly threatened with budgetary elimination, the records program of the NHPRC distributed its resources widely, achieving far-reaching results by means of active, aggressive planning. It supported the establishment of new archival programs in the public and private sectors, and these served as models for similar institutions. It intervened to support the rescue of "endangered records," particularly those that were threatened with destruction because no likely repository seemed available to take them. It underwrote a range of educational projects, both those for the education of professional archivists (including preparation of a set of basic manuals on archival procedures published by SAA in 1977—a first in America) and those designed to educate administrators on the importance of archival programs. Beginning in the early 1980s, it funded "assessment reports" in nearly every state, the first systematic attempt to take stock of the total American archival scene since the WPA Historical Records Survey. In the 1990s the NHPRC was a leader in sponsoring research on the management of electronic records. The commission has perhaps been a dominant influence in the enhancement of the modern American archival community, although the full range of its activities has yet to be critically evaluated.[59]

Finally, archival diversification was also evident in an expanding base of professional organizations. Since the 1930s, SAA had been the only association in which archivists met one another to discuss common concerns. By the 1970s, however, professional energy was seeking other outlets. As a result, new archival associations were formed across the country, organized around local, state, or multistate areas. These "regionals," as they came to be called, were less formal than SAA, but as their numbers grew their influence was substantial. Within fifteen years, there were more than fifty of them, some with membership approaching a thousand.[60] Smaller, less expensive to join, and perhaps less intimidating for beginning archivists, these organizations provided the benefits of professional membership to the growing number of archivists working in small, new archives. Because they were confined to specific geographic areas, their meetings were easy to attend. Most produced newsletters for the exchange of local archival information, and some even began publication of journals that provided additional sources of professional literature. Some embarked on educational programs that provided basic and advanced workshops. These regional archival associations made the tools and attitudes of professionalism more accessible, and they thus assisted in the ongoing democratization of American archives. Other new associations were formed around the concerns of managing particular kinds of records. The National Association of Government Archives and Records Administrators (1972) and the Association of Moving Image Archivists (1991) were established because of concerns that SAA was not providing sufficient attention to their special problems. These groups were helpful on their own terms, though they did make it more difficult to build a sense of professional community that encompasses the diversity of archivists and archival programs. This problem has been addressed in part by the creation of listservs and other online means for interaction, which have already proven to be important factors in the continuing consolidation of the archival identity.

Consolidation of Professional Identity

Even as the archival profession became more diversified, its identity began to consolidate in several critical ways. The recent past has witnessed many signs of this ongoing consolidation. A period of growth for archives, begun in the 1970s and 1980s, continues, as new repositories come into existence and new professionals are appointed to care for them. Archivists achieved both sufficient numbers and sufficient institutional stability so that they could turn their attention to solidifying the gains they had previously made. Discussion about what they did, how they did it, and why they did it was lively, a sign of intellectual dynamism. The growing numbers of archives, archivists, and users of archives fueled a renewed sense of direction for the profession and, amid the vagaries of particular issues, a consensus began to take shape, particularly focused on issues of standardization and professionalism.

Standardization had always been problematic for archivists because they placed such emphasis on the idea of uniqueness.[61] Their collections were unique by definition: each archives contained original records and documents that were necessarily different from those in any other repository. As a result, archivists often presumed that the procedures for managing their collections also had to be unique. Every archives collection was different, so it seemed unavoidable that every archives repository would have its own way of doing things. Archivists acknowledged certain general theoretical principles, to be sure, but they were always prepared to allow each repository the freedom to apply those principles in its own way. What is more, archivists tacitly accepted the idea that how any given repository applied those principles was pretty much its own business. Agreement on common standards might be desirable, but the applicability of those standards was thought to be limited. When archivists prepared published guides to their holdings, they generally worked in isolation, following the traditions and procedures developed within their own four walls. When archivists acquired new collections, they often operated unilaterally or competed with other repositories. In teaching courses about archives, they usually focused on their own institutions and sought primarily to attract students to work as interns within their own repositories.[62]

During the period of professional consolidation, this attitude began to change, as archivists realized that much standardization was possible without compromising the uniqueness of their holdings. An early move in this direction was the appearance in the late 1950s of the *National Union Catalog of Manuscript Collections (NUCMC)*, which was published in bound volumes until 1994, when it was replaced with an online version. Produced by the Library of Congress and patterned after its *National Union Catalog* for printed books, NUCMC attempted to gather standard information about archival collections from widely differing repositories and to reduce that information to a uniform catalog card format. The archives reporting to it might be large or small, well endowed or impoverished; the collections reported might possess national or merely local importance. Still, the same basic information—the creator or compiler of the papers, what kinds of records they were, their inclusive dates, their quantity, a brief description of their contents—was gathered about all of them so as to provide potential researchers, as well as other archivists, with systematic information about holdings. By the middle 1970s, SAA and other professional groups were actively exploring ways to expand these common efforts.[63]

Advancing technology aided this process. Libraries had great incentives for applying automated methods to their work, resulting in more efficient (and therefore cheaper) systems for acquisitions, cataloging, reference, and circulation. With increasingly sophisticated technology, archivists found that they, too, could take advantage of it for their own special problems. As archives faced the prospects and benefits of interinstitutional cooperation in automated formats—sharing information about related collections, for example, or even about large collections that were divided among more than one repository—they recognized the necessity of trying to ensure that everyone was speaking the same language.

After some early efforts toward developing a standard descriptive format for archival and manuscript materials, SAA in 1977 formed a National Information Systems Task Force, charged with searching for the common ground among unique repositories. The group eventually constructed an elaborate and expandable system of "data elements." Every archives might be unique, but each one wanted to know and disseminate the same information about its holdings. The same data elements were present in every collection regardless of size, content, or context. When tied to a system of "electronic pigeon-holes," these data elements became the basis for an automated format that all archives could use to control, describe, and share information about their holdings. This was finally given fixed form with the creation of what was called MARC AMC: the Archival and Manuscripts Control format of the United States Machine Readable Cataloging system. Thanks to this push from technology, the kind of standardization that had come to library book cataloging almost one hundred years before was now possible for archives as well.[64] Descriptive standards continued to develop thereafter, leading in 1995 to Encoded Archival Description (EAD), based on an international Standard Generalized Markup Language (SGML) and later updated to conform to the Extensible Markup Language (XML). This format made it possible for archivists to put detailed, searchable finding aids to specific collections on the World Wide Web, which was becoming popular just at that time, and this provided an added benefit to archival users that MARC records had been unable to provide.[65]

For all practical purposes, this movement in the direction of standardization resulted in a merger of the distinct public archives and historical manuscripts traditions out of which the archival profession had developed at the beginning of the twentieth century. Archives in the two traditions might contain very different materials, and they might serve very different types of users. Those differences did not justify entirely distinct procedures, however, and all archivists began to appreciate the similarities. Even the separate terminology that had grown up in each tradition seemed decreasingly significant. Public archives had been accustomed to producing "inventories" of their holdings, for example, while collections of historical manuscripts often described their finding aids as "registers." In the warming air of standardization, archivists acknowledged this to be a distinction without a difference, since all repositories wanted to know and record the same things about their collections in the effort to make them usable.[66] Some distinctions remained between collecting and institutional repositories, of course, and these differences often played out in debates about electronic records management, the education of entry-level archivists, and the relative importance of cultural and other values, such as evidence and accountability.[67] Even so, standardization showed that there was much common ground for archivists to explore.

At the same time, concern for standardization met concern for improved professionalism in an extended discussion of the nature

and quality of professional credentials, an important topic in any continuing professionalization process. What kind of knowledge and
skills should archivists have, and how should they acquire them? For
the early generations of American archivists, the answers to those
questions had often been informal and unpredictable. Archivists were
most often individuals who had fallen into their profession on the way
to or from something else. Many had entered the field through an
interest in historical research in a particular subject, while others had
come to it as a specialized form of librarianship. They had picked up
the specific tasks and techniques of their work, together with general
professional acculturation, as they went along, "learning by doing" in
apprenticeship arrangements within particular repositories. What
formal training there was came in the form of postappointment (that
is, after one was already working as an archivist) workshops or short
institutes, such as those sponsored jointly by the National Archives
and American University, directed for many years by Ernst Posner.[68]

Such an uneven approach to professional preparation had many
disadvantages, not least that it focused almost exclusively on archival
arrangement and description, just two of the principal archival functions. By the 1970s, however, a number of formal archival education
programs had begun to emerge in American universities. Situated
either in history departments or in library schools (and sometimes in
joint programs), this coursework attempted to provide an extended
and detailed form of preappointment education for budding
archivists. The number of courses devoted specifically to archival topics remained limited, though these offered more sustained attention
to archival matters than had been available in short workshops. Many
such education programs fell into a pattern of offering two courses,
usually a one-semester introduction followed by an advanced seminar. Most also had an internship or practicum component, in which
students got experience in organizing an archival collection by working in an archives. A few required a thesis that entailed a larger practicum project or, sometimes, research in a topic relating to archival
theory. These programs offered a less haphazard entry into the profession, but for many years archival education remained scattered and
small scale. Most programs relied on adjunct or part-time faculty,
usually working archivists with responsibilities in repositories of their

own (often the sponsoring university's own archivist) who also taught on the side.[69] The concurrent emergence of public history, broadly defined as the presentation of history to the public or the use of history in formulating public policy, paralleled the expansion of archival education, but it had less impact. In such programs, one or two courses in archives joined a smorgasbord of other topics (editing and museum management, for instance), and it was difficult for students to study much about any one of them. The rise of public history did little to strengthen the educational preparation of someone wanting specifically to be an archivist.[70]

Though formal archival educational efforts began in this somewhat halting manner, they did help the profession clarify its thinking about credentials and education in several ways. First, they effectively established a graduate degree, usually at the master's level, as the presumed qualification for beginning archivists. Those entering the profession might still bring to their work a variety of backgrounds, but a master's degree—in history or library science or both, and in any event with some specific archives coursework and experience—was proper for entry into the profession. Many archivists obtained both a subject master's degree and a master's in library and information science, with at least one of the two featuring a concentration of courses in archival studies. Second, the increasing number of archival education programs situated within different university settings raised the question of standardizing curriculum content. SAA first addressed this problem in 1977 by issuing a set of graduate education guidelines, a description of the subject matter to be covered in archives courses; more detailed versions of these guidelines were published in 1988, 1994, and 2002.[71] The process of refinement will no doubt continue in the future, though there has been little enthusiasm for the accreditation of archival education programs (similar to that for library education by the American Library Association) or for the development of a separate academic degree in archival studies, such as the one that emerged in Canada in the 1980s. Finally, the development of archival education led by the middle 1980s to the appointment of a handful of full-time archival educators, a number that rose to about thirty in North America by the end of the twentieth century. These were archivists who were freed from the responsibilities of managing repositories to devote themselves entirely to teaching and to research about their discipline.[72]

Progress in the field of archival education was never entirely smooth, and there were steps backward as well as forward. Well into the 1970s, it was possible for someone to enter the field by taking merely a course or two in either a history department or a school of library and information sciences.[73] By the 1980s, the appearance of full-time faculty was connected to the growth of the knowledge supporting archival work, but where archivists should be educated and who should teach them remained subjects for debate.[74] During the 1980s and 1990s, most of those joining the ranks of graduate archival educators had had long careers in the field, possessed a doctorate, and had a publication record (or the potential for one) befitting tenure-track faculty positions. By the end of the century, however, this supply had dried up. The posting of announcements for faculty positions teaching in archives had far outstripped the availability of qualified individuals to hold these posts, and the shortage of faculty threatened to weaken the further development of graduate archival education. This in turn threatened to limit the number of qualified individuals prepared for archival careers, even as it inhibited the continued development of the discipline's research literature.

At the same time, however, the profession explored two other efforts to improve archival professionalism. One was through a focus on institutional evaluation, in which archival repositories would be studied, either by their own staff or by archivists from elsewhere, and measured with a view toward improving their procedures. No formal program for rating or accrediting archival institutions took shape, and while SAA published successively more refined models for self-study that archivists could use in their own repositories, few took advantage of them systematically. On another front, SAA in 1987 established a procedure for certifying individual archivists, similar to the certification of other professionals, including accountants, records managers, and some kinds of specialized librarians. Making certification available first by "grandfathering" those who could present a specified level of professional experience, the plan was designed to shift the basis for certification to successful completion of an examination.[75] By 1989, a sufficient number of archivists had applied for grandfathering that an autonomous Academy of Certified Archivists had come into existence to oversee the administration of future exams and procedures, but the number of those sitting for the exam each year has remained small. Nor did employers typically demand this credential in filling archival jobs. Like institutional evaluation, individual certification had only limited effect.[76]

The theme in all these efforts, however, was the improvement of professional standards and credentials in the hope of improving archival practice. Channeling professional energy in this way produced other evidence of the consolidation of archival identity. In particular, for the first time since the 1930s, many archivists devoted sustained attention to studying and writing about archival theory, attempting to reexamine the existing intellectual basis for archives work and to push it in new directions. By the 1980s, what one observer called "the age of archival analysis" brought renewed intellectual vigor to the profession. The professional journals began to publish articles that questioned some of the most basic assumptions archivists had made about their work, a welcome change from a preponderance of articles that had merely described practice. One controversial essay, for example, argued that long-held archival collections be periodically reappraised and subsequently destroyed if they no longer seemed valuable. Others challenged the record group concept that had served as the basis for archival arrangement activities. More recent writings, grappling with the new digital technologies, have even questioned the very nature of what constitutes a record. For fifteen years, the most successful incubator of study was the Bentley Historical Library of the University of Michigan. With the support of public and private granting agencies, the Bentley summer fellowship program fostered the study of a range of subjects and contributed significantly to improving the professional literature.[77]

Other groups of archivists also came together around particular problems of archival research, and they produced studies that had implications beyond their own institutions. Two separate groups, for instance, studied the problems of preserving an adequate record of modern science and technology. Their conclusions about the problem of twentieth-century records in general—how to save enough in circumstances in which it was obviously impossible to save everything—

proved useful even to those archivists whose collections had nothing to do with science. A group of Canadian archivists addressed the problem of standards for archival description and finding aids, and a comparable body in the United States took up the same cause. Some professionals experimented with a more planned, deliberate approach to the problems of records appraisal and urged adoption of what they called "documentation strategies," an often-misunderstood phrase that evoked passionate discussion. Most ambitiously of all, SAA established a committee, expressly designed as a kind of "archival think tank" and called "GAP" after its mandate to propose "Goals and Priorities" for the entire profession, not just for individual repositories. The result was a succession of comprehensive planning documents that set forth a professional mission for archivists, as well as detailed recommendations for steps to realize that mission. Skeptics dismissed these efforts as too much introspection, absorbing energy that might better be applied to the concrete archival tasks of getting and organizing records. Others viewed the active reexamination of traditional theory and practice as essential parts of any living and growing profession.[78] In either case, most archivists agree that a great many questions and problems remain, requiring considerably more research and thought.

Current Issues

Describing the history of the archival profession is a safer, surer business than predicting its future. That it has a future, however, is beyond question. Dire predictions that rapid advances in the technology that produces recorded information will make obsolete earlier forms (and therefore make similarly obsolete the archivists who care for them) are exaggerated; we had these same predictions two and three decades ago, and archives and archivists are still here.[79] New technologies seldom replace older technologies completely, and professions that adapt to changed circumstances improve their chances of survival. Nevertheless, the implications of the new digital technologies on the archival profession and its mission are serious. Linguists studying the death of languages suggest that one reason for language death is "immense pressure on the people to speak the dominant language—pressure that can come from political, social, or economic sources," followed by a "period of emerging bilingualism" and then a period when the "younger generation becomes increasingly proficient in the new language, identifying more with it, and finding their first language less relevant to their new needs."[80] One wonders if the sense of "the record" is being lost, and whether this might be a kind of death of archival language.

Despite the risks of prediction, some assessment of current and future issues facing the archival profession may be ventured. The number of archives will continue to grow. The trend in the 1980s and 1990s was toward the establishment of archival programs in institutions that had been producing archival records for some time but had never had trained archivists to care for them. Particularly in the business community and among cultural institutions, new archives were established. This trend eventually leveled off, but the continuing use of digital technologies by all sorts of agencies generated sustained interest in the archival function. The availability of well-qualified archivists who had deliberately chosen their careers and pursued their interest by means of formal graduate education provided this growing number of archives with capable personnel. Though it violates the laws of economics, the supply of educated archivists (especially those from more rigorous and comprehensive graduate programs) seems to have had a positive effect on the demand for them. Continuation of that trend will lead to a healthy, if not necessarily dramatic, expansion of the archival profession's public profile.

Communication and the exchange of information among archives will also be a feature of the ongoing consolidation of professional identity. The new automated databases of the 1980s were established to ease cooperation among repositories and to promote the sharing of knowledge about archival collections and procedures. By the 1990s, archivists had made these a normal part of their work. They were also employing online listservs for discussion, and they were building sites for their repositories on the World Wide Web. Such systems have obvious value for users of archives, who can more readily find collections, scattered around the country, relevant to their interests. These online tools have also proved useful to archivists themselves, who can share information about the acquisition, appraisal, organization, and management of their collections. The cost of participating in these kinds of networks goes down, while the benefits of participation bring in more archivists eager to cooperate with their colleagues. The hope for a single, universal database for sharing this information remains illusory, but pressures in the direction of standardization and cooperation will remain strong. Archivists are a long way from perfecting electronic systems for these purposes, but the sense of archival community has been significantly strengthened by enabling the rapid exchange of information. Archivists have not fully utilized the Web for more sophisticated exchanges of case studies and reports, but this is beginning to happen.

As archivists enhance cooperation among themselves, they will also work to define their role among other records professionals. The boundaries between different forms of recorded information— published and unpublished; current and noncurrent; eye-legible and machine-readable; written, oral, and visual—will continue to blur. New scholarship on public memory, cultural and literary studies, and material culture have all contributed to such blurring, highlighting the usefulness of other forms of evidence and expanding the context of traditional archival sources. As a result, archivists will necessarily search for the commonalities they share with librarians of all kinds, records managers, and information specialists. Like archivists, these other practitioners rightly claim to be in the "information business," and archivists will realize increasingly the importance of working with them. New permutations of information specialists, such as knowledge managers, also will stretch the disciplinary and organizational boundaries within which archivists have labored. Knowledge managers, who are concerned with the kinds of information often not captured in typical organizational functions (the knowledge held in the minds of longtime workers, for example), have much in common with those who manage archival records.[81] This pushes both archivists working within such environments and the broader profession to articulate a clear message about the value of archival documentation.

Similarly, archivists will have to enhance their connection to archival users. The solitary historical scholar seeking rare manuscript sources becomes less typical of archival clients every day. Researchers seeking the answers to a widening circle of questions care more about the information itself than they do about the form it comes in. Moreover, technology is already changing the way in which research is done. The Internet may stimulate more visits to archives, but it may also reduce them by generating demand for remote access to digitized documents. Since the use that archival records receive is the primary reason for preserving them in the first place, archivists will work to understand their users' needs better in the future, or they will risk irrelevance. Several challenges are still to be resolved. While the number of archival user studies has grown, archivists still know less about how and why archives are used than they ought. The demand by the users of archives for enhanced access to historical records brings with it problems of stretching resources and setting priorities.[82]

In large measure, a broadening base of knowledge for archivists will support a new outlook. Research and publication about archival topics is happily expanding, and a number of factors indicate that this will persist. What is more, archival thinking and writing have moved permanently beyond the genre of professional literature often characterized as "how we do it good" at a particular repository. Basic manuals like this one will always have their place, but scholarly monographs and provocative essays are now the more important locus of archival research and publication, and these are appearing in quantities no one would have imagined a decade or two ago.[83] While there will always be a need for a significant body of case studies, the archival literature of the future will be healthy to the extent that it promotes research into archival theory, archival practice, and archival history. The rise of a group of professional archival educators has already aided this trend, as these teachers are able to conduct their own research and publication—perhaps out of pure love of learning, though more likely because such scholarly activity is the measure of continuation and advancement in the academy. It will, of course, be necessary to keep this scholarship connected in meaningful ways to the practice of archivists.[84]

Finally, archivists will continue to devote considerable attention to projecting the professionalism that lies at the heart of their work and to demonstrating the usefulness of archives to society at large. There has been much concern over archival "image," over what the nonarchival world thinks about archives and archivists, if indeed it thinks of them at all. Some of this concern has come in the form of hand-wringing that is not particularly productive, but much of it has accustomed archivists to the necessity of telling others about the value of what they do. The transition from archival monks to archival missionaries is by no means complete, but archivists have come to realize the importance of sharing the excitement of what they do with those who use archives—or would do so if they understood them better. Growing media coverage with a particular focus on records is helping to transform the archival image. In the past decade, news about tobacco litigation, the assets of Holocaust victims, and the troubles of leading financial companies all produced remarkable coverage about the need to administer records properly.[85] Archivists will have to learn to use such public interest to their own advantage.

Conclusion

To be sure, the future is not uniformly bright; the half-full glass is also half-empty. The distribution of scarce resources and the acquisition of an appropriate share of them for archives will always be a challenge. Just as new archives are called into existence, others will be abolished by those parent organizations that consider them acceptable luxuries in good times but expendable in bad times. Some archival education programs will flourish while others fall by the wayside. Professional associations will face more demands from their members than they can meet. Technology will present as many challenges for managing new records as opportunities for organizing and using older ones.

Still, the American archival profession has achieved a great deal in less than a century of organized activity. It has grown both in numbers and in maturity to achieve all the characteristics of a profession, complete with a body of theoretical principles, a history of institutional and individual experience, and a committed body of practitioners devoted to and excited by their work. Archivists are professionals who acquire and make their own a broad base of knowledge. They derive a set of characteristic beliefs and values from that knowledge. As the very word suggests, they "profess" all of these in their professional lives and put them into practice in day-to-day responsibilities and duties. An understanding of archives and manuscripts rests ultimately on understanding archival knowledge, values, and responsibilities.

Chapter 3

The Archivist's Perspective: Knowledge and Values

Like the practitioners of other professions, archivists bring a particular perspective to their work. Just as doctors think like doctors and lawyers think like lawyers, so archivists think like archivists: they analyze and understand archives and records in their own particular way. Those who create and use recorded information have their perspectives, too, but archivists develop a way of looking at records that is peculiarly their own, different from that of others. Creators, for example, usually take a practical view of records: records help them accomplish a particular task and are viewed in that light.[1] To their creators, records are a means to a specific end. Once that immediate use is past, records have little further significance in themselves and can be ignored or destroyed. Records users, by contrast, often look on records purely as research materials, carriers of information that are valuable or not to the extent that they answer the question of the moment. For users, too, records are simply a means to some immediate end.[2]

Archivists have a perspective on records that is broader than either of these. They see a bigger picture. From the history of their profession and their own place in it, archivists develop habits of thinking and analyzing, together with characteristic attitudes that govern and guide their work. For the archivist, records perform not merely one service but a whole range of them, some of which cannot be anticipated in advance. Making that variety of use possible—indeed, encouraging it and making it easy—is the archivist's goal. To achieve it, archivists rely on a perspective that derives from a base of knowledge and a set of shared values, acquired and refined over the course of their careers and nurtured by the traditions and experiences of the archival community. Before considering the various activities that make up archival practice, therefore, it is necessary to understand the perspective from which those activities flow.

Knowledge

Archivists build up a store of knowledge, which they apply to their work through introductory archival education at the graduate level, on-the-job experience, and continuing professional education. This building implies change, of course, meaning that archival knowledge is elastic and its acquisition is an ongoing process. While in the past archivists often favored extensive apprenticeship approaches to learning their craft, it is now the case that the ideal basis for acquiring archival knowledge comes from all three sources. Comprehensive graduate education provides a systematic orientation to the theories and methods of archival work. While most graduate programs continue to include a practicum component, it is probably the case that the real orientation to practice comes in the archivist's first position. Continuing professional education, once nearly exclusively directed at an introductory or rudimentary level, is now increasingly meeting the needs of those in middle or even advanced careers. This is a sign of how the rapidly changing technologies, legal issues, and the social contexts of records systems are affecting the knowledge of archivists and other records professionals. In general, however, archival knowledge focuses on four broad categories: knowledge about the individuals, organizations, and institutions that produce records; knowledge about the records produced by those people and entities; knowledge of the uses to which records can be put; and knowledge about the principles best suited to the management of those records. This knowledge encompasses both the historical aspects of these categories and their contemporary manifestations.[3]

Knowledge of Individuals, Organizations, and Institutions. Because they live with the paper and electronic remains of human activity, archivists acquire a broad knowledge of the varieties and possibilities of that activity. Through the records over which they exercise control, archivists vicariously experience otherwise unfamiliar places and events, learning things they would not otherwise have known and expanding their sense of the possible. A pioneer's diary now preserved in a historical society describes in stark human terms the emotions of migration and settlement. The letters of a young woman in a collection of family papers describe the experiences of motherhood, child-rearing, and career choices. The founding documents of a charitable organization kept in the group's archives convey the original fervor that brought it into being. The financial records of a corporation provide glimpses into the decisions, wise or misguided, that have led it to success or failure. The archivist does not actually need to have any of these experiences personally to understand them through the records that are left behind. Even when working in a repository that has a relatively narrow collecting scope or in an institutional archives serving only the parent organization's needs, the archivist will be exposed through records to a wide range of people and groups, not all of them likable but each with a story to tell.

This exposure gives the archivist a sense of the complexity of life and the variety of its expressions. Through the records, the archivist is ideally situated to see how complex any activity is. Individual responsibility and action may lie at the heart of it, but individuals seldom operate entirely on their own. The delivery of social services, for example, whether by public or private agencies, is no longer a matter (if it ever was) of a few good-hearted people single-mindedly pursuing their goals. Rather, it results from the coordination of a great many individual and collective actions. Large bureaucracies emerge to make the effort possible, peopled in some measure by individuals who never come close to direct contact with those actually being served. The accountant who manages the financial resources and the personnel director who hires the staff have as much of a role to play as the social worker who visits clients. Even in the personal realm, the demands of modern life are multifarious: individuals undertake a great many tasks, join a number of voluntary associations, and expand their range of involvements. Archivists have long been aware that it is not only the great political leaders or the engaging ideas that cause new events or create great movements; with their orientation to the records of a wide array of people and organizations, archivists have long been open to a "microhistory" perspective, even before it became a scholarly fashion.[4]

Because archivists encounter the extensive, interconnected, and overlapping records of all these phenomena, they come to appreciate complexity and to look for collective activity and significance. In doing so, they recognize that context is all important: similar actions in different contexts have significantly different meanings. Archivists also develop a structural understanding of these phenomena, looking on them not as random productions of human interest but rather as the result of deliberate, often complicated processes that must be reconstructed and understood. These processes change with time, and the archivist is ideally suited to see their development through changes in the records. The records of an organization or the papers of an individual have as much to do with external regulations, policies, and traditions as with the immediate, peculiar circumstances of the single agency or person.

The nineteenth-century records of an orphanage, for example, may have been kept in large ledger books, with all the pertinent information about each child written on a single line divided into columns running across a double page. By the twentieth century, these volumes have been replaced by case files: fat, expandable folders in which all manner of documents concerning each child are kept. Today, these files are probably in digital form. In all instances, the records creator was concerned primarily with accounting for the children, keeping the records (whatever their format) to accomplish that fundamental, though increasingly complicated, purpose. The records' forms change with government regulations and social work practices, and the analysis of these regulations and practices enables the archivist to comprehend why and how the recordkeeping systems have changed. The records user of today is concerned principally with the content of the information recorded, consulting it to answer questions that are either particular (was a specific child ever in this orphanage?) or general (what were the broad demographic characteristics of orphans in certain periods?). Many others—lawyers, court-appointed investigators, the media—may also seek to use these records for their own purposes.[5]

The archivist asks very different questions. How were the records kept originally, and how can that original system be reconstructed so as to enhance rather than obscure meaning? How can the earlier recordkeeping practices be explained to present-day users so they can draw information from them, perhaps in answer to entirely new, unforeseen questions? Are the records worth keeping at all for the long term? Do the potential uses outweigh the financial costs involved in maintaining the records in an archival repository? There are other practical considerations as well. Since a row of bound volumes will be more compact than a stack of boxes containing hundreds of case files, how much space will have to be set aside to store the records? What physical condition are the records in, and what steps will have to be taken to stabilize or restore it? Do the records contain sensitive information that might have to be withheld from use for a certain time? How have changing laws and regulations affected the records? The archivist lives with the evolving nature of the records themselves and must therefore be prepared to understand them as a whole in a way that is not so critical for either creator or user. That wider view is the measure of the differing perspectives of archivists, creators, and users of records.

The archivist can thus see not merely that the record becomes more complex with time, but also that the structures, systems, and activities from which the record derives become more complex. In the orphanage case files, careful testing and detailed psychological analysis have replaced the quick, seemingly off-hand remarks of the earlier ledger books. The record left behind is thus more detailed, but it is also more clearly the result of formal, articulated procedures in which larger goals are achieved through a succession of smaller steps. This pattern of development will not be quite so noticeable to one who lacks the archivist's singular perspective.[6] On the one hand, the records creator focuses mostly on the immediate tasks to be accomplished, with the records almost an afterthought. On the other hand, the records user may miss the larger organizational context from a desire to answer only one or two of the thousands of questions that might possibly be asked. The archivist learns to see through the records to larger insights that ultimately help explain the records, the actions that produced them, and the information they contain. The archivist can see how individuals and organizations reveal themselves, knowingly or not, through their records.

The archivist seeks the fundamental connections between the producers of records and the records themselves. What are the characteristics of the records produced by different activities? How did those processes change over time? What evidence can we find of those changes in the documents that will lead to a better understanding of the phenomena? How clear, in other words, are the windows to other experiences that the records offer? How do these particular records relate to other sources of information and evidence? A knowledge of how and why individuals and institutions produce records leads the archivist to recognize all these as crucial questions.

Knowledge of Records. If archivists know something about the structures and processes that produce records, they also come to know a great deal about the records themselves, both in general and in particular. Fundamentally, archivists become scholars of records and recordkeeping systems—not merely their content, but also their cultural and symbolic meanings.[7] Two specialized branches of archives work devote scholarly attention to records as ends in themselves. *Paleography* studies the changing nature of writing, while *diplomatics* studies the forms that documents take and the impact their style has on their content.[8] More generally, archivists inevitably learn something about the subject content of their collections. Archivists do not, of course, spend their working hours simply reading historical documents for their own amusement or edification, any more than librarians spend their days reading books. Still, in the course of acquiring, organizing, and helping others use records, archivists learn a great deal, even if they enter a position with little previous subject knowledge. A state archivist, for instance, develops a detailed knowledge of the state, even if not a native. The archivist in a repository devoted to the records of a particular religious or ethnic group learns a great deal about that group, even if from another background. Constantly surrounded by the subject matter, archivists develop a detailed knowledge of the historical and other issues raised in their collections. While such subject knowledge enhances the archivist's ability to work with the records, it is expertise about the records and the systems creating and supporting records that is the special contribution of the archivist.

More important than any specific subject knowledge, however, is a broader understanding of how records function and what they do, whether in an organizational setting or in personal life. Archivists frequently express this understanding by speaking of a *life cycle of records*. Developed first and most fully by records managers, this notion expresses the idea that, like the people who produce them, records pass through a life cycle of different phases. The records life cycle is often thought of as having four stages—creation, use, storage, and disposition—and archivists believe that they can best manage the records they encounter by understanding them at each stage of their life cycle and the effects each stage has on the others. More recently, some archivists have also spoken of a *records continuum*, arguing that archival records are never really "disposed" of, and that a continuum metaphor thus takes better account of records in time and space. The distinction between current and noncurrent records is artificial, in this view, since "records are 'fixed' in time and space from the moment of their creation, but recordkeeping regimes carry them forward and enable their use for multiple purposes by delivering them to people living in different times and spaces."[9] The concept suggests that the value of records has little to do with any element of time and everything to do with their function, characteristics, and compliance attributes. The records continuum concept may also enhance the connection between archival and records management responsibilities, and this strengthens the focus on the importance of records in any organization.[10] Both concepts support the notion that records are integral to the lives of organizations, individuals, and societies.

When records are created, they are made by a given technology in a particular form in order to carry out certain functions. While archivists may have become preoccupied with the implications of recent digital technologies—probably because they change so rapidly, are so fragile, and are the creation of software engineers who have a culture and mission of their own—records have always been the products of sophisticated technologies. The creator, however, usually does not stop to reflect on either the form or the function: the record is merely a tool, and the job that the tool does is more important than the tool itself. The archivist, however, sees the necessary connection and knows that decisions, conscious and unconscious, made at the time of creation will affect the future meaning and usefulness of any record. The information in a document may be laid out in an unusual manner, for example, making its use or even its intelligibility problematic. The record may be in such a form that it cannot be read by the unaided eye, requiring a microfilm enlarger, a projector, or varying kinds of computer hardware and software. Some records may be created in very large formats, making their handling and storage difficult. Some may be created with long-term or permanent retention in mind, but constructed out of very impermanent materials that work against that goal. Since many of these records are eventually included in the archives, archivists live with the results of the decisions made during the creation of records. It is thus important for them to know the circumstances of that creation. Some archivists even contend that they are as much in the business of tracking and implementing policy as in shepherding records, since records are the expression of laws, regulations, best practices, conventions, and traditions. This is a valuable insight, since it reemphasizes the archivist's responsibility to become expert in all dimensions of recordkeeping systems.

Records are necessarily created with a particular use in mind, and that period of use represents the second stage of the life cycle. A record's usefulness may be immediate or long term, and it may also change with time. Archivists are predisposed to value the usefulness of records (or rather the usefulness of the information in them), but they also understand some of the problems that use entails. Who, for example, has the right—legal, moral, or other—to see certain records, and which records must, for whatever reasons, be restricted from use? In this era of ever-shifting privacy and security concerns, how does the archivist administer access to records fairly? What once was perceived to be a mundane record of uncertain value but worth maintaining because of its connection to an important event or project may now be seen as presenting security problems. The archivist may find the old building blueprint or weekly statistical report needs to be maintained with extra care. What should be done with documents that are so heavily used that they begin to wear out physically? How might usefulness change? This is not as simple as it may seem. In some instances, the value of the records may remain constant for a very long time: the blueprints of an old building remain, in some senses, current and active as long as the structure stands. In other cases, the useful life of records may be very brief: the weekly report becomes outdated as soon as its statistical information is superseded by next week's report or by the monthly report.

Whether records are in constant or less frequent use, they need to be filed and stored somewhere, and a necessary part of the archivist's perspective is a concern over the problems of storage even before records actually get to the archives. In particular, the archivist must be concerned with the questions of how to store records efficiently and how to find them when they are needed. What kinds of storage equipment (filing cabinets, boxes, shelves) are the most cost effective, and how can records be stored so as to take maximum advantage of the available floor space? How high off the ground can records be stored and still permit ready retrieval? What weight of records will the floor safely support? How do environmental conditions in the storage areas affect the long-term physical survival of the material? Should the format of the records be altered (through microfilming, for example) in order to store a greater volume in a smaller space or for other reasons? How complicated is the arrangement of the records, and how easily can one locate information when required? While these kinds of issues remain relevant concerns even with digital records, additional considerations are involved in their maintenance. Should archivists take physical custody of records, and what kinds of decisions will have to be made about emulation or migration, thereby transforming archival appraisal from a one-time decision into a continuous process?[11] Neither the records creator nor the records user worries much about such considerations; for them, having the information stored close at hand for convenience when needed is likely to be the principal concern. They need not, as the archivist and the records manager must, see storage as a problem of its own, one that must be addressed in a planned and systematic way.

When records have fulfilled their immediate purposes, they arrive at the disposition stage of their life cycle. For the records creator, *disposition* usually means precisely that: throwing the records away to make room for new ones. This has always been problematic for archivists, since modern organizations have tended to see paper records as bureaucratic (in the pejorative sense of the word) barriers to efficient operation. The archivist applies a broader meaning to the term *disposition,* viewing both temporary transfer to interim, bulk storage (often called a records center) and long-term storage in the archives as forms of disposition. The original meaning and usefulness of the records may have passed, but in disposing of them the archivist knows that other uses are possible and that those potential uses must affect any decision to retain or destroy them.[12] The archivist thus sees a wider range of disposition options and can select the most appropriate one in any particular case. Understanding all the previous stages of the life cycle of records provides the archivist with information necessary to make proper judgments at the disposition stage, offering a knowledgeable basis for deciding which records will survive and which will not.

Beyond this broad knowledge of what records go through before they ever find their way into archival custody, archivists also develop a detailed knowledge of certain technical matters. Foremost among these is a knowledge of what records are made of physically and how they are put together. Archivists learn how to recognize the different types of record material. They are familiar with the various kinds of systems that have been used for recording and filing information. They understand, for example, the circumstances that produced press-book copies of letters, file drawers filled with carbon copies, or systems of electronic mail. They also know the forms and types of documents that are characteristic of different periods, and this allows them to fix approximate dates for records with reasonable accuracy. By looking at a document—the kind of paper and ink, the size and format of the information, the style of handwriting, in some cases even the feel or the smell—the archivist knows something about it, readily distinguishing an eighteenth-century letter from a twentieth-century letter, for example. The archivist is also now becoming an expert in understanding the digital means for producing records, from word processing to electronic mail to Web-based records systems. Given the complexities of modern records, archivists not only have had to expand the scope of their own knowledge, but they have had to work with other professionals responsible for records and information systems.

With the same knowledge, the archivist is able to judge the authenticity of records, distinguishing those that are genuine from fakes or forgeries. Something is obviously amiss when a document with eighteenth-century physical characteristics speaks of twentieth-century subjects, and the archivist recognizes anomalies in a way that someone else might not. The distortion and deliberate faking of records is all the more difficult to detect in digital systems, of course, but archivists certainly have the opportunity in these circumstances to demonstrate their knowledge of records and recordkeeping systems.[13] Their technical knowledge is also sufficiently detailed so that archivists can understand what causes records to deteriorate; this allows them to make plans to retard or reverse that deterioration. Naturally, well-trained and experienced archivists can make these judgments more readily and with greater assurance than novices. Still, all archivists learn to examine records in this way, adding to their knowledge and reinforcing a perspective that is uniquely their own.

Knowledge of the Uses of Records. If archivists know something about where records come from and how they are produced, they also know from daily experience that records can and will be used for a wide range of purposes. Indeed, it is the expectation of enduring and continuing usefulness that explains all the effort and energy archivists expend on the materials in their care. In the archivist's view, saving and organizing the unique, original recorded information from past and present are not ends in themselves. Rather, they are warranted only to the extent that someone—indeed, a large number of some-ones—will use that information. What the archivist does makes that use possible.

The archivist differs from others who use records, however, in that the archivist's perspective takes in a wider range of possibilities. Where the creator or user of records usually sees only the current value of recorded information—the task or the inquiry of the moment—the archivist sees a more open-ended potential. One person may ask one set of questions of archival holdings this morning, but the archivist knows that someone else will ask an entirely different set of questions of those same materials tomorrow—or maybe even this afternoon. The certainty that this process will go on indefinitely drives the archivist's desire to facilitate the work of all the questioners, not organizing the collection in a way that will satisfy one while making usability or understanding difficult for the others. The diversity of potential uses also challenges archivists in conducting appraisal for known current uses and unpredictable future uses and in creating finding aids for a wide array of researchers.

The reasons why users call on the information in archival records are thus constantly shifting, and the archivist's perspective entails a predisposition to appreciate these shifts. Government census data or the records of births, marriages, and deaths maintained by counties and towns offer good examples of the unpredictable multiplicity of uses that archives may receive. The information they contain is recorded in the first place to serve wholly practical, instrumental purposes. These records offer legal proof of age and personal status (of existence, even), and many benefits depend on them. The rights to vote, to drive an automobile, or to purchase certain products, for instance, all depend on proving that one has achieved a certain age. Representation in local and national legislatures depends on the aggregate information of the census. Passports offer proof of citizenship, but they also adapt to broader uses in an era of civil unrest, war, and terrorism. The changing technology of passports—including biometric information, for example, in addition to physical description and photographs—expands their possible uses even further.[14]

As important as they are, these immediate uses of records are transitory. The archivist knows that most records will lose their original usefulness but that they will take on a secondary usefulness, one that will make them important for different reasons. A genealogist will ask new questions of the records, trying to find information about particular individuals at particular times. A lawyer will seek to reconstruct families in the settlement of estates. Government and private-sector planners will look for population trends and movements that will affect the shape of cities and the landscape. Historians will connect the rise or decline of population to other factors in assembling a complete picture of what happened in the past. Even quite ordinary records—cancelled checks and insurance policies—have been placed in archives because of their association with horrific events, such as the Holocaust, and have taken on importance as instruments of accountability.[15] No one of these eventual uses was in the mind of the creator of the records, but the archivist is prepared for all of them.

The changing utility of records is no less evident in the case of private manuscripts and papers. Diaries and personal letters may not have the same practical purposes as census records, but they none-theless fix and hold information reliably for their creators and recipients. The originators of personal papers count on them to communicate with others at a distance or simply to remember things they might otherwise forget. Subsequent readers of those same items, however, will find different uses for them and will be able to answer previously unimagined questions. By "reading between the lines," these later users will be able to reconstruct and understand the inter-personal dynamics between correspondents. They will be able to watch an intellect or a personality develop over time, seeing a change so gradual that it would not have been apparent to a contemporary. They will be able to see conscious literary productions take shape and grow from draft to masterpiece. The classic example of this type of records use may be seen in a prize-winning study of a woman's diary. Martha Ballard, a midwife in frontier Maine in the era of the American Revolution, maintained a diary that subsequent generations ignored as little more than an account of routine chores, weather, and other insignificant matters. A later historian used the diary to create a rich tapestry of social life and women's roles in early America, seeing it as a kind of unofficial town archives.[16] Such users may be exploring any of these potential topics for scholarly, academic purposes, or they may pursue them simply in the interests of understanding their family or themselves. In either case, the recorded information is being put to uses quite different from those originally intended.

The archivist is in a better position than anyone else who comes into contact with the records to see this kind of broad and constantly changing usefulness. The wider perspective demands that all sorts of uses, including many that are not obvious, be accommodated. Not all possible uses of records are created equal, of course, and archivists generally try to avoid the trap of thinking that "somebody, some-where, someday" might be interested in a given topic, no matter how trivial or obscure. Still, when archivists look at records, they see a greater number of possibilities, and they go about their work in a way that encourages diversity and adaptability. By committing themselves to assisting all possible users of the information in their custody, archivists assume the ongoing responsibility to gather systematic information about their holdings and to pass that information on to those who have a need or a desire to use it.

Knowledge of Archival Principles. These three areas of the archivist's knowledge—of the organizations and individuals that produce records; of the nature of records themselves; and of the possible uses of records—become most relevant when they are combined with a knowledge of the principles best suited to organizing and managing those records. Most important are those that focus on making all records, produced for various and often unpredictable reasons, comprehensible and therefore useful. Materials that have a logical order at the time of their creation may lose that order as time goes on. Restoring the original coherence thus becomes a critical task, one that will be especially difficult if the original orderliness has been replaced by chaos and disorder. Archivists thus share with librarians and museum curators the mission of organizing the materials in their care in some systematic manner and then codifying and communicating that order to users who want to retrieve information.

Archivists designate this as the process of establishing *intellectual and physical control* over their holdings. Intellectual control means knowing what the pieces of an archival collection are, where they come from, and how they fit together. To achieve intellectual control is to be able to answer, with reasonable specificity, the questions, "What is this?" and "How did this come to be?" Such an understanding can operate on its own, without immediate reference to the actual physical location of the material: it is possible to know what an archival collection or group contains without necessarily being able to state the precise order or place of it. Just as one can tell that a jigsaw puzzle is a lovely pastoral scene before actually putting it together, so the archivist can know, in the aggregate or even in some detail, what an archival collection is before fully understanding how all its pieces relate to one another. Thus, establishing intellectual control is mentally prior, the necessary first step. The process is, as one archivist has said, a case of "mind over matter," an understanding of the records, the systems supporting them, and the regulations and conventions shaping them.[17]

It is always necessary, of course, to take the next step. Basic intellectual control may come first, but archivists must always establish physical control as well. It is not sufficient merely to know intellectually what the pieces of the archival jigsaw are; it is also necessary to know where they are so they may be retrieved when needed. Knowing what parts make up an archival whole is useless unless it is possible to find and retrieve those pieces, and only those pieces, rather than all of them. Establishing intellectual and physical control lies at the heart of the organizing function, whether in museums, libraries, or archives. Archivists know that they must be able to achieve this control over their holdings, even those portions that are difficult to understand. Archivists hope that when the records arrive at their repositories they will be in the original order of their creation and use by the records creator, thereby preserving important evidence. In organizational or institutional archives, this is why archivists often have records management responsibilities or work closely with records managers, focusing on external requirements, auditors' practices, legal considerations, and administrative use—usually identified in records retention or disposition schedules. Personal papers may present more challenges in establishing control, but there has been a growing recognition that such papers have evident structures critical to understanding them. Intellectual and physical control are not always accomplished sitting in a room full of recently acquired records; they are done through ongoing research about the functions and activities, people and organizations, generating the records.

For librarians, intellectual and physical control are always intimately connected. For any library system to work properly, the books will have to be on the shelves (physical control) in the order of the numbers assigned them in the catalog (intellectual control). The same can be said for museum collections, in which registration or accession numbers substitute for classification or call numbers. Because of the differences in the nature of the materials in their care, however, archivists approach these organizational tasks in a different way. Library materials usually exist in multiple copies that are all more or less the same. The way that one library catalogs a book, therefore, can be adopted, perhaps with minor modifications, by other libraries. This is true whether the classification schema is based on an expandable a priori outline of all conceivable subject fields (like the Dewey Decimal System) or simply on the organizational plan of the largest, most comprehensive library available (like the Library of Congress System). At the same time, most published materials address one topic or a limited range of topics, and they do so deliberately, following an author's conscious intention. Librarians can therefore rely on subject categories as the basis for their organizational effort. A book may be about Impressionist painting or about nuclear engineering, but it is unlikely to be about both. Individual library materials may thus be organized and kept with items that pertain to the same subject. In fact, there is a positive advantage to doing so because it enables library users to browse, finding items that interest them in physical proximity to one another.

Archivists cannot profit from either of these advantages. In the first place, each archival collection is, in the strictest meaning of the term, unique: the materials held by the National Archives are and always will be distinct from the collections in a local historical society. Attempting to devise a single classification framework that will work equally well for both is thus futile.[18] Furthermore, since manuscript and archival materials are often produced as an unconscious byproduct of human activity, they may pertain to a myriad of subjects. A single letter may speak of family matters, business affairs, avocational interests, and random thoughts of no apparent significance. When archivists deal not with a single letter but with thousands of them in large files, this problem becomes even more difficult. Determining just exactly what topic a file is "about" may be no easy task. Which of the many subjects should be used for classification purposes? If the archivist chooses one, what happens to the other subjects discussed in the records? How many hundreds of cross-references will be required to provide equally easy access to information by very different users asking very different questions?[19]

Because these characteristics are inherent in the nature of archival materials, archivists need a more reliable principle for organizing their collections (similar to principles held by other professionals, such as museum curators and archaeologists). This principle, which archivists call *provenance,* is based on the deceptively obvious insight that the person or organization producing the records determines their content.[20] A nuclear engineer will produce files and documents that are essentially different from those produced by an Impressionist painter, even if both of them talk about a whole range of subjects in their letters. Thus, the archivist can adopt the individual or corporate entity that created the records as the central organizing standard, keeping all the records produced by a particular origin or source—that is, a single provenance—together. By knowing something about the point of origin of the records—who the person was and what that person did or was interested in; what the corporate body was and how it was structured and operated—the archivist lets the records fall into the natural groupings they had when they were created.[21] This approach eliminates the necessity of imposing on them predetermined subject categories that may not be entirely fitting. The archivist is still intent on gaining intellectual and physical control but chooses means for accomplishing this that are best suited to the material at hand, extending from analysis and understanding of the records and recordkeeping systems.

To this reliance on provenance, the archivist adds a closely related principle that is flexible and well suited to maintaining control over records. This is the principle of *original order.* When the records of any given provenance are created, they come into existence with a certain order already imposed on them, identified more than a century ago as the "organic" nature of records.[22] The records creator divides them into logical groupings, often based on different functions or activities: the personal correspondence is kept together in one place, the financial records somewhere else, and so on. In organizations, this practice is even more apparent and beneficial: the president's office records are all kept together, separate from those of the heads of the various departments. What is more, within the files themselves, there is another level of order, again established at the time the records are created. In a set of letters, the documents are filed chronologically; in a series of personnel files, they are alphabetical by the employee's name; in a collection of medical records, they may follow some sequential numbering system. Whatever arrangement is there has been chosen by the creator of the records because the very order itself is an effective means for keeping the records straight. The physical arrangement of the records gives fundamental clues as to why they have been created and how and why they may have continuing use.

Archivists know that maintaining this original order is as important as maintaining provenance in understanding and controlling the records after they pass into archival custody. Relying on the natural order allows the records to stand on their own as much as possible, without introducing any other variables from the archivist. No matter how logical outside, subject-based schemes may appear, they always have a limited usefulness. What is more, they are unnecessary, since an original order of some kind is always present, even if it has been partly obscured through misfiling or other carelessness. This is equally true for electronic records, even if they are never printed out into a physical form. Like provenance, the principle of original order provides an objective rather than subjective way of treating the records: the archivist accepts the order and arrangement the records already have, rather than trying to make one up after the fact. Not only is time saved when archivists are involved with descriptive work, but essential aspects of the evidence in records are preserved as well.

Thinking of records in terms of their provenance and original order and then applying those principles to a particular body of records are critical components of the archivist's way of looking at things. Others have a different perspective. When creators and users look at records, they "see" other things, either the task to be accomplished or the subject matter being investigated. When archivists look at records, what they see first and foremost are provenance and original order. This perception permits the establishment of a context that will serve as the basis for everything else the archivist does.[23] It establishes the point of origin and the natural, original arrangement of the records as the fixed reference points for archival organization, eliminating the necessity for the archivist to concoct such schemes from scratch. Archivists thus know how to identify provenance and to discern original order in particular collections, no matter how ostensibly disorganized those collections may at first appear.

All archival knowledge is acquired by archivists through a combination of means. Foremost of these is formal academic study at the graduate level. Through lectures by instructors, extensive readings in the professional literature, classroom discussions, student research and projects, case study exercises, and other means of introductory and advanced professional education, students acquire the foundations of their knowledge. The graduate classroom is the place where future archivists have the opportunity to study and to question archival knowledge and practice, apart from the pressures of organizational assignments and responsibilities. As such, it is a crucible for thinking about archival administration and its application in any organizational or cultural setting. Upon this base, all archivists next build a growing body of professional experience by actually working with records. This experience adds to each individual archivist's storehouse of applications and examples, instances of problem solving that offer numerous demonstrations of how the general principles apply in particular cases. Some of these experiences come in the form of internships or work-study opportunities, often while beginning archivists are still receiving their introductory education. Similar insights continue to build over the course of a career. Finally, the archivist's knowledge is refined and developed through continuing professional education, which is necessary for all archivists, no matter how experienced. Continuing education expands the connections between theory and practice beyond the necessarily limited range of one's own experiences, drawing useful examples and lessons from the experience of others. This "life-long learning" also permits archivists to keep abreast of important changes and developments in their work, particularly in areas (such as automation and preservation technology) that are changing constantly. Participating in the activities of professional associations and attending continuing education workshops and academic programs are valued means for keeping abreast of the growing body of archival knowledge. All these forms of education are important; to have one without the others is to have a limited grounding.

There is also another critical area, and that is building a foundation for lifelong reading across a variety of disciplines for insights into records and recordkeeping systems. Although archivists have many textbooks, the substance of archival knowledge is far more complex than can be covered in a single volume. The idea that all archival knowledge can be summarized neatly in two or three hundred pages is false. There are many books far removed from the production of practice-oriented basic textbooks. Some are, of course, intended to be studies about records or archives (they all have very different purposes), but taken together they provide insight and inspiration about how archivists can approach the documents of the past. We can add to these kinds of books layer after layer of works from anthropology, sociology, political science, and other fields providing both a deeper and broader scholarship on archival matters. Enriching this is the work of a new generation of scholars studying archives from inside the field, perhaps best represented by the growing number of dissertations on archival subjects. All of this makes reliance on the single-volume archival text-book more problematic. Textbooks provide an introduction to the field, but archival knowledge is broader and deeper.[24]

Values

Drawing on their base of knowledge and building on their practical experiences, archivists also develop a characteristic set of values about what they do, why they do it, and why it is important to do. This professional value system includes a commitment to ethical behavior as an archival professional, but it also goes well beyond ethics to include a broader set of beliefs. These values embody what archivists think is good and bad, proper and improper, and they provide the foundation for making decisions in countless professional situations. The values archivists share may be summarized in a number of propositions.

1. **Archival records exist to be used and not merely saved for their own sake.** Archivists are charged with the responsibility to preserve records, indeed to preserve them for the indefinite future. This responsibility requires that archivists employ certain safeguards to ensure that the records in their care will survive, including establishing and enforcing procedures that will guarantee the physical survival and integrity of the records. Connected to this is the responsibility to organize the records in a coherent and understandable way. All those activities are not carried out for their own sake, however; rather, they are necessary only because they serve the larger purpose of making the records usable. Archivists are not hoarders or packrats. They are preservers of evidence and information and, just as important, they are sharers of that evidence and information. The reasons for which records will be used are practically unlimited, from "pure" historical research to government and corporate accountability. Archivists see in the uses that their collections receive the real reason for keeping them

in the first place and for lavishing their time and professional attention on them. The public at large may equate archival work merely with preserving records; for archivists, however, preservation is always done for a purpose, and that purpose is use.

2. Some records ought to be preserved long term, even after their immediate usefulness has passed. Archivists take a long view of the usefulness of information. This perspective is probably even more important in the contemporary era, with its emphasis on speed, change, and instant gratification, an age in which computer specialists speak of "archiving" records—meaning that they might keep them for as long as six months. Archivists accept the value of preserving records into a longer future, well beyond the limit of their own careers. They commit themselves to that care and maintenance, even though they may not be able to predict, much less control, the use those records will receive in the future. Nevertheless, archivists' role as preservers of evidence and information is a particularly important responsibility in our modern age of ephemeral media. At the same time, archivists balance preservation with other responsibilities. They approach the universe of documentation with the assumption that everything will *not* be saved. They are, then, destroyers as well as keepers, although they destroy records in a controlled and careful manner. Expanding digital memory will not change this reality, especially as the fear of being swamped by information continues to grow. One conservative estimate suggests that about "800 MB of recorded information is produced per person [in the entire world] each year. It would take about 30 feet of books to store the equivalent of 800 MB of information on paper."[25] Obviously, with this growth rate, archivists will continue to balance preservation and destruction and will adopt more competent approaches to selection.

3. Archival records ought to be preserved as completely and coherently as possible, with critical information about context and connections preserved. Archivists work toward this goal actively, helping destroy records that do not have any ongoing significance; in large measure, this is a "forest-and-trees" problem, ensuring that the forest of meaning will become visible through selective clearing of some of the trees. Still, for those records that will be chosen for survival, archivists believe that they ought to be preserved as fully and as carefully as possible, without gaps or omissions, either deliberate or inadvertent. What is more, archivists understand the value of making their selection choices on the basis of a reasoned, articulated set of criteria rather than on whim or on vague, intuitive feelings about what distinguishes informative records from less valuable ones. With the shift of large portions of the information professions to the idea of "content management," the business of preserving records in a manner that maintains their integrity becomes both more important and more difficult, and archivists have to relate their objectives to the new demands of the digital era.[26]

4. Archival records ought to be organized properly and in a timely way so they can be used. Every archives has a backlog of work, a portion of its holdings that its staff has not quite gotten around to yet. In any archives that continues to grow—and growth is necessary and healthy in virtually every repository—a backlog is inevitable. That condition notwithstanding, archivists remain committed to the value of organizing their collections, if only at an aggregate level, as quickly as possible so the information in them can be understood and used. The archivist approaches collections in a manner that refines them progressively, organizing all holdings in a summary way before

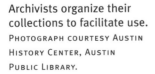

Archivists organize their collections to facilitate use.
PHOTOGRAPH COURTESY AUSTIN HISTORY CENTER, AUSTIN PUBLIC LIBRARY.

treating any single collection in detail. What is more, archivists believe implicitly in the value of sharing knowledge about the materials they hold. Some information in records may have to be guarded, but archivists believe that information about records should always be shared. Archivists seldom value secrecy about their holdings, recognizing instead the responsibility to spread the word about what they have and welcoming those who desire to study it. At the same time, archivists must be careful that this principle of timely processing and access does not lessen commitments to other responsibilities.[27]

5. Sensitive information and information given in situations presumed to be private should be protected from use as long as that sensitivity remains. The belief that records exist to be taken advantage of does not imply that archivists should disregard legitimate concerns for the rights of privacy and confidentiality. In fact, archivists are frequently in the forefront of protecting these rights by restricting the use that their collections may receive. Archivists are committed to balancing the maximum use of records with the necessity of safeguarding confidential information. They take this responsibility seriously, and they place a positive value on doing so fairly and consistently. In an age of increasing concerns about personal privacy, especially in matters of national security, it is critical that archivists hold to administering their collections in a way that protects privacy but that ensures that records are not unfairly restricted.

The society in which contemporary archivists live and work may challenge this value. Controversial government legislation, corporate misconduct, and media attention have changed forever the world of archivists, complicating matters related to sensitive information and privacy. The Internet, cable television, and other factors have created both new threats and opportunities for archivists. While they can now make information about their holdings more quickly and more widely available, archivists must also be more sensitive to potential breaches of privacy and to the difficulties of balancing personal privacy and the greater public good. A generation ago, archivists might have been able to approach such matters by posting notices in their reading rooms and distributing policies to their researchers. Today, archivists are working collectively through their professional associations and other venues to change laws and public policy threatening their traditional values in preserving and making available historical records.

6. Archivists should administer their collections equitably and impartially. Archivists place a fundamental value on minimizing distinctions among users of their holdings, trying insofar as possible to treat their users equally. In some instances, certain distinctions are appropriate. The archives of an institution or organization will undoubtedly permit wider access to users from inside the organization (the present staff of an office whose earlier records are in the archives, for instance) than to users from outside the organization. Archivists are disposed to keep such distinctions to a minimum, however, and in particular they should not attempt to distinguish so-called serious users from others or otherwise discriminate on the basis of academic qualifications. If access to archival records cannot always be precisely equal, archivists believe that it should always be equitable.

7. Archival repositories ought to cooperate in preserving historical records. Archivists place a high value on cooperation rather than competition in assembling and administering their collections. In particular, in those archives that collect materials from sources other than a parent organization—historical societies or university archives that collect materials from private individuals and donors, for instance—archivists believe that it is wrong to compete with one another in dividing a single collection among several repositories. Likewise, they believe it is improper to bid up the price of collections that are purchased, a problem that has taken on renewed seriousness with the appearance of online auction sites. Acceptance of the value of cooperation also means that archivists place great importance on designing and refining their collecting policies so that they will not knowingly compete with other archives. Archivists in a number of states, starting in the late 1960s, for example, developed regional systems encouraging coordination and cooperation within their jurisdiction. A decade later, many archives became participants in the establishment of regional conservation centers as well. By the 1980s, appraisal methodology had been refined to encompass cooperative efforts such as documentation strategies; even the drafting of an institution's own acquisition policy by necessity featured a cooperative aspect. During these decades, there were also a number of efforts at melding distinct archival programs into one, most notably among local governments (such as when adjacent city and county governments merged archives and records management programs into one entity).[28] Despite these successes, it is hard to say that the cooperative spirit is as strong as it should be in American archival work, even when professional codes of ethics address such matters. Competition is perhaps still too prevalent in the profession. Even with helpful exchanges of information on archives listservs, the placing of ample information on archival websites, and the continuing exchange of views at conferences, institutes, and workshops, a sense of competition which seems out of place in the archival universe too often remains. Archivists must continue to minimize its effects.

Conclusion

Like archival knowledge, archival values are acquired through a combination of introductory education, professional experience, and continuing education and reflection. These values play themselves out in the everyday practice of archives, where (as with any system of values or ethics) general principles are applied to specific cases. Still, these values are at least as characteristic of the archivist's perspective as a specialized body of knowledge. Just as archivists see records, the objects of their work, in a particular way, so they place a special set of values on their work that distinguishes them from records creators and users. Creators may be much more eager for the deliberate destruction of potentially embarrassing records, for instance, or they may be more likely to draw sharp distinctions between who may and may not have access to records. Users may be interested in reserving the use of certain records to themselves, excluding those who might be seen as intellectual competitors, or they may be tempted to rearrange archival organizational priorities to suit their own convenience at the expense of other users. If the knowledge of archivists gives them a different perspective from these groups, so the values of archivists support that different perspective.

The knowledge and values that archivists possess are the foundation of their professional activity, but archivists do not spend their time merely reflecting on them for their own sake. Rather, archivists constantly apply their knowledge and values to particular situations in particular archival collections. An archivist knows and values certain things, but what does an archivist actually do? One may identify larger intellectual concerns for archivists, but those archivists still live in the real world in which there is work to be done, collections to be acquired and organized, and users to be served. The archivist's perspective is important because it helps archivists do certain things. A consideration of the archivist's task, the duties and responsibilities archivists face as professionals, provides additional understanding of what archives and manuscripts are all about.

Chapter 4

The Archivist's Task: Responsibilities and Duties

Regardless of their size, contents, staffing, or organizational placement, all archives share a common task. Archivists work in an assortment of settings with a diversity of materials. They are employed by large state archives and small private historical societies. They manage the scarce documents of the remote past and the more voluminous records of recent times. They care for bureaucratic business records and personal diaries. They handle records made exclusively of paper and ink as well as large numbers of photographs, movies, sound recordings, and collections of electronic data. Even so, they are all members of the same profession because their goals are ultimately identical. No matter what the institution served or how varied the collection, the archivist has responsibility for the valuable records of society and its people, and that responsibility requires certain common activities and duties. Just as lawyers, librarians, and accountants are all part of unified professions regardless of the organizations they work for, so the commonality of purpose among archivists stands out amid the variety of individual cases that seem to separate them one from another. Such common goals have only been strengthened as archivists have formed national, regional, and thematic associations. Their common purposes have also been aided by the emergence of the World Wide Web and Internet, providing mechanisms for mutual sharing of information.

This commonality of purpose has been challenged anew in recent years by changes in the technology of recordkeeping and by constantly shifting political, economic, and social factors. The distinction between the work of different kinds of archives—those that stress cultural and historical values, for instance, and those that provide institutional continuity and accountability—continue to provoke professional discussion, and these distinctions are important ones.[1] Various forces may threaten to fragment the archival community, but they actually reflect healthy growth and diversity. Specialized listservs and print journals continue to expand in number, and research of interest and value to the broader archival community can seem to get lost in the cacophony of voices and communication channels. Even as the appearance of basic archival manuals remains steady, the publication of specialized studies (on particular archival functions, different archival program types, and different records forms) has grown appreciably. Despite debates about their orientation and work, however, the majority of archivists can still agree on a broad mandate to identify, preserve, and provide access to archival records.

What specific responsibilities and duties do archivists carry out in their many professional settings? What tasks occupy their professional lives, and what are the activities to which they apply their professional knowledge and values? Archival activity is nothing if not varied, a reality that only enhances the appeal of the profession to many of its practitioners. This morning the archivist may acquire a new and interesting set of records; this afternoon a researcher with intriguing questions wants information from another collection. Tomorrow plans must be made for microfilming, digitizing, or preserving deteriorating documents. Next week an exhibit or a program for school children opens; a month later the archivist is lobbying for new legislation or participating in a capital fund campaign. In the majority of American archives (which employ only one or two professionals), all these tasks may be performed by the same individual, though in larger programs with more archivists on the staff, there is greater opportunity for specialization. Although the type of records, scope of researchers, and other aspects of their work may vary, the tasks in their management of the records are consistent.[2]

Planning

Amid this diversity of tasks, keeping priorities straight demands that archivists plan the structure of their work carefully. Organizing the archival effort itself is the first step toward organizing the archives. This requires that the archives have a clear mission or vision statement, together with the endorsement of that mission by the parent organization. Records cannot be transferred to the archives until some basic decisions have been made about how it will be established and what it will do. Thus, before giving any attention to records at all, the archivist must lay an organizational foundation for the archival program and its continuing maintenance. *Planning* for the archives is the task that must precede all others. This requires archivists to be both astute observers of the larger institutional culture of which they are a part and articulate advocates of the archival mission. The need to do this has become even more pressing as many outside the archival field, working with digital documents and information resources, have taken on archival functions.

This programmatic planning focuses on a number of areas, beginning with fundamental questions of policy and purpose. Why has the archives been established? What is it intended to accomplish? If the archival program is placed within a library or a research institution, these purposes may seem self-evident, but it is still necessary to express them in a concise way. If the archives is located within an organization whose primary purpose is something other than preserving information and promoting research—a business or religious organization, for example—the value of stating the archives' mission will be even greater. In either case, settling these fundamental questions at the very beginning, perhaps long before any records actually come through the door, is essential. It is not enough for archivists to know what their mission is; they must be able to articulate and justify it, even amid changing circumstances.

Next come questions of organizational structure. Where will the archives be placed within the parent body? Who will it report to, and what position does that office have within the organization? By what authority will the archives be established? The archivist's concern here is in laying as firm a basis as possible for the archives, not relying on the whim or interest (however enthusiastic) of a superior. Archival programs must have a clear line of reporting to the organization's chief administrative officer, primarily because archival responsibilities cut across all the units of the institution. In public settings, the archives should be formally established in law, preferably with specificity in such areas as program elements and even the qualifications of staff. In private settings, the archives should be established through whatever formal organizational process is available internally. Making clear the lines of authority at the outset is necessary if the archives is to determine its proper jurisdiction over records.

Beyond these concerns, the archives will need a clear statement about the scope of its holdings. What kinds of records documenting what kinds of people and activities will the archives assemble and hold? What subject areas will be the special purview of this archives, thereby distinguishing it from others? Is the archives intended to gather only the records of the parent body, or will it collect other materials as well? Will it acquire its holdings only when someone freely gives them, or will it in some (or even most) circumstances purchase them? In a public repository or that of a private institution, will the archives have the authority to compel offices or individuals to deposit the institution's records? The initial planning process should include a collecting policy that addresses these questions. The policy should be reviewed periodically as the archives extends its work into the future, accommodating changing institutional demands, research interests, and information technologies.[3]

The archivist must also plan for the space the archives will occupy and for the facilities and equipment it will contain. Is space being specially constructed for the archives, or is existing space being renovated? What special considerations need to be taken into account to make that space suitable for use as an archives? How will the areas for staff, for users, and for the collections be differentiated from one another so as to take maximum advantage of the fixed limits? What kinds of equipment and supplies will be required? Ideally, planning for the space in which archival records will be managed comes before any actual records are acquired. In many instances, however, archival programs have been established and records gathered without adequate facilities, making use of whatever space, good or bad, is available. No archivist ever has (or ever admits to having) enough space, and any growing collection constantly faces the prospect of exhausting its space, either now or in the future. Space planning has become more complex with the increasing number and complexity of digital recordkeeping systems. One might expect the amount of paper records to decline, but the so-called paperless office remains one of the great myths of modern times.[4] Thus, archivists have to plan spaces for storing an increasingly mixed set of record formats.

Arranging space and buying equipment naturally cost money, and the archivist must therefore include budgetary planning in any initial deliberations. How and where will the archives get the funds it needs to carry out its activities? Will funding come entirely from the parent organization, or will it also be necessary to rely on outside support? In either case, how can the archives be assured of steady, reliable funding—support that does not wax and wane with an administrator's or benefactor's interest? Beyond that, how will the archives apportion its resources internally? What percentage of the budget will be needed for salaries, for equipment, for security and physical preservation needs, and for other activities? Finally, what kind of accounting procedures will be needed so that the archives will know at any given moment where it stands and whether it can afford to do what it hopes to do?

Planning must also include a consideration of the personnel who will embody the archives. How many and what kinds of people will make up the staff? What educational background will they need, and what sorts of things should they be able to do? What will their responsibilities be within the archives, and what specific tasks will they perform? What procedures will be established to judge their performance, reward them when they do well, and promote them to greater responsibilities? What will be the lines of supervision given and received? These matters, too, must be addressed at the beginning of any archival effort. Fortunately, with the strengthening of graduate archival education, it is easier today to identify qualified applicants for archival positions. The directors of archival programs bear the responsibility to continue to promote the professionalism of the staff.[5]

Planning is not a one-time-only activity, undertaken only when a new archival program is established or a new archivist appointed. Rather, the planning process must be accompanied by ongoing *evalu-*

ation of the archival effort. This begins with the archives collecting systematic data about itself and its operations in the form of user statistics, processing costs and rates, and other measurements. Progress toward the completion of particular projects—the ramping up of activities in anticipation of a significant institutional anniversary, for example—should be charted, and the impact of unexpected obstacles noted. More systematic evaluation tools are also available and, while these can be time consuming, they reveal dimensions of the archival program which may not be apparent in day-to-day practice. There are good models for collection analysis, in which the archivist studies not merely the quantity of holdings but, more important, their quality. Has a religious archives, for instance, fulfilled its mission to document church life if all it holds are registers of baptisms and marriages? Where are the records of congregational associations, social service programs, and the prayer life and religious practice of the members? There are also useful models of detailed studies of the users of archives. Most archivists think they know who their "typical" users are, but are those perceptions accurate? Isn't something amiss if an archives gears its descriptive media toward the scholarly historical researcher if 80 percent of the people who come through the door are amateur genealogists?[6] Armed with the information derived from such evaluation techniques, archivists can periodically adjust their mission statements, priorities, and other activities.

On the face of things, some of these tasks may not seem like archival questions or responsibilities. They relate not to records as such, but to broad management functions as they apply to archives. Still, failure to address these issues at the outset guarantees that the archivist will never even have the chance to address the archival questions. Once proper planning has been undertaken, however, archivists can proceed to perform the tasks that constitute their own particular expertise. Those activities may be encompassed under three broad headings: saving and acquiring archival records; organizing archival records; and making archival records available.

Saving and Acquiring Archival Records

1. Identification. Once the archives has been established, the archivist turns to the task of saving and acquiring records of enduring value: the basic *identification* of those records. This is the activity that establishes an initial level of intellectual and physical control over the records, and it does so by applying several fundamental questions to archival materials. Who produced them? What are they? What are the reasons and purposes for which the records were created? When were they produced, and what period do they cover? How many of them are there? Where are they? Why are they in a particular form and order? What have they been through before coming into the control of the archives? How have their technologies changed, if at all? What kinds of established user clienteles would be interested in these records? How do these records relate to the mission of the archival program?

To answer these questions, the archivist analyzes the background of the records and then actually examines them, putting the pieces of the puzzle together. For many archivists, this is one of the most enjoyable of their duties, for it entails an extended discovery process, frequently requiring the solution to a succession of mysteries. It is also the single most critical archival function, since all other archival work hinges on its success. The questions are asked, often through the instrument of a survey, field work, or scheduling, in which the archivist seeks out records in what may be considered their "original habitat" (a working office, the attic of a family home, a personal computer's memory, or a storage room of some kind).

2. Appraisal and Acquisition. Not all records will have sufficient value to justify inclusion in the archives, and, once the records have been identified, the archivist makes decisions about which of them to acquire. Archivists call the process of making those decisions *appraisal,* and it entails establishing procedures for analyzing records in order to make sound and consistent choices. Archival theory has evolved detailed standards for making appraisal judgments. These standards have become all the more important as the quantity of records has increased and their quality has generally decreased. Appraisal theory proposes a set of criteria, analytical tools, and techniques for archivists to apply in a systematic way. Because appraisal thus represents a doorway into the archives through which all records must pass, it is critical. The transfer of a document into an archival repository imbues it with particular value, not unlike a work of art in an art museum or an artifact in a history museum or historic site. For that reason, appraisal has been the focus of intensive research and thought by archivists, especially in recent years.[7]

Many different intellectual frameworks have been developed for archivists to use as they approach the task of appraisal. Some stress the identification of what are called *evidential and informational* values in records: evidence of the existence and activities of record creators, and information about people and things mentioned in the records. Others call for systematic planning and interinstitutional cooperation in detailed and evolving documentation strategies. Still others recommend functional analysis, studying first the personal and collective activities that produce records and then examining the records themselves. Finally, some approaches stress analyzing the quality of already-existing documentary holdings before seeking to add to them, so as to fill gaps better. Archivists today have considerable latitude in adapting a range of appraisal methods best suited to their repository's needs.[8]

Once appraisal decisions are made, the archivist can initiate specific plans to transfer the records to the custody of the archives, a process archivists call *acquisition.* This, too, is a form of intellectual and physical control, and it takes place on both levels simultaneously. Intellectually, the archivist maintains the knowledge of what the records are and secures full control over them undisturbed. In many archives, especially those that collect records from outside the parent organization, this requires a formal transfer of legal ownership, not only of the records themselves as physical objects, but also (insofar as possible) of their contents. Physically, the acquisition process includes concern for the actual transfer of the records from their original location to the archives facility. This process is deceptively simple, since great care must be exercised in making the transfer. A wise old archivist once stated as a maxim that, for destruction of records, "three moves equals a fire." All archivists must therefore ensure that the records puzzle has the same number of pieces after acquisition as before. An accession record must be made by the archives to ensure that this has been done. The advent of electronic recordkeeping systems presents further challenges to the archivist to maintain both the records and the systems that support them.[9]

3. Physical Preservation. "Saving" archival records often means just that, and archivists must therefore be concerned with issues of physical *preservation* and care. Through their education and experience, archivists come to know something of the physical (and now digital) characteristics of the records they encounter, as well as the factors that cause those records to deteriorate. They must therefore be on guard against physical damage and make plans from the very beginning of their work to prevent, retard, arrest, or reverse it. Most important of all is a systematic effort to maintain a stable environment in the archives, with reasonably constant temperature and humidity and control of light. It may be necessary for the archivist to intervene, usually with the help of preservation specialists, to check further degradation or to reverse deterioration that has already occurred. The archivist may also have to consider transferring records from one format to another so that the information will survive even if the records themselves do not. For archivists working with digital records, this may mean experimenting with procedures such as emulation and migration of data. The concept of preservation is expanding, and it is more complicated now than ever before.[10]

Safeguarding the physical integrity and survival of archival records begins the very first time the archivist acts to save and acquire them. Archivists also increasingly recognize the need to intervene in the creation of records and information systems if they hope to have much chance of saving anything. Just how intrusive archivists should be remains a matter of ongoing debate, but the preservation of records in fact begins with their creation. Moreover, archivists often have to make decisions to preserve one aspect of an archival record (usually its content) knowing that other elements (such as its physical container) will be lost. Preservation is a nuanced responsibility.

Organizing Archival Records

1. Arrangement. Once valuable records have been saved and acquired by the archives, the archivist shifts attention to the work of organizing them in a systematic and useful way. These organizational efforts lie at the heart of archival activity, and they are the special focus of the archivist's knowledge and skills. This work begins with the *arrangement* of records, the process of refining intellectual and physical control over them. Applying the principles of provenance and original order, the archivist discerns the proper intellectual arrangement of the records and then puts them physically in that order.

The actual work of arrangement proceeds at the theoretical and practical levels simultaneously. First, the archivist determines how this body of records is organized and what its various component parts are. A state government archives, for example, will hold the records of many government agencies, complete with their various subdivisions, officers, commissions, and employees. The arrangement of those records requires separating them organizationally, and grouping together those that have come from one particular office or function within the agency. The intellectual work of arrangement consists of determining the groupings for each set of archival records. In the case of a collection of personal papers, the archival work is much the same, though the precise questions may vary slightly. What different activities was the creator of the papers involved in during the course of life, and how are those activities reflected in the papers? Personal correspondence may represent one activity, writings or speeches another, financial affairs a third, and photographs yet another. The intellectual work of arrangement in that case likewise consists of determining what those groupings are—not making them up according to the archivist's own inclination, but trying to discover and reestablish the natural order that is already there, even if it has been obscured.

Physical arrangement proceeds at the same time, if the archivist is working with paper (rather than electronic) records. This is the point at which the archivist actually puts the pieces of the collection into the order of the intellectual arrangement. This step in archival activity is often called *processing*. The intellectual and physical arrangements are brought together. Other activities connected with the physical preservation of the records may also be undertaken at this time. Folded documents are flattened out; rusting staples and paper clips are removed; fragile or valuable items that require special handling are treated; in general, neatness and order are effected. The records are placed in folders and boxes, and these are labeled to identify their contents. More refined processing in the future is always a possibility, but in the majority of cases it is unlikely. Thus, the processing that the records receive at this stage of arrangement is often the only processing they are likely ever to get. Where available, archives technicians, student interns, or volunteers can carry out this kind of work under the supervision of a professional archivist.

   2. Description. Once the records have been arranged, the archivist must proceed to the next logical step and describe what that arrangement is. *Description* is the archival activity that fixes and records information about the organized collection in some medium other than the archivist's own head and serves as a guide to any potential user.[11] The archivist produces various descriptive media to accomplish this task. Librarians, too, produce comparable and more familiar "descriptive media," traditionally in the form of the card catalog and now the online computer catalog. In library terms, arrangement corresponds roughly to the structure of the classification scheme, while description corresponds to the actual public catalog itself, used by librarians and library patrons alike. Allowing for the differences between library and archival materials, description in archives is designed to accomplish the same purpose of letting users know what materials are available and how they are arranged.

   The precise forms of descriptive media that archivists use to convey knowledge about their records will vary, and several different levels of description may overlap. Descriptions may include online catalogs, written inventories of considerable detail, indexes, or even lists of individual documents or groups of documents. Many archives still publish general guides to their holdings, although this has become less common with the ability to describe holdings on the World Wide Web. All of these are known collectively among archivists as *finding aids,* and the phrase itself is telling: they are aids to both the archivist and to any potential user of the records in finding information in those records. Each archives produces some or all of these finding aids—often more than one, embodying different levels of detail, for the same collection—for use inside the archives. A single collection may have a brief, summary entry in the general catalog, for instance, as well as a more detailed inventory or list of box and folder contents. Archives also produce such descriptive media for use beyond the walls of the archives by reporting their holdings to published multirepository guides or national computerized directories. Many archivists report on potential research by preparing articles for various print journals, or they monitor listservs on the Internet where researchers discuss their work.[12] Proceeding on all these levels at once, archival description codifies what archivists know about their collections as the result of working with them and then passes that knowledge on to others.

Making Archival Records Available

1. Reference. As they have come increasingly to appreciate, archivists are not savers of records for their own sake; rather, they save so that archival records can be made available and used. The clearest example of the use of archives and manuscripts comes in the *reference* process, when someone other than the archivist looks for information in them. This contact with archival records may come in person, over the telephone, via electronic mail, or by the traditional route that is now called "snail" mail. Like the librarian in a similar setting, the archivist is in the position of helping the user locate information. The reference interaction is the point at which all other archival activity begins to pay off. What happens in the reference room also ought to be the chief measure of the archivist's success. Experience in the reference room may also be analyzed to measure the effectiveness of the archives program, becoming in effect a laboratory for archivists to gather data about their work, to experiment with new approaches, and to test long-standing assumptions.[13]

The reference process may seem simple, but in fact it is complex and multilayered. What question has the researcher asked, and is that really what the user wants to know? Most archivists can recite examples of users who, with perfectly good intentions (frequently trying to be "helpful" or not to appear unknowing), asked about one matter when they really wanted to know something else altogether.[14] In the same way, many researchers can relate cases in which they asked one question but the archivist (again, with good intentions) heard and answered a different one. The reference process must therefore begin with the archivist and researcher communicating clearly to be sure that each understands the other. This can be challenging, given the diversity of researchers who use archival records. The archivist one minute may be working with a genealogist who is looking for very specific evidence about an ancestor and the next counseling a graduate student fishing for a dissertation topic. Researchers bring a wide variety of backgrounds, skills, and disciplinary methods into the reference room, and the archivist must become adept at discerning their differing needs. Researchers also bring a wide range of personalities, and the archivist must be prepared to work with all of them, particularly those who lack experience in using archival records.

Next, the archivist makes available to the researcher any descriptive media about the archival holdings that will provide clues to the possible locations of the desired information. By looking at the finding aids, the archivist and the user are able to narrow the search, finding the points of intersection between subject interest and the information in the records. The archivist, who knows more about the nature of the records and recordkeeping systems, will often have an advantage over the researcher, and archivists therefore play a more active role in reference than in a library, where many users are able to locate holdings on their own. In a private archives, more than one collection may have letters of the particular individual under study, and the finding aids provided in the reference interview will make that apparent. In a public archives, another researcher will be guided to look at the records of one government agency rather than another in seeking answers to the particular questions of the moment.[15] In an institutional archives, the archivist might be expected to do considerably more for the researcher, such as more initial searching, to find pertinent records for the institutionally based researcher.[16] While archivists need always to be working to make the reference process as independent and user-friendly as possible, especially as they design online guides, they must always be prepared to help researchers more rather than less.

Finally, the archivist actually makes the records themselves available to the user, retrieving those materials that will be helpful. Though the archivist is interested in making this use as open and easy as possible, there are certain constraints that must be taken into account. Many of these have to do with the simple security and safekeeping of the records, and most archivists adopt rules of use best fitting the circumstances of their own reference room. Unlike most libraries, all archives have what are known as closed stacks: the archivist rather than the user is the one to go and retrieve the records from the storage area and bring them to the place where they will be studied. This is one reason why archival finding aids strive for utmost clarity; it is also why archivists almost always will be intermediaries between the researchers and the records. Only in rare circumstances do the documents leave archival custody, although many finding aids will guide researchers to records held by other archives or by the originating office. The user will study the records under controlled conditions in the presence of the archivist to guard against physical abuse or, in extreme cases, damage or theft. This is especially important in the case of archival records that have great financial value, as in the case of autographs, for instance.[17] Archivists include the drafting of policies and procedures to govern use of the collections in their general planning for the archives. Archivists also must be careful to instruct researchers, especially those who are novices in the use of archival records, about how to work with such sources. Researchers are asked to sign forms agreeing to abide by the research rules of the repository, and it is usually a good idea to regularly remind researchers of these regulations.

2. Access. With many records, particularly those of relatively recent date, the archivist must also be concerned with questions of privacy, confidentiality, and sensitivity. The archivist's general interest is in making the maximum amount of information available to users, but some records must be restricted from use, at least for a certain time. The problems presented by such records are identified by archivists as questions of *access:* who has the right to see which records, and which need to be withheld? The archivist has the responsibility to strike an appropriate balance here, promoting the maximum amount of use of records that is consistent with the protection of legitimate rights to privacy and confidentiality. This is most successfully done by focusing on the particular requirements of each archival collection or fonds. Archives usually specify that certain records are closed for a stated period, such as five years, ten years, or a specified time after the donor's death. Most archives avoid procedures that impose across-the-board access dates, opening all records before a given year and closing everything after it, regardless of content. Such an approach "over-protects" some records that are not sensitive, even as it "under-protects" those that have to be guarded longer. Access restrictions must be drawn carefully, sometimes by the archivist alone, sometimes in consultation with the donor or originating office, sometimes with the donor's family. Most users recognize the need for such restrictions, and archivists approach their work in this area with care so as to balance conflicting interests and to avoid creating the impression that they are "hiding something." Clearly established procedures whereby researchers may ask for a review and reconsideration of access restrictions also help overcome that perception.

Archivists have learned to be particularly astute about privacy and security. Some archivists have developed specific procedures for researchers to request access to restricted records,[18] and it is important that all archives have clear and appropriate procedures for providing access to the records they hold. If records cannot be used, it is appropriate to ask why the records are in the archival repository to begin with; this same logic questions excessive delays in archival processing, whereby certain collections or fonds are essentially blocked from use. Archivists realize that family members can be sensitive to what the records of a relative might reveal about them, and archivists might face some candid and awkward negotiations with them about such matters.[19] Unfortunately, there are enough cases in which archives have been careless in establishing guidelines for access (allowing donors or family members to have undue control over who gets to use the records, for example) that the professional community is becoming more careful in matters of access. One of the worst things that an archives can experience is negative publicity about how it administers its records, with potential negative consequences for soliciting new collections and in working with researchers.[20]

3. Ethics. In administering access, the archivist must be especially concerned with professional *ethics*, but in fact ethical conduct must pervade all archival work. This begins with honest treatment of potential donors of records and the fulfillment of commitments to timely arrangement and description. Professional ethics are particularly important, however, when records are made available. The archivist must endeavor to treat all users equitably, not giving favored treatment to one over another and certainly not permitting one researcher access to materials that are closed to a comparable researcher. Many other archival activities also present ethical dilemmas.[21] Archivists are also cautious about conducting research in their own collections. When they do so, they are careful to avoid competing with their patrons and thus avoid the temptation to provide them with less than equal consideration. Finally, archivists make no attempt to influence the conclusions that users may draw from the information that is in their collections.

The scope of ethical conduct of concern to archivists has expanded. Within the past two decades, the ownership of the records and artifacts—they are often indistinguishable—of the world's indigenous peoples became a new issue, fought in the courtrooms, in the media, and in various protests.[22] Federal laws, such as the Native American Graves Protection and Repatriation Act of 1990 (NAGPRA) and the American Indian Religious Freedom Act of 1978, pose special problems for archives and archivists holding records of ethnographers and other researchers. Some archivists may just as likely discover that they are in possession of materials illegally removed from a Jewish family during the Holocaust or inappropriately acquired from a corporation in the name of a greater public good.[23] Others may discover that they are holding records that have been targeted by the federal government as being potential threats to national security. At the least, archivists should document carefully how they handle records that may prove to be controversial or contested.

4. Sharing Information. Archivists fulfill only half their responsibility to make records available if they simply sit and wait for users to come to them. Instead, archivists must be active in *publicizing* their *holdings*. This responsibility implies the necessity of sharing information about what is in each archives, as well as the knowledge of how and by whom it may be used. Archivists accomplish this by disseminating information about their collections in as many ways as they can. Reporting acquisitions or the opening of collections to scholarly journals is also useful. These same objectives are accomplished when archives report their holdings to subject-based, regional, or national guides. The *National Union Catalog of Manuscript Collections*, now incorporated into the Research Libraries Information Network, and the NHPRC *Directory of Archives and Manuscript Repositories in the United States* were the pioneers, and there were other early efforts to spread knowledge of archival holdings. The most dramatic change in sharing knowledge about archives, however, has come with use of the World Wide Web. Today, nearly every archives has a website, providing at least basic information about its mission, the nature of its holdings, location, hours of operation, and other information valuable to potential researchers.[24] Some archives have expanded these websites to include complete sets of what were formerly in-house finding aids, selective full text digitized copies of records, digital exhibitions, and self-paced tutorials on how to use the archives. The potential for expanding public knowledge of archives via the Web seems unlimited and, in comparison to other methods of publicizing archives, the costs are meager.[25]

5. Exhibits, Outreach, and Advocacy. Especially in recent years, archivists have devoted increasing attention to the importance of *exhibit and outreach programs.* They have come to recognize that archival treasures should not be hidden away but should be shown off. In an effort to promote a wider use of their collections, archivists have begun to plan more carefully for various kinds of public programs. Exhibitions of particularly valuable, intriguing, or important items from the collection; displays that commemorate significant events in personal, local, national, or organizational history; reproductions of items that will permit the wider community to remember and validate its own experience; popular publications highlighting the most important documents held by the archives and the services provided; newspaper columns and television productions that bring the past to life—these are all significant services that archives can perform.

At the same time, archivists have begun to plan even more active programs for nontraditional users of archives. The archives is not intended merely for the administrator, the scholar, or the supposedly "serious" student. Many other kinds of people can be introduced to the pleasures of archival records. School children, for example, can see history come alive through contact with original or copied archival

Even young students can be introduced to the uses and importance of archives.
Photograph courtesy Library and Archives Division, Historical Society of Western Pennsylvania.

records, which offer them an insight into the reality of the past that is too often absent from their study of the subject. The elderly can be aided in the recollection of their own past and rewarded with a sense that their individual lives have been worthwhile through programs that include original documents, photographs, and sound recordings. By actively taking portions of their collections to such groups, archivists not only broaden support for their programs, but also fulfill their responsibilities to make their holdings as broadly available as possible. An enhanced public profile of the archives or historical manuscripts program also lays the foundation for raising additional support for the programs preserving our documentary heritage. Many archival programs, both government and private, have created trusts and other venues to raise additional funds to support archival programs.[26]

Developing public programs is a natural extension of other archival tasks. In all the activities archivists engage in, they have always had one eye on the people who want to use their records. What has proved more challenging has been stepping beyond outreach to engage in advocacy. If public programs are intended to raise public awareness of archival programs and work, then advocacy activities to bring about specific results, such as new legislation, changes in public policy, or greater government financial support, are no less important.[27] This can be complicated, as the ability of archivists to provide the critical role in explaining the importance of records has been weakened somewhat by our era's generalized emphasis on information. Records may seem old-fashioned, even though every organization creates and maintains them, or obstacles to efficient administration and competitive advantage. Just as in public programming, advocacy requires that archivists have a clear mission and a specific objective. The difference, of course, is that advocacy requires archivists to participate in a political process, and most archival programs have not been equipped or allowed to do this. Advocacy, however, is one of the functions clearly uniting archivists on the local level with their national professional community. Advocacy brings archivists face to face with the limitations of their resources, message, and public profile, but it is necessary if they hope to change the various stereotypes plaguing their work.[28] It is part of the price archivists must pay if they are to be effective in preserving the documentary heritage in the real world.

Conclusion

The archivist's task is to carry out a full range of responsibilities. Like a juggler who keeps several balls in the air at one time, the archivist keeps several activities going simultaneously. The very number of those duties is obvious proof that archival work is multifaceted and demanding. It requires many skills. Some of these are acquired at first as a part of introductory archival education; most develop fully only after the archivist has acquired a certain body of experience against which to measure the theoretical understandings of the classroom and continuing study. Some skills are strengthened only as archivists try new approaches, fail, and start again, sharing their experiences with others as a part of the professional community. Being a professional archivist means that one never stops learning and improving both the theory and the practice of the task. The job is never really done.

If the archival task is never quite finished, however, it has its genuine rewards nonetheless. Most archivists find immense satisfaction in their work. They are genuinely oriented toward people of all kinds and toward working with them in a friendly and cooperative manner. Creators, donors, and users of records all have stories to tell and needs to be met, and archivists look forward to working toward shared goals. Archivists are interested in discovering the stories in archives and manuscripts and in sharing those stories with others for the knowledge, insight, understanding, entertainment, and pure enjoyment that they convey. What is more, in an age in which the technology of mass culture has attenuated the sense of reality in human experience, archivists are surrounded by the real stuff of real life. The records in their custody are genuine; they are carriers of information that speak, from one person to another, across the barriers of time, distance, and experience. It is this larger vision that archival work provides. In preserving and transmitting the record of human experience, archivists approach their task with enthusiasm.

Chapter 5

Archivists and the Challenges of New Worlds

The work of the archivist is always challenged by societal forces and trends. Archivists need to be experts not only on records and record-keeping systems; they must also understand the larger organizational cultures that produce and sustain records systems. These offer both opportunities for greater insight into archival documentation and potential threats that undermine the archivist's mission and work. Archivists have always been aware of some challenges, such as the needs for financial resources and professional status. Other challenges are newer and more subtle, the products of the particular demands and developments of the contemporary world. Several of these are especially important for archivists to consider.

Postmodernism

We live in a postmodern world—or, at least we hear people saying that we do. What does this ubiquitous term mean? Definitions are contested, and the disagreements themselves may help elucidate the concept. One dictionary says that postmodernism is the "cultural condition prevailing in the advanced capitalist societies since the 1960s, characterized by a superabundance of disconnected images and styles—most notably in television, advertising, commercial design, and pop video." Postmodernism is "a culture of fragmentary sensations, eclectic nostalgia, disposable simulacra, and promiscuous superficiality, in which the traditionally valued qualities of depth, coherence, meaning, originality, and authenticity are evacuated or dissolved amid the random swirl of empty signals."[1] Postmodernism conjures up relativism, the end of history, the equality of all cultural ventures regardless of their merit, and ultimately the loss of meaning. None of these are attributes that archivists should accept lightly.

Postmodernism has been credited—or blamed—with having many influences: on architecture, writing, education, and other fundamental aspects of society. The concept has certainly influenced the ways in which cultural objects are identified, chosen for long-term maintenance, and interpreted over time.[2] Archives are among those newly challenged cultural objects. One group of archivists exploring this topic has asserted that "the central professional myth of the past century that the archivist is (or should be) an objective, neutral, passive . . . keeper of truth" has become unsustainable. While "archival professionals and users of archives have been slow to recognize the nature of archives as socially constructed institutions, the relationship of archives to notions of memory and truth, the role of archives in the production of knowledge about the past, and, above all, the power of archives and records to shape our notions of history, identity, and memory,"[3] it may well be that archives have become a postmodern phenomenon. But does this postmodern archives share anything with real archives or the day-to-day work of archivists?

No doubt the concept of postmodernism has helped many archivists in their efforts to understand records and archives. One archivist, reflecting on the Vatican Archives (which would seem immune from postmodern tendencies), has said that "we have moved from a rigid sense of positivist notions of history to a more complex sense of the past, a sense that sees pasts plural, and pasts separate but interconnected—pasts derived not only from the archives but derived from a collective memory producing a sense of social memory."[4] Others have noted the same impact, arguing the need for archivists "to (re)search thoroughly for the missing voices" in their archives, "for the complexity of the human or organizational functional activities under study during appraisal, description, or outreach activities, so that archives can acquire and reflect multiple voices, and not, by default, only the voices of the powerful."⁵

Postmodern sensibilities suggest that archival records are not immobile or static, that their meaning is not fixed and transparent. They are not objective sources, but rather documents constantly going through changes and changing interpretations. Nevertheless, records cannot be simply dismissed as sources for accountability; of their very nature, archives cannot cease to be places where evidence resides and some degree of truth can be found. Postmodernism, as a form of interpretive criticism of texts, offers much to archivists in their work with the documentary heritage, but it must be used thoughtfully.

Internet Time

In only a little more than the decade in which it became widely available, the Internet/World Wide Web has changed the world, influencing virtually every aspect of contemporary life. While archives and historical manuscripts have often been seen as ways of stopping time, the Internet seems to demonstrate that time always passes and passes quickly. While archives have apparently been all about fixity, the Internet suggests that change is the only real constant, and the speed of change is quickening as never before. The result of this is what one observer has called "Internet time," the idea that, especially in the business world, "product development and consumer acceptance were now occurring in a fraction of the time that they traditionally took." Whoever was first to use the Internet for marketing would have an advantage over those who did not. The fundamental characteristic of this new medium was that it offered "a potent communication tool, offering unprecedented speed and reach. It does change everything, just as the telegraph, the telephone, and electricity eventually did." These changes would be ongoing because "people do not operate on Internet time—and therefore the truly large implications of this new technology are likely to take many decades to unfold."⁶ Just how archives will function in this sped-up world remains to be seen.

Because they have the mandate to preserve their holdings for the very long term, archivists have tended to view time on an extended scale. Traditionally, this meant that they encountered records at the end of their life cycle, sometimes years or decades after the records had been created and performed their original use in their originating offices. Archivists who collected personal or family papers frequently had to wait a century or more before the documents came into their intellectual and physical control. Virtually every archivist can tell a story of "discovering" old records, stashed and forgotten in closets, basements, or attics, awaiting their own leisurely examination. The emergence of Internet time means that many archivists no longer have this luxury. Archivists increasingly recognize the need to be involved in the early stages of the records life cycle or continuum, both for traditional kinds of records and for those in digital formats. The need to be involved in the design of records and records systems is now apparent if archivists ever hope to get aboard the train that runs on Internet time. Thus, archivists will have to take on more and more of a policy role in order to fulfill their responsibilities to their parent agencies.

The passage of time has sped up on other fronts as well. Archivists have become accustomed to working with researchers inquiring into holdings via the Web and electronic mail, and expecting almost instantaneous answers. When the authors of this book entered the profession more than three decades ago, the process of requesting information from or about an archives was positively genteel: a reference exchange conducted by what is now derisively called "snail" mail might take several weeks or even months, and everyone seemed content with that pace. Today, archivists are expected to respond to all inquiries within hours. They are expected to maintain attractive websites with detailed information about their holdings and with user-friendly interfaces which encourage immediate interaction with researchers. Increasingly, researchers want fully digitized copies of records to be available—what? you mean I actually have to *go* to the archives?—and that these records should be fully searchable, word for word. There is no use in hoping that these trends will simply go away. As more and more Americans go online, they will only intensify.[7] Archivists will have to get used to living, like everyone else, in Internet time.

.

The USA PATRIOT Act, signed by President George W. Bush, had a profound effect on questions of access to records. WHITE HOUSE PHOTO BY ERIC DRAPER.

Ethics and Security

The development of codes of ethics has been one of the hallmarks of the growth of the archival profession. While few archivists spend much time consulting such codes in dealing with specific practical problems, archivists now find that ethical problems are more likely to appear in everyday practice. Questions of acquisition of records, of how to provide equitable access to them, and of how to navigate the shifting currents of law and policy present new challenges.

The autograph and manuscript marketplace is particularly problematic, forcing archivists to operate in a world governed by values different from their own. The emergence of online auction houses—eBay is the best known—has only intensified this problem. The professional associations of archivists and records managers have joined together in asking these outlets to provide information about public records, alienated into private hands, which are offered for sale. "As documents of all types have become increasingly collectible," a joint statement of the professional organizations said, "the number of official government records appearing for sale through online venues such as eBay has grown. Their disappearance into private hands deprives the public of access to important historical details concerning the development of property rights, taxation, judicial actions, and community growth, as well as the enduring impact of human beings upon their surrounding environments."[8] The steadily rising prices that such historical documents and artifacts can command, together with the ease of bartering and selling them online, will only exacerbate this problem for archivists in the future.

Ethical problems for archivists specifically related to questions of national security are also more complicated than ever before, producing significant changes in government regulations, particularly those regarding access to public records and information. In the years since the attacks of 11 September 2001, these questions have taken on a new urgency, portending a new era of government secrecy, perhaps best represented by the USA PATRIOT Act. This has only reinforced dispositions toward secrecy that are always characteristic of those in power. Archivists will increasingly find themselves in the middle of disputes of this kind: formerly quiet archives may now be sites of information that is crucial to national security, or they may be repositories where terrorists will be able to find information useful in planning further attacks. We know, for example, that ours is an age in which Boy Scouts can build nuclear breeders in their backyards, using information in the public domain and their old high school chemistry books.[9] In such a world, all archivists must think again about how they approach these issues.

Archivists working in government settings are particularly apt to face difficult decisions about preservation and open access to the records for which they are responsible. The reliance on e-mail for all matters, great and small, offers a particularly telling case. Even in tiny Vermont, the state archivist reported in 2004, the disappearance of e-mail became a serious problem. The state's governor had taken to responding to e-mail at home, apparently thinking that any of his communications would thereby be considered personal rather than official. At the same time, the statehouse network server became so overwhelmed with accumulated e-mail from and to members of the legislature that it threatened to crash. To prevent this, the archivist said, the system "was programmed to automatically delete email messages once they had been on the system ninety days." As a result, "another [archival] resource vanished, not because of an appraisal of its legal or historical value, but because of limited network storage capacity. Storage space, whether virtual or physical, constantly limits our capacity to preserve resources."[10] For all the advantages the new digital means of communication bring, they may also help to erode government accountability even further and to reinforce new levels of government secrecy.

If such predicaments face government archivists, those confronting archivists who work in corporate settings are perhaps even greater. New regulations concerning corporate records are well intended and even necessary, but they may also have the effect of reinforcing poor attitudes that some businesses have toward archives and records management. Too many executives look on records as obstacles to efficiency and competitive agility: records are seen as impediments to corporate re-engineering, best replaced by chimerical "paperless" offices. Worse, corporate leaders often look on stricter recordkeeping requirements, best represented by the Sarbanes-Oxley Act of 2002 passed in response to scandals in the accounting industry, as incentives to keep only the minimal amount of documentation required. Corporate archivists have had to continue to struggle against such attitudes, and the struggle is getting harder all the time.

Symbolism and Technology

In making decisions about which records to preserve and in building their holdings, archivists have long had to assess different kinds of value. Evidence, information, accountability, and public and corporate memory have traditionally been the practical characteristics of records archivists appraised, but they have also considered the symbolic and cultural significance of archives. On their face, these latter values seem irrelevant in a world of electronic information technology. Perhaps someone will one day study the symbolic value of disks of various sizes, computer screens and CPUs, or the various editions of computer manuals, but it is difficult to imagine that these will ever be approached with the same romanticism with which handwritten manuscripts or early printed books are sometimes treated. Even so, will the ongoing preoccupation with technology strip archival work of these aesthetic and emotional satisfactions?

For all their trumpeting of brave new worlds, technologists themselves are not immune to the attractions of traditional documents and documentary forms. Even magazines such as *Wired*, which is devoted to the promotion of high technology, still produce glossy, attractive editions which, the editors apparently hope, will be smuggled into some library or archives and preserved for the long term among other physical artifacts. Elsewhere, we find persistent paeans to traditional forms of print and manuscript. Authors such as Sven Birkerts and Nicholson Baker have received wide notice for extolling records as artifacts and for their assertion that the preservation of these originals should supersede all other responsibilities for archivists and librarians. Old books and papers seem to represent a stable, timeless form, which is the more reassuring in a time when all else seems subject to constant and rapid change. Of course, these attitudes tap into a much older tradition—that of Ned Lud and his fellow loom-smashers in nineteenth century England—but they are still a forceful backlash against the apparent sterility of the digital age, in which information seems to be everywhere and nowhere at the same time. To forego use of the personal computer in favor of the typewriter or pencil, however, is merely to exchange one set of technologies for another. All records and archives are produced by some generating technology or other, and archivists must work with all of them. Since all records and recordkeeping systems are the product of technology, all archivists are technologists. Emphasis exclusively on the cultural mission of archives and an insistence that archivists are more like museum curators than software engineers misses this important point.

Advocacy and the Archival Mission

Archives are more than symbolic repositories that help in the construction of public memory. They are more immediately useful for historians and other academics in scholarly research. Beyond that, most archivists today also want to see their holdings used more widely

Exhibits demonstrate that archives have something for everyone. PHOTOGRAPH
COURTESY SPECIAL COLLECTIONS LIBRARY, PENN STATE UNIVERSITY.

by public-policy makers, by school children studying the history of
their town, by news media covering the events of the present, and by
many other users. This has demanded that archivists be clear about
the messages they send and the resources they make available to society.

In the last few decades, the professional associations of archivists
and records professionals have formed the habit of issuing statements
on controversial and timely topics. Regardless of the particulars of any
given issue, this trend helpfully establishes the notion that archivists
have something to say on important matters. They have, for example,
issued statements on the apparent alienation of public records into
private hands, as in the case of the papers of Mayor Rudolph Giuliani
of New York, which were temporarily given to a private consulting
group for processing in 2003, rather than to the city's Department of
Records and Information Services. A year later, the Society of
American Archivists joined with other groups in a lawsuit to open
previously restricted records of the vice president of the United States
pertaining to the formation of energy policy. The society also continually monitors interpretation of the Presidential Records Act, protesting

executive orders that seem to run counter to the law's predisposition in favor of the opening of records as soon as practicable.[11] These interventions by archivists and their professional associations have not always been successful, but they have become an accepted part of their mission.

Archives have also been featured in the courtroom, and archivists have to work on cogently expressing the nature of their mission and work. The defamation suit brought by David Irving against Deborah Lipstadt in London for her characterization of Irving as a Holocaust denier may be indicative of what is to come. A witness in the case, a prominent professional historian, said that the trial was "about how we can tell the difference between truth and lies in history," ultimately concluding that the ruling against Irving was a "victory for history, for historical truth and historical scholarship."[12] While journalists were often bored by the detailed testimony about the nuances of historical research, the critical analysis of documents, and the comparison of various sources in order to make conclusions about particular events in the past—all of which were at issue—we may yet see more historical records in prominent, high-profile court cases, with archivists on the witness stand. The better archivists can explain their work, the more likely it will be that the public and policymakers will understand both the power of records and the need for professional administrators of those records.

As it continues into the future, such advocacy will have to be strategically planned. To do this, archives must continually refer to their mission statement and organizational placement. Experts in strategic planning always stress the importance of doing environmental scans to identify competitors and allies in particular functions. Archivists may be seen, for example, as competing with records managers, knowledge managers, systems designers, software engineers, information officers, and others. Losing out to these professionals can have deleterious effects on the archival budget and the ability to perform the archival mission. As a result, the challenge for archivists is to transform competition with these groups into partnerships, and that task begins with the archivist's placing a higher premium on advocacy and public outreach. In any given archival setting, this may entail a significant shift in priorities and programs.[13]

Recordkeeping in the Digital Era

Working across disciplinary and organizational lines, of course, is always challenging, and perhaps getting more so. The digital world is changing so much, making it easier to gain both unlawful and broader access to information. The nature of individual privacy, together with the need for organizational and societal security, has been transformed in recent decades, and especially in the first years of this new century. Concerns about privacy and security, for example, vary from group to group, and archivists may find seemingly natural allies on the opposite side of important questions. Whether in matters of national security or in controversies over access to the records of business corporations, archivists may discover that the values they instinctively place on the availability and flow of information are not shared. Archivists thus find themselves in the position of having to study the contexts of records from perspectives other than their own, a task that is both intrinsically interesting and potentially frustrating. This must be done without allowing introspection to paralyze action. New technologies do not herald a new dark age, any more than they solve all previous problems, but they do call for innovative thinking and solutions.

Traditionally, archivists have placed great credence in the record's stability and protection. Archivists often take it for granted that the books, manuscripts, and artifacts in their repositories have great worth and are thus critical in shaping our historical memory. No matter how haphazardly assembled, virtually any collection of books, manuscripts, or historic sites will influence or even determine our public memory. Once housed in the repository, these materials are, in a sense, enshrined as objects central to our collective sense of the past, but the form and meaning of such housing is now seen differently in our digital age. Much has been written about the end of the printed book and the practice of reading as we know it, and archivists have speculated about the meaning of archives and archival repositories in this context. Some have predicted the disappearance of archives, while others have made claims about new roles and influences for archivists. The truth lies somewhere in between, of course, as it usually does: archivists have had to deal with technology transitions in nearly every generation.[14]

There is no question that the growing use of computers at all levels of society changes most aspects of recordkeeping. The industrial office has become the cybernetic office: the former "stressed uniformity, fragmentation, and specialization," while the latter "stresses diversity, integration, and the generalist approach of systems theory."[15] The challenge for archivists is that most of the concepts governing archival and records administration were formulated in that earlier industrial office. Yet, if archivists are pursuing one of their responsibilities to be students of records and recordkeeping systems, they should work toward making the appropriate adjustments. Of course, larger archival programs with enhanced resources may have a greater chance to do this than do small historical records collecting repositories. Regardless of the size of their institutions, archivists need to utilize all the resources available to them to build a true professional community, exchanging lessons learned, new approaches, failures and the reasons for these failures, and research about basic practices.

It is interesting that so many sites on the World Wide Web featuring archives and historical manuscripts are playing with the concept of "memory," such as the Library of Congress's major digitization effort, called simply American Memory. Could it be that we are worried that one of the main threats of the digital era is a loss of memory? The rise of scholarly interest in public memory, with its ever-changing contours and slippery slopes, may be another indicator of these concerns. The primary institutions contributing to our collective sense of memory are museums, historic sites and buildings, libraries, and archives. Scholars have long recognized their value for public memory, yet the public generally does not comprehend how institutions such as libraries and museums determine what goes into their repositories. Despite their consistent visits to and use of the materials housed in these places, scholars studying public memory are only beginning to consider the implications of archives.

Other disciplines are taking notice of the challenges presented in maintaining the increasing portion of the documentary heritage that is in digital form. A historian's essay on digital preservation in the *American Historical Review*, describing the litany of challenges in managing electronic archives that are well known to archivists and records managers, lamented the increasing professional distance residing between archivists and historians. This commentator indicated that, while there has been considerable discussion about the problem of digital preservation, historians have "almost entirely ignored them," attributing some of this to a widening chasm between historians and archivists.[16] The only way this will change is if archivists come out of their stacks to explain their work, serve as expert witnesses, write letters to newspapers about cases and controversies involving records, and educate not just established researchers about their work but expand their horizons as far as possible. This requires a rethinking of how archivists have traditionally looked at themselves as professionals.

Professionalism

People are attracted to archives work for many reasons: because they love old things; because they see the value of records for social order; because they understand the importance of records in establishing and maintaining continuity. Many of these reasons echo the values that others see in archives. The connections between archives and history endure, and archivists will probably always be reexamining their relationship to this "parent" discipline. Debates about the appropriate education of archivists—primarily in history or primarily in library and information sciences—continue, though with somewhat less intensity than previously. The emergence in the 1970s of public history as a professional subspecialty renewed these debates, though the twin foundations of history and library science remain largely in place.[17]

The last few decades have seen increased debate on the relationship of archives to records management, and the lack of clarity about the boundary line between the two professions continues to cause confusion. Records managers have come more and more to identify themselves as information managers: they have changed the name of their journal from *Records Management Quarterly* to *Information Management Journal*, and they have tried to focus more attention on the technical dimensions of information science. In the process, they have apparently moved away from a focus on records as such, even as archivists have worked harder to define the nature of records.[18] More troublesome are several studies and cases that seem to indicate that a records management program within an organization does not guarantee that systematic efforts will be made for the identification and maintenance of archival records.[19] At the very least, the rise of more complex and pervasive digital systems in all institutional settings demonstrates the need for a holistic approach to records management.

There is a need for a new kind of professionalism, one in which archivists do not work unilaterally, but rather that propels them to join forces with all interested in the preservation of the documentary heritage, from traditional documents to innovative and complex digital objects. To be responsible for identifying the key sources in society's documentary heritage requires archivists to get their hands dirty and operate fully and visibly in the real world. They need to communicate and work across disciplinary lines, and archivists must consider carefully all the ways in which society and its organizations document themselves. There is no reason why archivists should not be the ones who take the lead in generating such cooperative activity, and it would do much to transform their societal image if they did precisely this. Society needs to understand archives and manuscripts because it is in its best interest to know that such records are essential to the public good. Archivists are the only ones who can make this clear.

Conclusion

No job is ever really done. The current and future issues enumerated here are important as we write, but other issues will have occurred to readers already. When the first edition of this volume appeared, in those seemingly ancient days before the widespread availability and use of the World Wide Web, it seemed possible to think that a reasonably complete understanding of archives and manuscripts could be accomplished in a few pages. Today, we recognize that a volume such as this can only provide the barest of introductions, even as it points to ongoing research and discussion within the archives profession. We hope to participate in those discussions ourselves, but we also look forward to the contributions that new generations of archivists will make. Helping society at large understand archives work is an important task, even if it is challenging—as all worthy activities tend to be.

Bibliographic Essay

Fifteen years ago the author of the first edition of this volume wrote, "Any effort to summarize the vast professional literature about archives in a few pages is so foolish an enterprise that it ought to deter a sensible person from even trying." What follows is more than a "few pages," reflecting some significant changes in the nature of what constitutes professional knowledge, but this bibliographic essay is still not intended to be comprehensive.[1] As practitioners of one of the learned professions, archivists have not been reluctant to write about what they do and why they do it. In monographs both long and short and in journal articles, they have considered a wide range of issues; the World Wide Web has expanded the quantity of introductions to and analyses of archival work. Not only are archivists writing even more than before (from basic, practical manuals to scholarly monographs), but they have been joined by doctoral students writing dissertations and other disciplines speculating (both broadly and sometimes wildly) about the nature of archives.

The results of that research, thought, and writing are on the whole readily available, and readers of the present volume are encouraged to explore more deeply in areas of particular interest to them. The other volumes in this *Archival Fundamentals Series* contain references to works that touch on specific aspects of theory and practice (in fact, in a number of the revised volumes in this series the citations to the literature also have expanded considerably), but some general citations may not be out of place here. The following suggestions, arranged generally to follow the five chapters in this volume, are offered merely as *initial* guidance through the archival literature. Rather than trying to be comprehensive, we have opted to focus on general texts providing an introduction to archival work and other writings focused on key aspects critical to *understanding* archives and manuscripts (and writings that have been useful in the preparation of the present volume). While the number of bibliographical references is larger, what follows should still be understood as merely introductory; in many instances, we have included some representative examples of the kinds of scholarship archivists and others can consult in their quest to understand archives and manuscripts. We have opted to stress recent works reflecting current thought and practice, classic writings with continuing insights to offer individuals desiring to understand archives and archival work, and some exceptional or controversial writings reflecting changing knowledge and practice in the field.

Recording, Keeping, and Using Information

We could fill a volume with descriptions of scholarly and other inquiries about the basic human impulses to record, maintain, and use information. Perhaps what is most important to note is that so much valuable and interesting research with implications for understanding archives and manuscripts has come from outside the archival discipline itself. At the least, this broadened scholarly inquiry has led to the creation of some works, such as John Seely Brown and Paul Duguid, *The Social Life of Information* (Boston: Harvard Business School Press, 2000), and David M. Levy, *Scrolling Forward: Making Sense of Documents in the Digital Age* (New York: Arcade Publishing, 2001), that have engaged researchers, the public, and others with a sense of the importance of the document in our so-called modern Information Age. These observers, certainly not archivists, have surprisingly similar or compatible views about the nature of the record. Some archivists have written compelling assessments of what the archival record represents that could be read in conjunction with the writings of commentators such as Brown/Duguid and Levy. One such work is the exceptionally useful publication by Anne J. Gilliland-Swetland, *Enduring Paradigm, New Opportunities: The Value of the Archival Perspective in the Digital Environment* (Washington, D.C.: Council on Library and Information Resources, February 2000), also available on the website of the Council on Library and Information Resources (CLIR). Gilliland-Swetland reviews evidence and archival principles such as provenance, records life cycle, the organic nature of records, records hierarchy, and metadata.

Some rather monumental efforts in understanding writing and related communication systems have enriched our understanding of aspects of records. Steven Roger Fischer's trilogy, *A History of Language* (London: Reaktion Books, Ltd., 1999), *A History of Writing* (London: Reaktion Books, Ltd., 2001), and *A History of Reading* (London: Reaktion Books, Ltd., 2003) is a massive, but useful, assessment of language, with some perspective on the nature of records and the idea of an information age. The trilogy not only provides a rich historical context for working with records but the volumes include many references to the creation, use, and maintenance of documents of interest to the records professional. Fischer's volumes provide little in the way of practical applications for archives and records management, but they do provide an understanding about the origins and nature of documents that can enhance the work of records professionals. Records are a kind of universal language, even in the present digital era. We have to learn how to read these documents just as we have had to learn to read the languages that are in them. Fischer's scholarship even reminds archivists and records managers that the importance of records is all the more remarkable given their original and still often mundane purposes. His histories of language, writing, and reading suggest that, in a larger global, historical sense, we can claim not just to be an information age but a records age.

Orality and Literacy. Archivists have become interested in the nexus between oral and written cultures, that is, between societies that produce archives and those that do not. Albert B. Lord's *The Singer of Tales* (Cambridge, Mass.: Harvard University Press, 1960) explores the connection between the oral and written traditions in Homer. Other important studies on the transition from orality to written systems include Eric A. Havelock, *The Literate Revolution in Greece and Its*

Aftermath (Princeton: Princeton University Press, 1982); Jan Vansina, *Oral Tradition as History* (Madison: University of Wisconsin Press, 1985); and M. T. Clanchy, *From Memory to Written Record: England, 1066–1307* (Cambridge, Mass.: Harvard University Press, 1979; rev. ed. 1991, Blackwell). Patrick J. Geary, *Phantoms of Remembrance: Memory and Oblivion at the End of the First Millennium* (Princeton: Princeton University Press, 1994) provides an interesting contrast to Clanchy's work, especially in the view of how medieval scholars and chroniclers often fabricated evidence; for more on how the concept of forgery and fabrication has changed, also consult Anthony Grafton, *Forgers and Critics: Creativity and Duplicity in Western Scholarship* (Princeton: Princeton University Press, 1990). Walter J. Ong offers a philosophical view in *Orality and Literacy: The Technologizing of the Word* (London: Methuen, 1982), a study that has been the starting point for many scholarly inquiries into the notions of orality and literacy.

 Reasons for Recording Information. A reinvigorated interest in the history of writing has produced a literature offering many insights into the nature of records and archives, especially helping us to understand why information and evidence are recorded. Jack Goody, *The Logic of Writing and the Organization of Society* (London: Cambridge University Press, 1986) and many of his other writings look at this topic the most broadly, discerning interesting connections to religion, culture, government, and other socio-economic factors with the emergence and subsequent use of writing and recordkeeping systems. One of the most comprehensive volumes is Henri-Jean Martin, *The History and Power of Writing,* trans. Lydia G. Cochrane (Chicago: University of Chicago Press, 1994), providing a panoramic sweep of the origins of writing (with many references to recordkeeping) in human society. Denise Schumandt-Besserat's *How Writing Came About* (Austin: University of Texas Press, 1996) provides a convenient summary of her controversial but useful study of the evolution of counting tokens into scripts and writing systems. A sampling of other important investigations into the origins and characteristics of writing include William V. Harris, *Ancient Literacy* (Cambridge, Mass.: Harvard University Press, 1989), Jean Bottero, *Mesopotamia: Writing, Reasoning, and the Gods,* trans. Zainab Bahrani and Marc Van De Mieroop (Chicago: University of Chicago Press, 1992), and Elizabeth

Hill Boone and Walter D. Mignolo, eds., *Writing Without Words: Alternative Literacies in Mesoamerica and the Andes* (Durham, N.C.: Duke University Press, 1994), each emphasizing different aspects with ample references to records and recordkeeping systems.

Why records are created leads the inquirer into this topic into many possible areas for exploration. Thomas Richards, *The Imperial Archive: Knowledge and the Fantasy of Empire* (London: Verso, 1993) may not seem, for example, to have much directly to do with the reality of archives, but the volume provides another lens for viewing the nature of records, evidence, and their cultural meaning that has not always been widely understood within the community of archival practitioners. How and why individuals create and use documents is increasing as a topic of study by scholars. Thomas Augst in his *The Clerk's Tale: Young Men and Moral Life in Nineteenth-Century America* (Chicago: University of Chicago Press, 2003) considers the purpose of diary writing, letter writing, and penmanship, in the process of self-discovery, identity, and acquiring a moral consciousness and authority. Augst is attentive to how the creation of personal documents expanded as writing technologies and supplies became cheaper and more accessible to the middle class. Augst also suggests how these clerks and their particular uses of document creation disappeared by the end of the nineteenth century as new office technologies emerged. Indeed, we can discover important insights into the motives for recordkeeping in unlikely places, such as in H. J. Jackson, *Marginalia: Readers Writing in Books* (New Haven: Yale University Press, 2001), whereby books become personal documents because of annotations, and Anne L. Bower, ed., *Recipes for Reading: Community Cookbooks, Stories, Histories* (Amherst: University of Massachusetts, 1997), whereby accumulations of recipes, often in unique manuscript form, become symbolic centers for community and identity.

Impulses to Save and Destroy Records. When we think of the impulse to save records, we generally think of professionals such as archivists and their role in society and through the past. Luciana Duranti, "The Odyssey of Records Managers," *Records Management Quarterly* 23 (July 1989): 3–6, 8–11 and (October 1989): 3–6, 8–11 provides the broadest portrait of the roles of archivists and other records custodians. This is too simple a way of considering these human impulses. We need to consider, on the saving side, matters such as the history and psychology of collecting, leading to assessments such as Leah Dilworth, ed., *Acts of Possession: Collecting in America* (New Brunswick, N.J.: Rutgers University Press, 2003); Werner Muensterberger, *Collecting: An Unruly Passion: Psychological Perspectives* (Princeton: Princeton University Press, 1994); or Nicholas A. Basbanes, *A Gentle Madness: Bibliophiles, Bibliomanes, and the Eternal Passion for Books* (New York: Henry Holt and Co., 1995) (the latter considering the collecting of manuscripts as much as books). We also learn when we consider how often archives, libraries, and museums are destroyed, generally revealing the immense symbolic and cultural importance of records for nations and various population groups, such as is chronicled in Rebecca Knuth, *Libricide: The Regime-Sponsored Destruction of Books and Libraries in the Twentieth-Century* (New York: Praeger, 2003) and James Raven, ed., *Lost Libraries: The Destruction of Great Book Collections Since Antiquity* (New York: Palgrave Macmillan, 2004).

    Record-Making Technology. Some historians of information technology have provided a historical context for understanding the more recent development of records and recordkeeping systems. James R. Beniger, *The Control Revolution: Technological and Economic Origins of the Information Society* (Cambridge, Mass.: Harvard University Press, 1986) is the best known of such histories, examining the development of office technology (among other things) from the eighteenth to the twentieth centuries. Information on the history of recordkeeping can be found in unlikely places. The classic study of a particular information technology and its implications for society and the recording and preserving of human knowledge is Elizabeth L. Eisenstein, *The Printing Press as an Agent of Social Change* (Cambridge: Cambridge University Press, 1979), an important study with many commentaries and critiques by other scholars. We have many fine examples of the importance of particular kinds of recording devices. Henry Petroski, *The Pencil: A History of Design and Circumstance* (New York: Alfred A. Knopf, 1990) demonstrates that examples of information engineering are not confined to the digital computer but can be seen in the humble wood pencil. Tamara Plakins Thornton, *Handwriting in America: A Cultural History* (New Haven: Yale

University Press, 1996) considers the cultural implications of handwriting manuals, instructors, and practice with numerous implications for early recordkeeping and autograph collecting.

Humans have consistently tried to develop better and faster means of creating documents, as seen in the classic study of the typewriter, Michael H. Adler, *The Writing Machine* (London: Allen and Unwyn, 1973). Likewise Silvio A. Bedini, *Thomas Jefferson and His Copying Machines* (Charlottesville: University Press of Virginia, 1984) is an interesting study of an early and well-known effort to create a device for easing the copying of manuscripts, and it is interesting to compare Jefferson's work to that of the later developer of the electrostatic copying machine in David Owen, *Copies in Seconds: How a Lone Inventor and an Unknown Company Created the Biggest Communication Breakthrough Since Gutenberg: Chester Carlson and the Birth of the Xerox Machine* (New York: Simon & Schuster, 2004).

None of these recording technologies have been neutral, however, and there is an increasing scholarship on the social and cultural implications of them in such books as Lisa Gitelman, *Scripts, Grooves, and Writing Machines: Representing Technology in the Edison Era* (Stanford, Calif.: Stanford University Press, 1999); Margery W. Davies, *Woman's Place Is at the Typewriter: Office Work and Office Workers 1870–1930* (Philadelphia: Temple University Press, 1982); Sharon Hartman Strom, *Beyond the Typewriter: Gender, Class, and the Origins of Modern American Office Work, 1900–1930* (Urbana: University of Illinois Press, 1992); and Hillel Schwartz, *The Culture of the Copy: Striking Likenesses, Unreasonable Facsimiles* (New York: Zone Books, 1996). The ever-growing and broadening scholarship provides new ways for archivists to understand their work and its societal and organizational implications and mandates.

The technology of record making and keeping also can be understood by considering studies of specific types of records, especially diaries. One of the best introductions to diary writing is Thomas Mallon, *A Book of One's Own: People and Their Diaries* (New York: Hungry Minds Publishing, 1984), an informative account of the various types of diaries kept, their purposes, and why some were published and others not. Suzanne L. Bunkers and Cynthia A. Huff, eds., *Inscribing the Daily: Critical Essays on Women's Diaries* (Amherst:

University of Massachusetts Press, 1996) considers diary writing as part of an activity assisting women in maintaining their own private space and in fostering their unique identities. Andrew Hassam, *Sailing to Australia: Shipboard Diaries By Nineteenth-Century British Immigrants* (Melbourne, Aus.: Melbourne University Press, 1995) is an interesting study about how diaries were created not just to document experiences but to help others in their journeys to this new world. Alexandra Johnson, *The Hidden Writer: Diaries and the Creative Life* (New York: Anchor Book, Doubleday, 1997) provides a literary perspective, considering how writers use diaries to support their writing or how they write diaries as a form of literary expression. James G. Moseley, *John Winthrop's World: History as a Story, The Story as History* (Madison: University of Wisconsin Press, 1992) considers the nature of Winthrop's journal in the settlement of seventeenth-century Massachusetts. The most outstanding exploration of diary writing, showing the promise for archivists in using this literature, is Laurel Thatcher Ulrich, *A Midwife's Tale: The Life of Martha Ballard, Based on Her Diary, 1785–1812* (New York: Vintage Books, 1990), a study emphasizing the extraordinary insights very ordinary documents can provide. Ulrich describes Ballard as an unofficial town historian, as well as exploring the very personal reasons why she keeps her diary. Ulrich's depiction of Ballard's role as an unofficial town historian ought to play a substantial role in how such ordinary journals are considered by archivists, and it would be interesting to know just what sort of impact it has had through the past decade.

We are discovering much more about how early Americans used and thought of records and information, and this knowledge is helpful for understanding archives in the present. Jill Lepore, *The Name of War: King Philip's War and the Origins of American Identity* (New York: Vintage Books, 1999) is not about records but it is about paper, books, ink, and volumes forming a critical part of being white, colonial, and English. Lepore demonstrates that waging war is also about writing about the war's meaning, providing an excellent context for the development and importance of literacy and recordkeeping. Another study concerning seventeenth-century records, and one of the most intriguing historical studies on recordkeeping to appear in years, is Donna Merwick, *Death of a Notary: Conquest and Change in Colonial New York* (Ithaca, N.Y.: Cornell University Press, 1999). Merwick's study follows the life of Adriaen Janse van Ilpendam, a Dutch émigré to New Netherland, whose career as a notary leads him to an uncertain existence after the English take over and to his suicide in 1686. The historian provides many insights into the importance and nature of records in the seventeenth century. In addition to describing the work of a notary and the sources for a notary's authority, Merwick discusses how the notary's papers form a sort of archives and uses considerable iconographic evidence to reveal how a notary's activities supported both government and private life in the colonial era. Merwick relates an ironic tale as writing and recordkeeping become more important in the growing colonial settlement, but the Dutch notary's form of records service fades in significance.

Studies on government and recordkeeping also provide many insights into the relationship between technology and record making. Both James H. Cassedy, *Demography in Early America: Beginnings of the Statistical Mind 1600–1800* (Cambridge, Mass.: Harvard University Press, 1969) and Patricia Cline Cohen, *A Calculating People: The Spread of Numeracy in Early America* (Chicago: University of Chicago Press, 1982) reveal the degree in which all levels of government and other organizations generated a massive documentary emphasis in society. Simon A. Cole's history of fingerprinting—*Suspect Identities: A History of Fingerprinting and Criminal Identification* (Cambridge, Mass.: Harvard University Press, 2001)—is also a history of the modern state and the evolution of recordkeeping to sustain the growth of government, culminating a process started at least a thousand years before with the Domesday Book, well described in Elizabeth M. Hallam's *Domesday Book Through Nine Centuries* (London: Thames and Hudson, 1986). Besides court records, criminal records, and other statistical systems, we can see the development of government control through the creation of particular forms of records, such as maps, as described in G. Malcolm Lewis, ed., *Cartographic Encounters: Perspectives on Native American Mapmaking and Map Use* (Chicago: University of Chicago Press, 1998) and Roger J. P. Kain and Elizabeth Baigent, *The Cadastral Map in the Service of the State: A History of Property Mapping* (Chicago: University of Chicago Press, 1992).

Studies about how particular kinds of organizations administer recordkeeping also provide ample insights into the nature of records and their generation. One of the preeminent examples of this historical analysis is Barbara Craig, "Hospital Records and Record-Keeping, c. 1850–c. 1950 Part I: The Development of Records in Hospitals," *Archivaria* 29 (Winter 1989–90): 57–87 and "Hospital Records and Record-Keeping, c. 1850–c. 1950 Part II: The Development of Records in Hospitals," *Archivaria* 30 (Summer 1990): 21–38. The classic and most cited study is JoAnne Yates, *Control Through Communication: The Rise of System in American Management* (Baltimore: Johns Hopkins University Press, 1989), examining how four American corporations developed sophisticated recordkeeping and communications systems in the 1850–1920 era. Donald Albrecht and Chrysanthe B. Broikos, eds., *On the Job: Design and the American Office* (New York: Princeton Architectural Press and the National Building Museum, 2000), a companion to an exhibition at the National Building Museum, provides considerable explanation about how new information technologies impacted the layout, functioning, and social life of the American office over the past hundred or so years. The latter study is especially important for an understanding of archives as it provides a visual sense of the environment in which records were created and maintained.

Particular kinds of recording technologies have been sufficiently analyzed to suggest how advances in technical developments influence the range of recording efforts, successes, and challenges. Sound recordings often have challenged many archives and archivists because of their fragility, technical requirements, and problems with providing access, and it is a topic that has been recently accorded interesting new scholarship with much to offer anyone interested in the matter of understanding records. Jonathan Sterne, *The Audible Past: Cultural Origins of Sound Reproduction* (Durham, N.C: Duke University Press, 2003) is a marvelous study providing some historical background on these challenges, examining how sound reproduction developed and the role it played in the culture of the late nineteenth and early twentieth centuries. *The Audible Past* focuses on the technologies of sound and hearing as well as the social and cultural aspects of how people defined or approached sound, noting how over the course of a century, people became accustomed to the sound reproduction systems. The notion of the reliability or authenticity of the capturing of sound is an interesting matter Sterne explores in his book, including consideration of how sound recordings came to be seen as historical documents, covering the employment of the technologies by anthropologists, the placement of the recordings into archival repositories, and increasing concerns about audio preservation (the latter more a "Victorian fantasy"). For an assessment of the resurgence of new scholarly inquiries in sound, refer to Mark W. Smith, ed., *Hearing History: A Reader* (Athens: University of Georgia Press, 2004).

There are also many fascinating studies of photography and its technology—far too many to comment on in an abbreviated bibliographic note such as this—providing insights into the connection between technology and record making. Peter Burke's *Eyewitnessing: The Uses of Images as Historical Evidence* (Ithaca, N.Y.: Cornell University Press, 2001), examining photographs, portraits, the meaning of iconography and iconology, and images as used by religious groups, political and governmental bodies, and how images reflect material culture and other aspects of society, opens up many questions about how such recording technologies must be examined. Burke weaves a middle ground between "positivists who believe that images convey reliable information about the external world, and the sceptics or structuralists who assert that they do not," and as a result, *Eyewitnessing* addresses some of the same debates about evidence occurring within the archival community. Many historians are re-examining the role of visual record making, such as photography, with particular values for understanding records in general. A recent book on nineteenth century American Western photography provides an extended essay on photographs as evidence. Martha Sandweiss argues in her beautifully illustrated *Print the Legend: Photography and the American West* (New Haven: Yale University Press, 2002) that "photographs can, indeed, be rich primary source documents; they deserve and reward the careful sort of historical attention more often lavished on literary texts." Her study examines the daguerrean era and the transition to the wet-plate negative process expanding the technical and commercial possibilities of photographs. There are many interesting analyses of records forms such as photographs done by archivists. Joan Schwartz, building off her long career working with photographs and other visual images at the National Archives of Canada, published a breakthrough article in the analysis of photographs as documents—"'We make our tools and our tools make us': Lessons from Photographs for the Practice, Politics, and Poetics of Diplomatics," *Archivaria* 40 (Fall 1995): 40–74. Unlike earlier efforts by archivists and historians alike to recognize photographs as more than visual accompaniment to text, Schwartz argues that "photographs are documents, created by a will, for a purpose, to convey a message to an audience" and, moreover, that "diplomatics has the potential to shed new light on both informational *and* evidential value and thus increase visual literacy."

Moving image and sound records represent some of the most dynamic changes in twentieth-century recordkeeping. There is extensive research and publishing on the topic of the history of moving images and associated media, for example, that is far beyond the scope of this essay. For the purposes of archival work, Steven Davidson and Gregory Lukow, *Administration of Television Newsfilm and Videotape Collections: A Curatorial Manual* (Los Angeles: American Film Institute and Wolfson Media History Center, 1997) and *The Film Preservation Guide: The Basics for Archives, Libraries, and Museums* (San Francisco: National Film Preservation Foundation, 2004) are good sources to start with to gain some understanding of this media. Sam Kula, *Appraising Moving Images: Assessing the Archival and Monetary Value of Film and Video Records* (Metuchen, N.J.: Scarecrow Press, 2002) is also helpful for this purpose. The journal, *The Moving Image*, has rapidly established itself as the primary source for understanding this part of our documentary universe.

A somewhat more perverse, but quite intriguing, means for understanding the nature of record making and keeping technology is to explore something of the nature of forgery. Like so many dimensions of archives and manuscripts, the scholarly and professional literature on this topic has also expanded considerably. Anthony Grafton provides an interesting introduction to this topic in his *Forgers and Critics: Creativity and Duplicity in Western Scholarship* (Princeton: Princeton University Press, 1990). For examples of the increasingly sophisticated analysis of documentary forgeries, three more recent studies are insightful—Arthur Freeman and Janet Ing

Freeman, *John Payne Collier: Scholarship and Forgery in the Nineteenth Century* (New Haven: Yale University Press, 2004), 2 vols.; Ingrid D. Rowland, *The Scarith of Scornello: A Tale of Renaissance Forgery* (Chicago: University of Chicago Press, 2004); and Simon Worrall, *The Poet and the Murderer: A True Story of Literary Crime and the Art of Forgery* (New York: Dutton, 2002)—all providing an explanation of the motives, techniques, and careers of forgers. Kenneth W. Rendell's *Forging History: The Detection of Fake Letters and Documents* (Norman: University of Oklahoma Press, 1994), the work of a well-known autograph dealer, is also extremely useful for understanding the nature of forgery.

    Modern Record Making and Keeping. Surprisingly, the one area that has not led to a substantial scholarship reflecting on the relationship between records and technology, at least with a strong archival sensibility, is that of electronic records. Archivists, records managers, and other records custodians tend to dote on the challenges of preserving and maintaining the cultural record in the era of the computer, participating in efforts leading to reports such as *Committee on the Records of Government: Report* (Washington, D.C., March 1985), sounding an alarm about the potential loss of records and information in digital systems *if* new approaches and strategies are not developed, or speculating about the potential demise of the archival discipline, as in Richard Kesner's "Automated Information Management: Is There a Role for the Archivist in the Office of the Future?" *Archivaria* 19 (Winter 1984–85): 162–72. David Bearman, *Electronic Evidence: Strategies for Managing Records in Contemporary Organizations* (Pittsburgh: Archives and Museum Informatics, 1994) is an argumentative, stimulating, and controversial set of essays on how archivists and others need to reexamine and rethink their most cherished notions on electronic records management. A newer work by Charles Dollar, *Authentic Electronic Records: Strategies for Long-Term Access* (Chicago: Cohassett Associates, 1999) reflects more recent research and debates, updating his earlier *Archival Theory and Information Technologies: The Impact of Information Technologies on Archival Principles and Methods* (Macerata, Italy: University of Macerata Press, 1992). The shifting nature of archival attitudes toward digital media can be seen in Terry Cook's impressive analyses, "Electronic Records, Paper Minds: The Revolution in Information Management and Archives in the Post-Custodial and Post-Modernist Era," *Archives and Manuscripts* 22 (November 1994): 300–28 and "Easy to Byte, Harder to Chew: The Second Generation of Electronic Records Archives," *Archivaria* 33 (Winter 1991–92): 202–16. Richard J. Cox, *The First Generation of Electronic Records Archivists in the United States: A Study in Professionalization* (New York: Haworth Press, 1994) considers the same issues from the vantage of their impact on the archival community as profession. However, as of yet, there has not been the emergence of a scholarly literature, building on the growing scholarship on the history and nature of information technology and its use,[2] that secures a place for archives and records and an understanding of their significant role. Even though the literature on the nature and characteristics of the present Information Age is limitless, there is still a lack of writing on the meaning of new digital documents that can assist archivists to place this in a historical context. Instead, the scholarship and commentaries tend to stress the challenges or dangers, such as with personal privacy or corporate and government security.

The History of Archives and the Archives Profession

Surprisingly little attention has been paid to the history of a profession that has for so long been associated with history and historical research. An understanding of the nature of the archival community's interest in its own history is described in Richard J. Cox's cluster of essays, "American Archival History: Its Development, Needs, and Opportunities," *American Archivist* 46 (Winter 1983): 31–41; "On the Value of Archival History in the United States," *Libraries and Culture* 23 (Spring 1988): 135–51; "Library History and Library Archives," *Libraries and Culture* 26 (Fall 1991): 569–93; and "The Failure or Future of American Archival History: A Somewhat Unorthodox View," *Libraries and Culture* 35 (Winter 2000): 141–54. Cox is just one of many commentators about this matter, but the point is that much of the substantive research on the history of records, record making, and recordkeeping is being done in disciplines ranging from history to anthropology, sociology, and communications.

Old World Antecedents. There is an interesting and useful literature on archives in the ancient world. Ernst Posner's *Archives in the
Ancient World* (Cambridge, Mass.: Harvard
University Press, 1972), surveying archival history
from Mesopotamia through pharaonic Egypt to
imperial Rome, is the place to commence reading about this topic; a reissue of this out-of-print
volume was produced in 2003 by the Society of
American Archivists, with a new introduction
by James O'Toole. James P. Sickinger's *Public
Records and Archives in Classical Athens* (Chapel
Hill: University of North Carolina Press, 1999) is
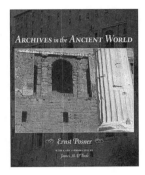
a response to Rosalind Thomas, *Literacy and Orality in Ancient Greece*
(Cambridge: Cambridge University Press, 1992), and Thomas is a
response to Posner's *Archives in the Ancient World*. Posner, the most
prominent archival historian of the twentieth century, stresses the
consolidation of archives and records operations into centralized and
authoritative organizations. Thomas, investigating literacy, believes
Posner superimposes modern ideas of records and archives onto the
ancient world. Thomas, instead of seeing the gradual change to more
efficient records programs, detects a more panoramic movement to
the fourth century's increased respect for the written word. Sickinger, a
Classics professor, sees the fourth-century establishment of an archives
building as part of a long, slow process that does not necessarily represent progress but instead reflects a mixed bag of approaches to the
administration of records. Sickinger's argument is more in line with
what Posner wrote three decades ago, except that Posner writes with a
greater authority about what ancient archives represented. Indeed,
many different perspectives are now in play about the nature of
ancient archives, best reflected in Maria Brosius, ed., *Ancient Archives
and Archival Traditions: Concepts of Recordkeeping in the Ancient World*
(New York: Oxford University Press, 2003). If nothing else, an immer-
sion into the new archival history wars suggests the need for those with
sensitivity to records and archives to investigate and question assumptions about their profession and institutions.

The other aspect of Old World antecedents that has often been
cited in discussions about the nature of archives and the archival pro-

fession has been the equating of the modern archives with the events of the French Revolution, best seen in Ernst Posner's seminal essay, "Some Aspects of Archival Development since the French Revolution," *American Archivist* 3 (1940): 159–72, a perspective challenged somewhat by Judith M. Panitch, "Liberty, Equality, Posterity?: Some Archival Lessons from the Case of the French Revolution," *American Archivist* 59 (Winter 1996): 30–47. Of course, writings about other dimensions of European archival history with a bearing on North American archives are limitless (some works relevant to other dimensions of the history of archives and the profession have been cited below, but to try to be comprehensive or even representative is outside the scope of this essay and book).

American Origins: The Two Traditions. Historical writings about specific aspects of American archives has not kept pace with the richer historical investigations about orality, writing, and recording technologies, described above. Some studies are worth special mention, especially on the formation of pioneering historical agencies, such as Henry D. Shapiro, "Putting the Past Under Glass: Preservation and the Idea of History in the Mid-Nineteenth Century," *Prospects: An Annual of American Cultural Studies* 10 (1985): 243–78. The development of American archival programs has been well, but not thoroughly, described. Classic explorations of this topic include Leslie W. Dunlap, *American Historical Societies 1790–1860* (Madison, Wis.: privately printed, 1944); H. G. Jones, *For History's Sake: The Preservation and Publication of North Carolina History, 1663–1903* (Chapel Hill: University of North Carolina Press, 1966); and David D. Van Tassel, *Recording America's Past: An Interpretation of the Development of Historical Studies in America 1607–1884* (Chicago: University of Chicago Press, 1960). H. G. Jones, ed., *Historical Consciousness in the Early Republic: The Origins of State Historical Societies, Museums, and Collections, 1791–1861* (Chapel Hill: North Caroliniana Society, Inc. and North Carolina Collection, 1995) is an interesting collection of essays commenting on many of the same themes in these earlier studies.

The impetus for modern records administration, and what ultimately leads to the idea of two traditions—manuscripts collecting and government archives—can be seen in James Gregory Bradsher's trio of essays on the growth and control of federal records, "A Brief

History of the Growth of Federal Government Records, Archives and Information, 1789–1985," *Government Publications Review* 13 (1986): 491–505; "An Administrative History of the Disposal of Federal Records, 1789–1949," *Provenance* 3 (Fall 1985): 1–21; and "An Administrative History of the Disposal of Federal Records, 1950–1985," *Provenance* 4 (Fall 1986): 49–73. However, much remains to be understood about the distinctive characteristics of these traditions.

   Emergence of the Archival Profession. The emergence of the archival profession can be tracked through classic writings, works that helped define the scope of its activity and served as practical and theoretical standards for many years.[3] For English-speaking archivists, these classics begin with Sir Hilary Jenkinson, *A Manual for Archive Administration*, 2nd ed. (London: Percy Lund, Humphries & Co., 1966), a revision of the original edition of 1922, establishing standards for professional practice that remain significant today, including such matters as provenance and the importance of an unbroken chain of documentary custody.[4] Following closely behind Jenkinson in importance are two works of 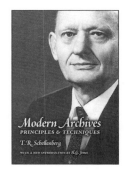 T. R. Schellenberg, *Modern Archives: Principles and Techniques* (Chicago: University of Chicago Press, 1956) and *The Management of Archives* (New York: Columbia University Press, 1965), both still in print, the former as a 2003 reprint by the Society of American Archivists with a new introduction by H. G. Jones and the latter in a 1981 reprint by the National Archives with a foreword by Jane F. Smith. Schellenberg's books were the first attempt to apply European archival principles to American records, and the first to consider how archival theory could be adapted to address the problems of large modern collections of records.

   There are other classic texts deserving mention. One was the work of three Dutch archivists, once referred to in archival circles as "the Dutch Bible": Samuel Muller, J. A. Feith, and R. Fruin, *Manual for the Arrangement and Description of Archives,* trans. Arthur H. Leavitt (New York: H. W. Wilson, 1968). Originally published in 1898, this book became widely available in America sixty years later. In a detailed, systematic way, it described the core functions of organizing archival collections. The Society of American Archivists reissued the volume in 2003 with new introductions by Peter Horsman, Eric Ketelaar, Theo Thomassen, and Marjorie Barritt. Thornton W. Mitchell, ed., *Norton on Archives: The Writings of Margaret Cross Norton on Archival and Records Management* (Carbondale: Southern Illinois University Press, 1975) provided a handy compilation of the extensive work of that important and influential writer. Emphasizing the practical value of archival records in public administration, Norton offered a corrective to the view that saw archives as merely an "auxiliary science" of esoteric historical scholarship. In 2003, the Society of American Archivists reissued the volume with a new introduction by Randall Jimerson. In 2004, the society also published a collection of Lester J. Cappon's essays, originally published between 1952 and 1982, discussing the nature of archival theory and historical scholarship, reflecting the emergence of archival theory and practice in the mid-twentieth century. Published with an introduction drawing upon Cappon's personal papers by Richard J. Cox, *Lester J. Cappon and the Relationship of History, Archives, and Scholarship in the Golden Age of Archival Theory* provides another window into the origins of the modern American archival community.

The archival profession continues to support the collecting of essays by or about archival pioneers, providing a unique set of writings on archival management with a historical perspective, especially the continuing formation of the profession. Terry Cook and Gordon Dodds, eds., *Imagining Archives: Essays and Reflections by Hugh A. Taylor* (Lanham, Md.: Society of American Archivists and Association of Canadian Archivists, 2003) brings together the important essays of one

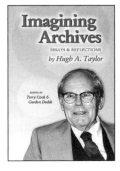

of the most original thinkers in the late twentieth century, particularly interesting for his reflections about the changing nature of documentation.[5] One of the best sources on Ernst Posner, one of the leading archival theorists and historians of the first half of the twentieth century, is Ken Munden, ed., *Archives and the Public Interest: Selected Essays by Ernst Posner* (Chicago: Society of American Archivists, 2006), conveniently collecting some of his seminal writings. Originally published in 1967, this new edition includes a new introduction by Angelika Menne-Haritz.

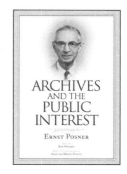

The Crucial Decade: The 1930s. Much of what has been written on American archival history has focused on the National Archives, the archival program established in 1934 and exercising immense influence on the subsequent development of the profession for decades. For a detailed overview, see Donald R. McCoy's *The National Archives: America's Ministry of Documents, 1934–1968* (Chapel Hill: University of North Carolina Press, 1978) and Victor Gondos, Jr., *J. Franklin Jameson and the Birth of the National Archives 1906–1926* (Philadelphia: University of Pennsylvania Press, 1981). Another common focus for the American profession's modern origins in this period has been the Society of American Archivists, founded in 1936; for some understanding about SAA and its role, see William F. Birdsall, "The Two Sides of the Desk: The Archivist and the Historian, 1909–1935," *American Archivist* 38 (1975): 159–73, and J. Frank Cook, "The Blessings of Providence on an Association of Archivists," *American Archivist* 46 (1983): 374–99.

There were, of course, other factors with importance similar to that of the National Archives in shaping the early development of the American archival profession. A general history of the Historical Records Survey (HRS) is provided in William F. McDonald, *Federal Relief Administration and the Arts* (Columbus: Ohio State University Press, 1969), 751–828. The legacy of the HRS was somewhat damaged by ill-fated maintenance of many of the survey records, described by Leonard Rapport, "Dumped from a Wharf into Casco Bay: The Historical Records Survey Revisited," *American Archivist* 37 (1974): 201–10. It must be remembered that the purpose of the HRS was not some lofty archives goal, rather it was part of a larger jobs relief program, an aspect well described in Burl Noggle, *Working with History: The Historical Records Survey in Louisiana and the Nation, 1936–1942* (Baton Rouge: Louisiana State University Press, 1981).

Diversification and Development. Some works providing benchmark assessments of critical aspects of archival work deserve to be considered as seminal writings, ones often marking critical junctures in the development of the profession. Four were done in the 1960s, considering the nature and development of historical societies, state government archives, the National Archives, and the use of archival sources in historical research. Walter Muir Whitehill, *Independent Historical Societies: An Enquiry into Their Research and Publication Functions and Their Financial Future* (Boston: Boston Athenaeum, 1962) is a massive analysis of the history, administration, activities, and prospects of private historical societies, institutions playing important archival roles in American society. Ernst Posner's *American State Archives* (Chicago: University of Chicago Press, 1964) was also a milestone work, one that was more significant than its apparent limitation to a particular kind of archival repository might suggest. Besides describing the condition of public records programs in the United States around 1960, Posner also provided an excellent summary of American archival history with a clear statement of what archival standards ought to be. Despite being four decades old, the book remains the clearest and most important assessment of state government archival programs ever published and deserves an updating. H. G. Jones, *The Records of a Nation: Their Management, Preservation, and Use* (New York: Atheneum, 1969) is a study about the National Archives conducted as part of the then-ongoing debate about the loss of independence of that institution and its placement under the General Services Administration in 1949. Finally, although somewhat different, Walter Rundell, Jr., *In Pursuit of American History: Research and Training in the United States* (Norman: University of Oklahoma Press, 1970) remains the finest study of how historians use archival sources. While there have been scores of studies on American historical writing and increased research by archivists on researchers' behavior since Rundell's work, none approach the in-depth consideration of how historians use archival records, the relationship between archivists and historians, and other aspects of the use of archival materials.

The growth in the archival profession can be seen in the development of many different types of institutional archives. Basic introductions to institutional types are well represented by volumes on college and university archives, government, nonprofit cultural institutions, and corporate archives, such as William Maher, *The Management of College and University Archives* (Metuchen, N.J.: Scarecrow Press and the Society of American Archivists, 1992); Bruce W. Dearstyne, *Managing Government Records and Information* (Prairie Village, Kans: ARMA International, 1999); and Richard J. Cox, *Managing Institutional Archives: Foundational Principles and Practices* (New York: Greenwood Press, 1992).  Maher's volume is both a basic "how-to" manage academic archives, as well as a serious effort in bringing together a considerable amount of information about the nature of these archival programs. Dearstyne provides a straightforward guide to thinking about government records and archives management, with chapters on the importance and nature of government records, issues and problems challenging such management, strategic approaches, promoting "responsible" recordkeeping environments, and the core elements for records management, electronic records management, and archival records management—along with a large group of appendices of practical guidelines. The Cox volume is built on the premise that the field needs to focus on the establishment and development of archival programs in corporations and other institutions. James M. O'Toole, ed., *The Records of American Business* (Chicago: Society of American Archivists, 1997) is particularly relevant for corporate records managers because it examines the value of business records from a variety of perspectives. Some older volumes, such as those on local government records, remain useful, such as H. G. Jones, *Local Government Records: An Introduction to Their Management, Preservation, and Use* (Nashville: American Association for State and Local History, 1980) and Bruce Dearstyne, *The Management of Local Government Records: A Guide for Local Officials* (Nashville: American Association for State and Local History, 1988).

Consolidation of Professional Identity. The archives profession has engaged in research about itself, resulting in some analyses reflecting the emergence of a stronger professional identity. These kinds of assessments include David Bearman, "1982 Survey of the Archival Profession," *American Archivist* 46 (1983): 233–41 and Paul Conway, "Perspectives on Archival Resources: The 1985 Census of Archival Institutions," *American Archivist* 50 (1987): 174–91, leading one commentator to declare the 1980s as the "age of archival analysis."[6] This was stimulated by the profession's major planning for itself, best marked by the Society of American Archivists' publications *Planning for the Archival Profession* (Chicago: SAA, 1986) and *An Action Agenda for the Archival Profession: Institutionalizing the Planning Process* (Chicago: SAA, 1988), partly inspired by the leadership of the National Historical Publications and Records Commission and its urging of statewide archival planning,[7] and assisted by a new focus on research.[8]

Additional efforts continue to the present day. The profession is gathering a considerable amount of data on itself, as is evident in the Council of State Historical Records Coordinators, *Maintaining State Records in an Era of Change: A National Challenge; A Report on State Archives and Records Management Programs* (n.p.: COSHRC, April 1996) and Victoria Irons Walch, *Where History Begins: A Report on Historical Records Repositories in the United States* (n.p.: COSHRC, May 1998), also available at http://www.archives.gov, a major resource on the state of affairs with nongovernmental historical records repositories. The report, with data from over two thousand repositories in about half of the states, includes considerable detail on repository types, acquisition policies, holdings, users, facilities and equipment, preservation and conservation, staffing, education and training, financial support, and needs and priorities. The 2006 publication of a massive census-taking effort will provide much greater data about the nature of the archival identity in the early twenty-first century.

The continuously developing professional identity includes debates about professional credentials. While the individual certification of archivists has led to little research about professional identity, the flavor of the concerns about such credentials can be seen in William J. Maher, "Contexts for Understanding Professional Certification: Opening Pandora's Box?" *American Archivist* 51 (1988): 408–27. One of the keys to consolidating professional identity, and another aspect of the credentialing discussion, has been the development of graduate archival education, especially in the past quarter of a century. The earlier development of education can be seen in Richard C. Berner, "Archival Education and Training in the United States, 1937 to Present," *Journal of Education for Librarianship* 22 (Summer/Fall 1981): 3–19 and Jacqueline Goggin, "'That We Shall Truly Deserve the Title of Profession': The Training and Education of Archivists, 1930–1960," *American Archivist* 47 (Summer 1984): 243–54. The present state of graduate archival education can be seen in Richard J. Cox, Elizabeth Yakel, David Wallace, Jeannette Bastian, and Jennifer Marshall, "Archival Education in North American Library and Information Science Schools: A Status Report," *Library Quarterly* 71 (April 2001): 141–94.

A segment of the consolidation of professional identity also stems from a variety of political, advocacy, and other movements engaging the profession, especially in the last few decades of the twentieth century. One of the most important, in terms of this identity, was the effort to gain the independence of the u.s. National Archives. For a very personal and unique contribution to this development, see Robert M. Warner, *Diary of a Dream: A History of the National Archives Independence Movement, 1980–1985* (Metuchen, N.J.: Scarecrow Press, 1995).

Current Issues. One could spend considerable time ruminating over the numerous issues facing the archives profession today, but here are a few major matters worth considering. The codification of professional knowledge continues to be one of the most important topics for discussion in the past few decades. The principal writing, one that called forth a number of responses, was Frank G. Burke's "The Future Course of Archival Theory in the United States," *American Archivist* 44 (1980): 40–46. Pointing up the paucity of theory in the profession, Burke poses a number of questions that budding theoreticians might explore, including those that touch on the reasons why archival material is made and saved in the first place. He also argues for archival educators, especially those with full-time academic appointments, to play an important role by undertaking basic research that would help advance professional theory. Burke's essay continued to receive comment until well into the mid-1990s, although by then the nature of the conversation about archival theory had shifted considerably.

From the reemphasis on electronic records has come a new interest in issues related to what constitutes a record, especially as developed as the result of two major research projects (located at the University of Pittsburgh and the University of British Columbia). While these projects generated a large number of essays in the professional literature, two books provide convenient commentary on the projects.[9] *The Preservation of the Integrity of Electronic Records,* by Luciana Duranti, Terry Eastwood, and Heather MacNeil and published in 2002 by Kluwer Academic Publishers, stresses theoretical and practical issues relating to the reliability and authenticity of electronic records drawing on diplomatic analysis; they updated their findings from this project in *The Long-term Preservation of Authentic Electronic Records: Findings of the InterPARES Project* (San Miniato, Italy: Archilab, 2004). Other publications reflecting the approach to records and recordkeeping systems can be seen in Trevor Livelton, *Archival Theory, Records, and the Public* (Lanham, Md.: Society of American Archivists and Scarecrow Press, 1996) and Heather MacNeil, *Trusting Records: Legal, Historical and Diplomatic Perspectives* (Dordrecht, Netherlands: Kluwer Academic Publishers, 2000). *Managing Records as Evidence and Information* by Richard J. Cox, published by Quorum Books in 2001, draws heavily on the research project at Pittsburgh and discusses defining records, how information technology plays into policy compiling, the fundamental tasks of identifying and maintaining records as critical to records and information policy, public outreach and advocacy as a key objective for such policy, and the role of educating records professionals in supporting sensible records policies.

Other book-length discussions about records and recordkeeping systems relate to the recent archival wrestling with modern records systems. Luciana Duranti, *Diplomatics: New Uses for an Old Science* (Lanham, Md.: Society of American Archivists and Association of Canadian Archivists in association with Scarecrow Press, 1998) is a description of the Renaissance science of diplomatics that has been used and reused in the discussions about the definition of the record, comprehending recordkeeping systems, and managing electronic records. There are other essays and writings on diplomatics, but Duranti's effort is directed right at the implications for modern archival work. The Australians have been especially adept in producing volumes of collected writings on similar topics, such as the two publications exploring fundamental aspects of the record and recordkeeping systems—Sue McKemmish and Frank Upward, eds., *Archival Documents: Providing Accountability through Recordkeeping* (Melbourne: Ancora Press, 1993) and Sue McKemmish and Michael Piggott, eds., *The Records Continuum: Ian Maclean and Australian Archives First Fifty Years* (Clayton, Aus.: Ancora Press in association with the Australian Archives, 1994). A similar volume on the contributions by Canadians on archival theory, with a focus on provenance, is Tom Nesmith, ed., *Canadian Archival Studies and the Rediscovery of Provenance* (Metuchen, N.J.: Scarecrow Press, 1993). A book with the title *Archives: Recordkeeping in Society* may be off-putting for many records managers, but ignoring this volume edited by Sue McKemmish, Michael Piggott, Barbara Reed, and Frank Upward and published in 2005 by the Center for Information Studies at Charles Sturt University in Wagga Wagga, New South Wales, would prove to be a loss for all records professionals, and it is especially helpful for archivists. Consisting of a dozen chapters by a dozen authors, mostly Australians, the book is introduced as providing a "conceptual base for archival science which coherently incorporates both established and emerging concepts within the discipline" and as a "valuable resource" both inside and outside the records professions, because it is "exposing leading archival thinking to scholars, thinkers and practitioners in many disciplines." True to the promises made for it, the volume brings together the "research and reflections" of a number of important thinkers and leaders in the field, providing an orientation to considerable debate evident in the field, and examining the "cultural conditions" of and "global approaches" to recordkeeping.

The Archivist's Perspective: Knowledge and Values

Individuals are not deemed to be archivists just because they are paid to do such work; they attain this professional distinction because of what they know and the values they hold. An array of interesting readings can assist us in understanding this knowledge and these values, while recognizing that debate continues about the nature of such knowledge and values.

Knowledge. To a certain extent, archivists speak their own language just as practitioners in other professions do, and both beginners and the more experienced often need a guide through that language. The current, and most substantive, effort in producing a glossary is Richard Pearce-Moses, *A Glossary of Archival and Records Terminology* (Chicago: Society of American Archivists, 2005) reflecting the immense changes in the archival profession that have occurred within the past couple of decades. (Reflective of the changes we have seen since the early 1990s, the Pearce-Moses glossary is offered as an updateable digital publication by the Society of American Archivists on its website.)

The efforts by archivists to define their knowledge, articulate their values, and codify their practice can be seen over the decades by volumes intended to serve as textbooks for courses and references for practicing archivists. Some efforts to compile sets of critical articles provide interesting reflections of the state of archival knowledge and practice, as in Maygene F. Daniels and Timothy Walch, eds., *A Modern Archives Reader: Basic Readings on Archival Theory and Practice* (Washington, D.C.: National Archives and Records Service, 1984); James Gregory Bradsher, ed., *Managing Archives and Archival Institutions* (Chicago: University of Chicago Press, 1988); and the Society of American Archivists' basic reader published in 2000 as *American Archival Studies: Readings in Theory and Practice*, edited by Randall Jimerson. In addition to such readers as these, the SAA's Basic Manual Series (1977–1985), the first Archival Fundamentals Series in the first half of the 1990s, and the present Archival Fundamental Series II all provide benchmarks for tracking trends, changes, and debates about archival knowledge and practice—all with a stress on capturing the consensus about what

archivists know and do. Peter Walne, comp., *Modern Archives Administration and Records Management: A* RAMP *Reader,* PGI-85/WS/32 (Paris: UNESCO, 1985) is a general volume worth consulting in comparison to the other archives readers and for its wider international perspective. Another important single-volume archival reader, with international perspective, is Judith Ellis, ed., *Keeping Archives,* 2nd ed. (Port Melbourne, Aus.: Thorpe in association with the Australian Society of Archivists, 1993), stressing the Australian perspective and incorporating ideas, concepts, and methods from other parts of the world—reconfiguring them for their own use.

While the SAA basic manual and archival fundamentals volumes certainly solidify archival practice and knowledge from the late 1970s into the mid-1990s, these series are not unique. We can find the historical precedent for the SAA publications in the brief basic manuals originally published by the United States National Archives as the National Archives Staff and Technical Series from the 1940s, some continuously cited to the present.[10] None can be read apart from the more recent archival literature, but they provide substantial insights into the development of archival description, appraisal, general management, and records management and the early role of the U.S. National Archives as the leader in the formulation of archival theory and methodology.[11] There are also international counterparts, as can be seen in the UNESCO Ramp Studies, whose nature and range Richard J. Cox describes in "RAMP Studies and Related UNESCO Publications: An International Source for Archival Administration," *American Archivist* 53 (Summer 1990): 488–95, with some remaining critical for the knowledge and practice of archivists.[12]

One of the profession's most persistent needs has been a records management textbook with a healthy archival perspective or presence, one consolidating the theoretical dimensions of all archival work. Elizabeth Shepherd and Geoffrey Yeo, *Managing Records: A Handbook of Principles and Practice* (London: Facet Publishing, 2003) comes closest to filling this need. Aiming at an international audience, this volume defines basic terminology, describes the objectives of records management, integrates sound management principles into developing and administering records management programs, and covers every basic function of records work (classification, creation and capture, appraisal and scheduling, storage, access, and planning and starting records management programs). One of the chief attributes of this book is the authors' success in bringing together disparate research and theoretical literature into a meaningful, coherent discourse about records management, emphasizing standards (ISO 15489); ideas about the authenticity, integrity, usability, and reliability of records alongside concise notions of a record's features of structure, content, and context; the records life cycle and records continuum; and evidence and accountability.

The role of faculty in building archival knowledge has been discussed by Paul Conway, "Archival Education and the Need for Full-Time Faculty," *American Archivist* 51 (1988): 254–65; Terry Eastwood, "Nurturing Archival Education in the University," *American Archivist* 51 (1988): 228–52; and Luciana Duranti, "The Archival Body of Knowledge: Archival Theory, Method, and Practice," *Journal of Education for Library and Information Science* 34 (Winter 1993): 8–24, among others. These earlier expressions of the need are predictions and expressions of hope, ones that are only beginning to show some results but likely to be major forces in the future development of archival knowledge.

Values. The nature of archival values—encouraging use, facilitating preservation, maintaining contextual evidence, providing timely and equitable use, and fostering cooperative ventures—permeates all the basic writings described in this essay, as well as those that consider ethical challenges. That not all is well can be seen in the declension of discussion within the professional literature about some of the critical activities that support building a stronger sense of such values. One example is the discussion about the centrality of cooperative ventures. The classic discussions about cooperation remain Richard A. Cameron, Timothy Ericson, and Anne R. Kenney, "Archival Cooperation: A Critical Look at Statewide Archival Networks," *American Archivist* 46 (Fall 1983): 414–32 and Frank G. Burke, "Archival Cooperation," *American Archivist* 46 (Summer 1983): 293–305. After intense consideration of such cooperative efforts a generation ago, the interest seems to have dissipated. The profession needs more intense study of how cooperative approaches work or do not work, especially in this highly networked era. The profession needs to reexamine in systematic fashion all of its essential values.

Perhaps the essential set of writings that raises issues about archival values is the one concerning planning for and managing archival programs. Some basic manuals of archival practice are as much about essential management issues as the basic tasks of archivists. Michael Kurtz's *Managing Archival and Manuscript Repositories* (Chicago: Society of American Archivists, 2004) is the most recent and comprehensive of the writings on this topic. Bruce Dearstyne's *The Archival Enterprise: Modern Archival Principles, Practices, and Management Techniques* (Chicago: American Library Association, 1993), directed toward librarians, is another useful volume. Gregory S. Hunter, *Developing and Maintaining Practical Archives: A How-to-Do-It Manual,* 2nd ed. (New York: Neal-Schuman, 2004) provides a very user-friendly description of the nuts and bolts of archival work and the administration of archival programs.

Some writings question as well as describe the underlying assumptions about the administration of archival programs. An important statement pointing out the problems with archivists and their views toward management is David Bearman's *Archival Methods* (Pittsburgh: Archives and Museum Informatics, 1989), a careful dismantling of archivists' assumptions about the core functions of their work and still a provocative read. Somewhat forgotten, but certainly illuminating about archival values, are the two-decade-old self-assessment guides (none are current), including Mary Jo Pugh and William Joyce, eds., *Evaluation of Archival Institutions: Services, Principles, and Guide to Self-Study* (Chicago: Society of American Archivists, 1982) and Paul H. McCarthy, Jr., ed., *Archives Assessment and Planning Workbook* (Chicago: Society of American Archivists, 1989). A more recent effort to assess some of the basic assumptions about archival administration is Richard J. Cox's *Archives and Archivists in the Information Age* (New York: Neal-Schuman, 2005).

The notion of archival management has expanded in scope over the past two decades. Individuals outside the archives field, for example, have taken up the topic in ways that raise concerns about archival values. Two very important companion volumes are Jed I. Bergman in collaboration with William G. Bowen and Thomas I. Nygren, *Managing Change in the Nonprofit Sector: Lessons from the Evolution of Five Independent Research Libraries* (San Francisco: Jossey-Bass Publishers, 1996) and Kevin M. Guthrie, *The New-York Historical Society: Lessons from One Nonprofit's Long Struggle for Survival* (San Francisco: Jossey-Bass Publishers, 1996), both focusing on the difficult fiscal management of such programs. Both aim to provide insights into nonprofit management. The Guthrie study is especially important as it relates the traditional collecting emphasis of this institution with its fiscal management woes. It should be read in conjunction with Sally F. Griffith, *Serving History in a Changing World: The Historical Society of Pennsylvania in the Twentieth Century* (Philadelphia: Historical Society of Pennsylvania, 2001), another assessment of an older historical society seeking to reevaluate its mission and collecting.[13]

The Archivist's Task: Responsibilities and Duties

Most associate the basic functions—appraisal, arrangement and description, and reference and access—with the identity of the archivist and archival and historical records repositories. Without question, these basic tasks have stimulated some of the most useful, engaging, and diverse writings.

Saving and Acquiring Archival Records. Particular aspects of archival work became the focus of theoretical reconsideration, with appraisal receiving the most attention at first. The several essays collected in Nancy E. Peace, ed., *Archival Choices: Managing the Historical Record in an Age of Abundance* (Lexington, Mass.: Lexington Books, 1984) wrestle with the problem of how to save the most important archival records in an era when there are obviously too many to save all of them. Clark A. Elliott, ed., *Understanding Progress as Process: Documentation of the History of Post-War Science and Technology in the United States; Final Report of the Joint Committee on Archives of Science and Technology* (Chicago: Society of American Archivists, 1983) is a benchmark perspective on the challenges of appraising complex modern records systems. It was followed by the equally important Joan K. Haas, et al., *Appraising the Records of Modern Science and Technology: A Guide* (Cambridge, Mass.: Massachusetts Institute of Technology, 1985) and Helen W. Samuels, *Varsity Letters: Documenting Modern Colleges and Universities* (Metuchen, N.J.: Scarecrow Press and the Society of American Archivists, 1992), both theoretical and practical guides to appraisal in these particular areas. Frank Boles, *Archival Appraisal* (New York: Neal-Schuman, 1991) was a pioneering effort to create a model for archival appraisal by studying *how* archivists think through the process of

selecting records, including a useful review of thinking about this function through the 1980s.

Other archivists began to argue for a more active, deliberate, and planned approach to appraisal, suggesting what they called "documentation strategies."[14] The theoretical underpinnings for this approach can be seen in Helen W. Samuels, "Who Controls the Past?" *American Archivist* 49 (1986): 109–24 and Larry J. Hackman and Joan Warnow-Blewitt, "The Documentation Strategy Process: A Model and a Case Study," *American Archivist* 50 (1987): 12–47. Many of these and other documentation planners point to the earlier writings of F. Gerald Ham as the source of rethinking archival appraisal and the broader issue of documentation, commenced by his "The Archival Edge," *American Archivist* 38 (January 1975): 5–13. Frank Boles, *Selecting and Appraising Archives and Manuscripts* (Chicago: Society of American Archivists, 2005) comments on and critiques many of these approaches, as does Barbara L. Craig, *Archival Appraisal: Theory and Practice* (München, Germany: K. G. Saur, 2004). A major aspect of the 1980s and following discussions about archival appraisal was the development of documentation

strategies, functional analysis, and macro-appraisal approaches, reflected in Richard J. Cox, *No Innocent Deposits: Forming Archives by Rethinking Appraisal* (Lanham, Md.: Scarecrow Press, 2004).

New manuals on preservation, some significant for their international perspective, have been published. John Feather, ed., *Managing Preservation for Libraries and Archives: Current Practice and Future Developments* (Burlington, Vt.: Ashgate Publishing Co., 2004) provides a group of essays discussing the basic principles and policies of preservation management, digital preservation issues (basic technical issues, selection, and long-term management), recent developments in paper preservation, sound recordings preservation, basic sources of information for preservation management, and future concerns in preservation management. The volume provides ample citations to resources and an overview of the most recent issues faced by preservation administrators, with discussion about work in Europe that might not be as familiar to North Americans. Feather has also coedited with Graham Matthews *Disaster Management for Libraries and Archives* (Burlington, Vt.: Ashgate Publishing Co., 2003), providing practical advice on disaster management. Essays by various authors, again reflecting an international perspective, concern planning, risk assessment, contending with fire and water damage, cooperation, human aspects of disaster response, war and terrorism, recovery, and additional sources for information (focusing on sources in English made available after 1995).

Some of the writings about archival functions such as preservation also reflect the changing nature of research and reflection about archival work. James M. O'Toole, "On the Idea of Permanence," *American Archivist* 52 (Winter 1989): 10–25, addresses how the idea of permanence has changed substantially through the decades. Most archivists, if asked to advise in designing and/or filling a time capsule, would view the task as an entertaining sideline to their more serious responsibilities. William E. Jarvis, *Time Capsules: A Cultural History* (Jefferson, N.C.: McFarland and Co., 2003) provides a serious analysis of the history, function, and image of time capsules that might have archivists rethinking their attitudes about time capsules (and it is handsomely illustrated as well). Jarvis states that "time capsules in a narrowly defined sense are deliberately sealed deposits of cultural relics and recorded knowledge that are intended for retrieval at a given future target date." Jarvis opens up the narrow definition to demonstrate how society has viewed time capsules and how the nature of time capsules has been extended to describe many preservation functions, including that of archives.

Preservation has been a long-time focus of archivists, superbly assessed by Paul Conway's "Archival Preservation Practice in a Nationwide Context," *American Archivist* 53 (Spring 1990): 204–22. Preservation sometimes has been a controversial matter as seen in Nicholson Baker's polemic about the misapplication of preservation approaches, *Double Fold: Libraries and the Assault on Paper* (New York: Random House, 2001), and responses such as Richard J. Cox's *Vandals in the Stacks? A Response to Nicholson Baker's Assault on Libraries* (Westport, Conn.: Greenwood Press, 2002) and James M. O'Toole, "Do Not Fold, Spindle, or Mutilate: *Double Fold* and the Assault on Libraries," *American Archivist* 64 (Fall/Winter 2001): 385–93. Other scholars, such as historian Roy Rosenzweig, "Scarcity or Abundance? Preserving the Past in a Digital Era," *American Historical Review* 108, no. 3 (2003): 735–62, are also beginning to scrutinize more carefully research studies and theoretical writings by archivists and preservationists, questioning their assumptions and approaches.

Organizing Archival Records. Archival arrangement has received considerable attention in the past few decades. Richard C. Berner's book, *Archival Theory and Practice in the United States: A Historical Analysis* (Seattle: University of Washington Press, 1983), is devoted almost exclusively to arrangement and description, its more inclusive title notwithstanding, and it describes how traditional archival practice developed. An interesting professional literature tracking the successive developments of the MARC AMC format and Encoded Archival Description (EAD) is captured in writings such as David Bearman, ed., *Toward National Information Systems for Archives and Manuscript Repositories: The National Information Systems Task Force Papers, 1981–1984* (Chicago: Society of American Archivists, 1987); the summer and fall 1997 issues of *American Archivist* (volume 60) devoted to the history, theory, and case studies of EAD; and Daniel V. Pitti and Wendy M. Duff, eds., *Encoded Archival Description on the Internet* (New York: Haworth Press, 2001). Kathleen D. Roe's *Arranging and Describing Archives and Manuscripts*

(Chicago: Society of American Archivists, 2005) is the most recent full analysis of this particular archival function.

Making Archival Records Available. A traditional approach to archival reference can be found
in Frank G. Burke, *Research and the Manuscript
Tradition* (Lanham, Md.: Scarecrow Press, and
Society of American Archivists, 1997) describing the
nature of evidence in archives and historical manuscripts, the evolution of archival finding aids, the
acquisition and appraisal of historical manuscripts
and archives, the nature of technology uses in and
challenges to the archival community, issues
concerning archival arrangement and description, the use and misuse of deeds of gift, security
and access approaches in archival repositories,
legal and ethical dilemmas, and changes in personal communications in our modern electronic age and the implications for archivists
and researchers. Laura B. Cohen, ed., *Reference
Services for Archives and Manuscripts* (New York:
Haworth Press, 1997) and Elsie Freeman Finch,
ed., *Advocating Archives: An Introduction to
Public Relations for Archivists* (Metuchen, N.J.:
Society of American Archivists and Scarecrow Press,
1994) both provide groups of writings adding to the
existing literature on reference and advocacy. The
Finch volume is the best set of writings on the
archival function of advocacy. Perhaps the most
important and fullest assessment of making archival
records available is Mary Jo Pugh's *Providing
Reference Services for Archives and Manuscripts*
(Chicago: Society of American Archivists, 2005).

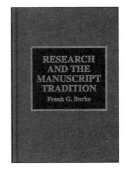

The use of archival records has generated some research, although
not nearly enough to enable the field to be able to discuss with confidence how individuals make use of records. The first major user study
was Richard H. Lytle, "Intellectual Access to Archives: I. Provenance
and Content Indexing Methods of Subject Retrieval," *American*

Archivist 43 (Winter 1980): 64–75 and "Report of an Experiment Comparing Provenance and Content Indexing Methods of Subject Retrieval," *American Archivist* 43 (Spring 1980): 191–206, an interesting contrast between how researchers utilize traditional finding aids versus automated guides. Not surprisingly, based on his model for conducting such research published as "Facts and Frameworks: An Approach to Studying the Users of Archives," *American Archivist* 49 (Fall 1986): 393–407, Paul Conway has made major contributions about understanding archival use. His *Partners in Research: Improving Access to the Nation's Archives* (Pittsburgh: Archives and Museum Informatics, 1994), a study of users in the National Archives, is the most comprehensive analysis of such use, drawing on interviews, surveys, and other data. Other user studies are scattered across the archival and library science journals. The problem with these studies, and others similar in approach, is trying to reconcile different data-gathering methods to develop some consistent knowledge about the use of archival records. Closely related to studies about archival use is a new and promising cluster of studies focused on the researcher's interaction with reference archivists, finding aids, national databases, and the World Wide Web. Examples of these studies include Timothy Hutchinson, "Retrieval Experiment Comparing MARC and EAD," *Archivaria* 44 (Fall 1997): 72–100; Helen R. Tibbo, "The Epic Struggle: Subject Retrieval from Large Bibliographic Databases," *American Archivist* 57 (Spring 1994): 310–26; and Wendy Duff and Elaine G. Toms, "'I spent 1 1/2 hours sifting through one large box. . . .': Diaries as Information Behavior of the Archives User: Lessons Learned," *Journal of the American Society for Information Science and Technology* 53 (December 2002): 1232–38. This is an aspect of archival work beginning to reflect a renaissance of interest, with great promise for the future.

Archivists and the Challenges of New Worlds

The world is changing, and so are the challenges to archival work. The notion of static archival principles seems to have disappeared as records have become dynamic, but the debates and controversies will continue. These tensions and challenges—postmodernism and its press on the notion of truth, the Internet and a complex networked world, ethics and security lapses and debates, the cultural role of archives in a technocratic society—all will push archivists to rethink their mission, professional status, and role in society, perhaps with some beneficial results.

Postmodernism. Postmodernism has led to more intensive ruminations about records and all documentary forms. The double issue of *Archival Science* on archives, power, and memory (guest-edited by Terry Cook and Joan Schwartz) is a provocative and extremely important collection of essays exploring the meaning of archives. In their introductory essay in the first part of this publication—"Archives, Records, and Power: The Making of Modern Memory," *Archival Science* 2 (2002): 1–19—Cook and Schwartz note that the "central professional myth of the past century that the archivist is (or should be) an objective, neutral, passive . . . keeper of truth" is the subject of exploration in all the essays. They believe that "archival professionals and users of archives have been slow to recognize the nature of archives as socially constructed institutions, the relationship of archives to notions of memory and truth, the role of archives in the production of knowledge about the past, and, above all, the power of archives and records to shape our notions of history, identity, and memory." The result is a group of readings encouraging new thinking and research about archives and archival records and examining the mythology of archival neutrality, the symbolic act of creating records, the implications of oral tradition and colonialism, archives as power, the evidence in the act of producing records, the definition of record, and the sense of knowledge and truth evident in archival practice, among many subjects explored.

Postmodern scholarship, or scholarship with a postmodernist tinge, on rethinking the nature of archives has become a persistent theme in recent efforts to understand archives and manuscripts. Carolyn Hamilton, Verne Harris, Jane Taylor, Michele Pickover, Graeme Reid, and Razia Saleh, *Refiguring the Archive* (Dordrecht, Netherlands: Kluwer Academic Publishers, 2002) is a grand example of postmodernists taking on the notion that an archives is a reasonably static place. *Refiguring the Archive* is an excellent compilation of the arguments about such issues, transforming the archives from static to ever-evolving accumulation. Drawing on the concept of archives in South Africa (the book emanates from an exhibition and seminar series hosted by the University of the Witwatersrand's Graduate School for the Humanities and Social Sciences, with the cooperation of four archival programs in that country), *Refiguring the Archive* examines every facet of archives, extending the definition of archives, considering the making of archives, and the expansion of the "boundaries" of archives. Many of the essays touch upon the connection between the public and the various objects constituting an archives, leading to speculations about the nature of truth, memory, information, knowledge, and evidence.

We can even play with one of the persistent stereotypes of archives: that of the dusty place, perhaps at a risk of losing the core perception of archives. Carolyn Steedman's *Dust: The Archive and Cultural History* (New Brunswick, N.J.: Rutgers University Press, 2002) plays with the idea of the archives in true cultural studies fashion, representing the idea of dust as belief system, the unifying "narrative principle" of historical inquiry drawing on archives, and as continuing joke. Steedman starts with a commentary on Derrida and then rambles through the nature of archives as memory, stories in archives, the silences in archival documentation, the deterioration of paper and leather and the dust produced as a symbolic means of representing archives. Still, does such scholarship, while broadening the parameters of how we see archives, really lead us to have a better understanding of what archives and manuscripts are about? It is the kind of question that has plagued many others in reflecting on the contributions of postmodernism—the best examples for those concerned about archives being Joyce Appleby, Lynn Hunt, and Margaret Jacob, *Telling the Truth about History* (New York: W. W. Norton, 1994) and Ernst Breisach, *On the Future of History: The Postmodernist Challenge and Its Aftermath* (Chicago: University of Chicago Press, 2003)—and that archivists need to be more reflective as they appropriate or critique the postmodern scholarship. The discussion will continue for a long time, and it needs to be put into the legacy of archival ideas, just as Terry Cook, in his "What Is Past Is Prologue: A History of Archival Ideas Since 1898, and the Future Paradigm Shift," *Archivaria* 43 (Spring 1997): 17–63, strives to do.

Internet Time. Besides the array of new scholarship about archives and archival work, the major change since the appearance of the first edition of this volume has been the emergence of the World Wide Web. The array of websites valuable for insights into archival work increases, and understanding archives now requires understanding the Web. The World Wide Web is a large and unruly place. It is growing and changing quickly, and with this growth comes both new additions and losses of older sites. The Web is a highly idiosyncratic place, depending on the personal interests and whims of individuals as well as the changing fortunes and objectives of professional associations, scholarly groups, citizens' groups, institutions, and government. That the World Wide Web has proved to be a positive asset in supporting research about electronic records management is a fitting irony for our digital age. The emergence of the Web not only launched the publication of hundreds of books about its impact on society, but it also led to great concerns about its fragility and potential loss of data. The formation of the Internet Archive (http://www.archive.org/) to build a "library of snapshots of publicly accessible Internet sites" and to "provide free access to researchers, historians, and scholars" is the best-known example of such concerns. "The Internet Archive is working to prevent the Internet—a new medium with major historical significance—from disappearing into the past."

While archivists at first seemed energetic in their efforts to discuss the nature and potential use of the Web—such as William Landis, "Archival Outreach on the World Wide Web," *Archival Issues* 20, no. 2 (1995): 129–47; Jenni Davidson and Donna McRostie, "Webbed Feet: Navigating the Net," *Archives and Manuscripts* 24 (November 1996): 330–51; and David Wallace, "Archival Repositories on the World Wide Web: A Preliminary Survey and Analysis," *Archives and Museum Informatics* 9, no. 2 (1995): 150–68—these kinds of reflections have receded, perhaps because archivists have become more comfortable with the Web and its values for disseminating information about their holdings and activities. More recent basic guides to building websites suggest this comfort zone as well, such as Frederick J. Stielow's *Building Digital Archives, Descriptions, and Displays: A How-To-Do-It Manual for Librarians and Archivists* (New York: Neal-Schuman, 2003). If archivists need to question the veracity of photographic images in their digital form, as suggested by William J. Mitchell, *The Reconfigured Eye: Visual Truth in the Post-photographic Era* (Cambridge, Mass.: MIT Press, 1992), then archivists need to more philosophically question what is happening with what is posted on the Web.

Ethics and Security. Ethical issues, along with other contentious challenges such as security to archives and manuscripts, may be the most serious matters for archivists to face in the next generation. Within the past two decades, for example, the ownership of the cultural artifacts of the world's indigenous societies became a cantankerous issue, turning the worlds of archivists and museum curators, along with individual collectors and dealers, completely upside down. These issues are now fought in the courtrooms, in the media, in protests, and by those pointing to ethical and economic dimensions as having equal weight in a manner really never before argued. Anthropologist Michael F. Brown considers these matters in his book, seeking a middle ground in the conflicts. *Who Owns Native Culture?* (Cambridge, Mass.: Harvard University Press, 2003) gives ample attention to archival issues, helping archivists navigate among the rocky shoals of intellectual property of contested documents and artifacts in an era of constantly shifting senses of the ethical and legal factors resonant in such matters. Brown makes repeated references to a number of relatively recent federal laws, such as the Native American Graves Protection and Repatriation Act of 1990 (NAGPRA) and the American Indian Religious Freedom Act of 1978, posing some special problems for archives and archivists.

Ethics and security concerns have also led to new thinking about these dimensions of archival work. Ethical issues challenging archivists in their work have received increased attention in the past two decades. Karen Benedict, *Ethics and the Archival Profession: Introduction and Case Studies* (Chicago: Society of American Archivists, 2003) provides a useful compendium of applied ethics cases, and it is an excellent starting point for considering such matters. Heather MacNeil, *Without Consent: The Ethics of Disclosing Personal Information in Public Archives* (Metuchen, N.J.: Scarecrow Press and Society of American Archivists, 1992) is an

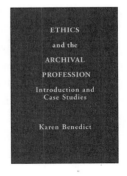

analysis of the problems of determining how to provide access to records possessing personal information, considering changing notions of research and evolving records systems, and setting out recommendations about how to allow research in such records. Generally, however, readings about the most interesting cases of archival ethics have been written by scholars and commentators outside the field. A classic example of this is Janet Malcolm, *In the Freud Archives* (New York: Alfred A. Knopf,

1984) concerning the controversy over the access to the papers of Sigmund Freud at the Library of Congress. H. Jeff Smith, *Managing Privacy: Information Technology and Corporate America* (Chapel Hill: University of North Carolina Press, 1994) is another example, providing a disturbing and detailed account of the adoption of information technologies without much regard for violations of personal privacy; despite a sizable number of archivists and records managers working in such corporate entities, this has not been an important topic in the professional literature. Kevin P. Kearns, *Managing for Accountability: Preserving the Public Trust in Public and Nonprofit Organizations* (San Francisco: Jossey-Bass Publishers, 1996) provides a general framework for thinking about accountability matters.

Security is an issue that has long been of interest to archivists, gradually emerging as a major concern in the 1970s and persisting through ever-increasing disquiet generated by national and international events (from wars to terrorism, all with major new types of legislation). Gregor Trinkaus-Randall, *Protecting Your Collections: A Manual of Archival Security* (Chicago: Society of American Archivists,

1995) is the standard reference, although it is in need of an updating. Again, some of the most interesting studies related to security in archives has come from the outside, such as Miles Harvey, *The Island of Lost Maps: A True Story of Cartographic Crime* (New York: Random House, 2000), an extremely important case study about security, collecting, and access to rare and valuable materials. Richard J. Cox,

Flowers after the Funeral: Reflections on the Post-9/11 Digital Age
(Lanham, Md.: Scarecrow Press, 2003), also provides a consideration
of security and other matters in his extended essay about the implications for archives and the information professions generated by the
terrorist attacks on America.

Other case studies about records, archives, and their value and use
in organizations and society, particularly government, stretch the
archivist's normal view of security. A landmark case concerning access
to government records is that of the Pentagon Papers, and there are
interesting perspectives on this case from both insiders and scholars,
such as Daniel Ellsberg, *Secrets: A Memoir of Vietnam and the
Pentagon Papers* (New York: Penguin Books, 2002); John Prados and
Margaret Pratt Porter, eds., *Inside the Pentagon Papers* (Lawrence:
University Press of Kansas, 2004); and David Rudenstine, *The Day the
Presses Stopped: A History of the Pentagon Papers Case* (Berkeley:
University of California Press, 1996). Shelley Davis, *Unbridled Power:
Inside the Secret Culture of the IRS* (New York: Harper, 1997) is a highly
personalized account by the former IRS historian of mammoth
recordkeeping problems at the Internal Revenue Service, where
records management had broken down and there was no archives
program at all. Bruce P. Montgomery, "Nixon's Legal Legacy: White
House Papers and the Constitution," *American Archivist* 56 (Fall 1993):
586–613 provides an interesting account of the history of these
records, a history continuing to unfold. Problems such as the ownership of and access to government records have emerged as among the
most troublesome issues of our modern era. A useful volume, written
primarily by researchers and public policy advocates, describing cases
of government records access is Athan G. Theoharis, ed., *A Culture of
Secrecy: The Government Versus the People's Right to Know* (Lawrence:
University Press of Kansas, 1998). Essays are included on the FBI's
resistance to the Freedom of Information Act, the CIA's secrecy, and
the National Security Agency, along with specific cases, such as getting
access to the FBI file on John Lennon, the FBI's Supreme Court sex
files, the continuing litigation over the Nixon tapes, the PROFS case,
the difficulties in producing the documentary series *Foreign Relations
of the United States*, and the work of the John F. Kennedy Assassination
Records Review Board.

An increasing array of studies from a variety of disciplines provides insights on records, recordkeeping systems, archives, and related topics, many of these presented as quite useful case studies. A number of these studies relate to issues of privacy and access in records, such as Timothy Garton Ash, *The File: A Personal History* (New York: Random House, 1997), a very personal view of the opening of the Stasi files in the former East Germany, and E. Wayne Carp, *Family Matters: Secrecy and Disclosure in the History of Adoption* (Cambridge, Mass.: Harvard University Press, 1998), an important study of how adoption and social service agencies have changed in regard to recordkeeping and access to these records. Many other books, similar to the Ash and Carp volumes, are appearing. A particularly powerful study about records management is Stanton A. Glantz, John Slade, Lisa A. Bero, Peter Hanauer, and Deborah E. Barnes, *The Cigarette Papers* (Berkeley: University of California Press, 1996), demonstrating how the management of records of tobacco companies was corrupted to support concealing information from the public and government about the health effects of cigarette smoking. For a volume examining the importance of records for accountability and commenting on many of these cases, with essays mostly by archivists, see Richard J. Cox and David A. Wallace, *Archives and the Public Good: Accountability and Records in Modern Society* (Westport, Conn.: Quorum Books, 2002). The National Security Archive has focused on particular accountability issues. An example of the publications is Peter Kornbluh, *The Pinochet File: A Declassified Dossier on Atrocity and Accountability* (New York: The New Press, 2003), a powerful example of the value of records for accountability, considering the story of the Augusto Pinochet overthrow of Salvador Allende's government in Chile and of the United States' role in the coup and its extended efforts to cover up its activities by keeping important records classified. This is one of a series of National Security Archive readers, including reports on the Bay of Pigs, the Cuban Missile Crisis, the Iran-Contra Scandal, Kissinger's secret talks with Beijing and Moscow, and South Africa-United States relations.

The Holocaust and recent concerns about looted art and property of its victims, as well as debates about the veracity of some aspects of this horrific period of modern history, has led to some interesting discussions of the value of archives, as seen in Stuart E. Eizenstat,

Imperfect Justice: Looted Assets, Slave Labor, and the Unfinished Business of World War II (New York: Public Affairs, 2003); Deborah Lipstadt, *Denying the Holocaust: The Growing Assault on Truth and Memory* (New York: The Free Press, 1993) and *History on Trial: My Day in Court with David Irving* (New York: Ecco, 2005); and Richard Evans, *Lying about Hitler: History, Holocaust, and the David Irving Trial* (New York: Basic Books, 2001).

Symbolism and Technology. Some studies reflect on the increasing concerns about elements of recordkeeping, such as personal privacy, brought about by the increasing uses of information technology. Janna Malamud Smith, *Private Matters: In Defense of the Personal Life* (Reading, Mass.: Addison-Wesley Publishing Co., 1997) includes, for example, a poignant chapter on the issues of privacy generated by the author serving as the executer of her father Bernard Malamud's estate (including his literary papers). That it is important to understand how the media thinks about archives and records can be seen in Barbie Zelizer, *Covering the Body: The Kennedy Assassination, the Media, and the Shaping of Collective Memory* (Chicago: University of Chicago Press, 1992), a study demonstrating how news reporters and their memories of this event became the official archive about it, rather than the records and other evidence compiled about it. Zelizer's study ought to be read in conjunction with David R. Wrone's *The Zapruder Film: Reframing JFK's Assassination* (Lawrence: University Press of Kansas, 2003) considering, among other things, the notion of this film footage as record and evidence and the ensuing fight over its custody and use, especially considering the battles over the ownership and copyright of the film (including the passage of two federal laws in 1965 and 1992). Menzi L. Behrnd-Klodt and Peter J. Wosh, eds., *Privacy and Confidentiality Perspectives: Archivists and Archival Records* (Chicago: Society of American Archivists, 2005) provides an excellent set of readings on the complex challenges of privacy and confidentiality, setting a larger context for cases such as those described above.

In the midst of research about electronic records considerable discussion developed about whether archival records must be physically maintained by real repositories, an interesting play with what virtual records had to do with this. David Bearman set the initial stage for the debate with his "An Indefensible Bastion: Archives as a Repository in the Electronic Age," included in his *Archival Management of Electronic Records* (Pittsburgh: Archives and Museum Informatics, 1991), 14–24. Luciana Duranti, "Archives as a Place," *Archives and Manuscripts* 24 (November 1996): 242–55 and Terry Eastwood, "Should Creating Agencies Keep Electronic Records Indefinitely?" *Archives and Manuscripts* 24 (November 1996): 256–67 respond with arguments that even electronic records must be maintained by archives, not by the creating agencies. The debate ultimately morphed into arguments about whether archives were more about evidence and accountability or cultural and symbolic bastions, leading to statements such as Adrian Cunningham, "Beyond the Pale? The 'Flinty' Relationship between Archivists Who Collect the Private Records of Individuals and the Rest of the Archival Profession," *Archives and Manuscripts* 24 (May 1996): 20–26 and Mark Greene, "The Power of Meaning: The Archival Mission in the Postmodern Age," *American Archivist* 65 (Spring/Summer 2002): 42–55.

   Advocacy and the Archival Mission. There are a number of articles and case studies about archival advocacy concerns, including some much outdated basic manuals, but it is also obvious that the notion of archival advocacy is due for a major rethinking. Here are some indicators of this potential change. The rise of studies on public memory has contributed considerably to our understanding of American archival activity and the importance of archives and manuscripts in shaping such memory, and a few examples demonstrate the value of the new scholarship. David Lowenthal's sweeping and pioneering analysis of how the past is understood, especially in its material representations including archives and historical manuscripts, *The Past Is a Foreign Country* (Cambridge: Cambridge University Press, 1985), provides an engaging framework for such purposes. Kenneth Foote, a historical geographer, gives an early example specifically targeted at understanding how archives serve a memory function in his "To Remember and Forget: Archives, Memory and Culture," *American Archivist* 53 (Summer 1990): 378–92. Roy Rosenzweig and David Thelen, *The Presence of the Past: Popular Uses of*

History in American Life (New York: Columbia University Press, 1998) provides an important perspective on Americans' interest in the past, with many references to the creation of diaries, photographic albums, and other such documents and the interaction of Americans at historic sites and history museums. This volume provides clues as to how Americans approach sources and the potential of archives to be used more widely.

Recordkeeping in the Digital Era. One of the most substantial changes in how archivists go about their business has been represented by the digitization of the world, reflected in the growing number of reports and studies about the selection of records and other materials for digitizing as well as how to maintain these digital holdings. Jeff Rothenberg, *Avoiding Technological Quicksand: Finding a Viable Technical Foundation for Digital Preservation* (Washington, D.C.: Council on Library and Information Resources, 1999) is an example of these reports, proposing an "emulation strategy," one that works "to emulate obsolete systems on future, unknown systems, so that a digital document's original software can be run in the future despite being obsolete." The National Science Foundation and the Library of Congress released a report on the research needed in digital preservation. *It's About Time: Research Challenges in Digital Archiving and Long-term Preservation*, published in August 2003 and available at http://www.digitalpreservation.gov/repor/NSF_LC_Final_Report.pdf, represents a wide range of organizations and disciplines, noting that "no acceptable methods exist today to preserve complex digital objects that contain combinations of text, data, images, audio, and video and that require specific software applications for reuse."

There are numerous reports about tests of new approaches and an increasing number of research studies. The administration of electronic records is not merely about technical issues, as difficult as these may seem at times, but also concerns matters of policy, law, and economics, as depicted in studies such as David A. Wallace, "The Public's Use of Federal Recordkeeping Statutes to Shape Federal Information Policy: A Study of the PROFS Case," (PhD diss., University of Pittsburgh, 1997)[15] and Mary Rawlings-Milton, "Electronic Records and the Law: Causing the Federal Records Program to Implode?" (PhD diss., Virginia Polytechnic Institute and State University, April

2000), and research on such matters by individuals outside the archives and records management fields, such as the important book by Abigail J. Sellen and Richard H. R. Harper, *The Myth of the Paperless Office* (Cambridge, Mass.: MIT, 2001). The latter changes are indicators of a healthier and expanded attention to records management and archiving concerns.

Professionalism. It is fitting to end this bibliographic essay with a final comment on the nature of archival professionalism. The notion of what constitutes a professional has long been a topic of concern for archivists, such as what has been written about the notion of the professional image—David B. Gracy, "Archivists, You Are What People Think You Keep," *American Archivist* 52 (1989): 72–78—and professional status—Richard J. Cox, "Professionalism and Archivists in the United States," *American Archivist* 49 (1986): 229–47. The latter essay is included in Richard J. Cox, *American Archival Analysis: The Recent Development of the Archival Profession in the United States* (Metuchen, N.J.: Scarecrow Press, 1990), seeking to explain the ferment of change characterizing the American archival profession in the 1970s and 1980s. Most of the writings described in this essay comment on, or assume, the notion of the archivist as a professional; indeed, this is essentially what this entire book is about.

Conclusion

As anyone familiar with the professional literature of archivists will recognize, this was a particularly hard chapter to include. It could have been several orders of magnitude larger and still not have satisfied everyone. We can quibble with what has been included—why is this old title mentioned and a newer work excluded—and we can fuss about the organization of the essay—since many of the publications mentioned here cross over topics, issues, and functions. The astute reader will also notice that references to sources on the World Wide Web are limited, both because these tend to change so often and because some parameters were needed to manage the discussion. It is certain that readers who plow through the numerous monographs, manuals, reports, and essays mentioned here will possess a better understanding of archives and manuscripts. Moreover, they will understand the needs for new research and exploration about such documentary expressions in order to continue to expand our understanding of this fundamental activity of humanity.

Notes

Chapter 1. Recording, Keeping, and Using Information

1 Ivan Illich and Barry Sanders, *The Alphabetization of the Popular Mind* (San Francisco: North Point Press, 1988), 15; Steven Roger Fischer, *A History of Language* (London: Reaktion Books, Ltd., 1999), 35, 189.

2 Robin Dunbar, *Grooming, Gossip, and the Evolution of Language* (London: Faber and Faber, 1996) and Jon Agar, *Constant Touch: A Global History of the Mobile Phone* (Cambridge, U.K.: Icon Books, 2003) are popular summaries of some of this research.

3 Scholars suggest that the notion of alphabetic writing as a hallmark of an advanced culture has been over emphasized. Historians studying cross-cultural contacts are now examining the problems in how views of language, communication, and writing contributed to misunderstanding and even violent conflicts. See Elizabeth Hill Boone and Walter D. Mignolo, eds., *Writing Without Words: Alternative Literacies in Mesoamerica and the Andes* (Durham, N.C.: Duke University Press, 1994); Jorge Canizares-Esguerra, *How to Write the History of the New World: Histories, Epistemologies, and Identities in the Eighteenth-Century Atlantic World* (Stanford, Calif.: Stanford University Press, 2001); and Jill Lepore, *The Name of War: King Philip's War and the Origins of American Identity* (New York: Vintage Books, 1999).

4 By far the best general guide for understanding the world of oral storage and transmission of information is Walter J. Ong, *Orality and Literacy: The Technologizing of the Word* (London: Methuen, 1982). For the use of these oral memory techniques in particular cultures, see Eric A. Havelock, *The Literate Revolution in Greece and Its Aftermath* (Princeton: Princeton University Press, 1982) and the classic Albert B. Lord, *The Singer of Tales* (Cambridge, Mass.: Harvard University Press, 1960). Jan Vansina's *Oral Tradition as History* (Madison: University of Wisconsin Press, 1985) provides an interesting commentary on how oral testimonies fare as historical evidence.

5 Carolyn Hamilton, Verne Harris, Jane Taylor, Michele Pickover, Graeme Reid, and Razia Saleh, *Refiguring the Archive* (Dordrecht, Netherlands: Kluwer Academic Publishers, 2002).

6 David Crystal, considering the death of languages, writes, "When you are the only one left, your knowledge of your language is like a repository, or archive, of your people's spoken linguistic past." David Crystal, *Language Death* (Cambridge: Cambridge University Press, 2000), 2.

7 Juliet Fleming argues that the "writing that survives from the Elizabethan period was produced by people who had the technological and financial resources for the laborious procedures of securing paper, pen, and ink. The poor, the hurried and those (it may have been practically everybody) unconcerned with the extensive circulation and long survival of their *bons mots* wrote with charcoal, chalk, stone and pencil" (but they all wrote, with graffiti on walls and objects of all sorts as testimony). Juliet Fleming, *Graffiti and the Writing Arts of Early Modern England* (Philadelphia: University of Pennsylvania Press, 2001), 50.

8 The classic study about the elaborate mechanisms, other than writing, created for aiding memory is Frances A. Yates, *The Art of Memory* (Chicago: University of Chicago Press, 1966).

9 Ong, *Orality and Literacy*, 11–12; Havelock, *Literate Revolution in Greece*, 87.

10 Jack Goody, *The Power of the Written Tradition* (Washington, D.C.: Smithsonian Institution Press, 2000).

11 Steven Roger Fischer, *A History of Reading* (London: Reaktion Books, Ltd., 2003), 97.

12 One can think of the audio recordings made of the Bible, or of particular references within this religious text suggesting reading out loud. John's Revelation is a clear case, noting in the very beginning, "Blessed is the one who reads aloud the words of this prophecy, and blessed are those who hear, and who keep what is written in it, for the time is near" (Revelation 1:3, English Standard Version).

13 Some of these fears have been expressed in the worries about the demise of reading and reflection, such as represented by Sven Birkerts, *The Gutenberg Elegies: The Fate of Reading in an Electronic Age* (Boston: Faber and Faber, 1994). The emerging reliance on more visual systems, such as the World Wide Web, some argue, also poses corresponding dangers in the weakening of memory based on textual literacy.

14 M. T. Clanchy, *From Memory to Written Record: England, 1066–1307* (Cambridge, Mass.: Harvard University Press, 1979), 21–22, 203–4, 220. On the importance of writing to the Roman Empire, see William V. Harris, *Ancient Literacy* (Cambridge, Mass.: Harvard University Press, 1989), 232.

15 Brian Stock, *Listening for the Text: On the Uses of the Past* (Philadelphia: University of Pennsylvania Press, 1997).

16 Steven Roger Fischer, *A History of Writing* (London: Reaktion Books, Ltd., 2001), 147.

17 Lawrence J. McCrank, "Documenting Reconquest and Reform: The Growth of Archives in the Medieval Crown of Aragon," *American Archivist* 56 (Spring 1993): 256–318 is a detailed exploration of the growth of early records, a growth that

mirrors what happens in later centuries in other countries. And through these centuries we have a shift in the concept of memory from the oral repeating of traditions to more elaborate and complex writing systems, supplemented by the powerful emergence of printing, to the algorithmic-driven systems of the modern computer where memory is cheap, a measure of power and potential, and sometimes more fragile than ancient ways of capturing information; see Michael E. Hobart and Zachary S. Schiffman, *Information Ages: Literacy, Numeracy, and the Computer Revolution* (Baltimore: Johns Hopkins University Press, 1998).

18 Quoted in Lisa Jardine, *Worldy Goods* (New York: Macmillan, 1996), 111.

19 For an introduction to this idea, see Wendy M. Duff, "Harnessing the Power of Warrant," *American Archivist* 61 (Spring 1998): 88–105.

20 Anne L. Bower, ed., *Recipes for Reading: Community Cookbooks, Stories, Histories* (Amherst: University of Massachusetts, 1997).

21 John Seely Brown and Paul Duguid, *The Social Life of Information* (Boston: Harvard Business School Press, 2000) is the preeminent example of this.

22 Jean Bottéro, *Mesopotamia: Writing, Reasoning, and the Gods* (Chicago: University of Chicago Press, 1992), 49. Especially important is Denise Schmandt-Besserat's contention that cuneiform writing gradually emerged from an accounting device; see her *How Writing Came About* (Austin: University of Texas Press, 1996).

23 Henri-Jean Martin, *The History and Power of Writing*, trans. Lydia G. Cochrane (Chicago: University of Chicago Press, 1994).

24 See James M. O'Toole, "The Symbolic Significance of Archives," *American Archivist* 56 (Spring 1993): 234–55. Recent debates about the need to administer electronic records (often resorting to other purposes such as evidence and accountability) have seen a resurgence of interest in the symbolic value of records, with some arguing that this is the core of what identifies an archival record and others seeing symbolism as part of a complex array of values that are constantly shifting as different issues and concerns emerge. For example, much of the discussion about how to commemorate the site and remember the victims of the September 11, 2001, terrorist attacks on the Pentagon and the World Trade Center, often seems to confuse the nature and purpose of institutions such as archives, museums, and libraries. Richard J. Cox, *Flowers After the Funeral: Reflections on the Post-9/11 Digital Age* (Lanham, Md.: Scarecrow Press, Inc., 2003) muses about this.

25 This is most dramatically seen in Nicholson Baker, *Double Fold: Libraries and the Assault on Paper* (New York: Random House, 2001). Responses include Richard J. Cox, *Vandals in the Stacks? A Response to Nicholson Baker's Assault on Libraries* (Westport, Conn.: Greenwood Press, 2002) and Nicholas Basbanes, *A Splendor of Letters: The Permanence of Books in an Impermanent World* (New York: HarperCollins, 2003).

26 Kenneth E. Foote, "To Remember and Forget: Archives, Memory and Culture," *American Archivist* 53 (Summer 1990): 378–92; David Lowenthal, *The Past Is a Foreign Country* (Cambridge: Cambridge University Press, 1985), especially chapter 5.

27 Nicholas Basbanes, *Among the Gently Mad: Perspectives and Strategies for the Book Hunter in the Twenty-First Century* (New York: Henry Holt and Co., 2002), 3.

28 Priscilla B. Hayner, *Unspeakable Truths: Facing the Challenge of Truth Commissions* (New York: Routledge, 2002).

29 Just as often, of course, rulers try to control and shape the past to cover their misdeeds or to fabricate an image in history undeserving for their role in it. It is reported that when King Leopold of Belgium was forced to give up his colony in the Congo, he endeavored to destroy all the evidence of his activities, claiming a privilege that this was his personal business and no one else's. Adam Hochschild, *King Leopold's Ghost: A Story of Greed, Terror and Heroism in Colonial Africa* (Boston: Houghton Mifflin Co., 1998).

30 More remarkably, the controversies in the 1990s about the looting of Holocaust victims' assets and the laundering of funds and other assets through Swiss banks brought a renewed attention to the fact that even a government committed to genocide is likely to document fully its atrocities. There are many accounts of the Holocaust victims' assets, but for a good introduction see Stuart E. Eizenstat, *Imperfect Justice: Looted Assets, Slave Labor, and the Unfinished Business of World War II* (New York: Public Affairs, 2003).

31 For a full perspective on this, see John Prados, *The White House Tapes: Eavesdropping on the President* (New York: The New Press, 2003).

32 Barbara Ley Toffler, with Jennifer Reingold, *Final Accounting: Ambition, Greed, and the Fall of Arthur Andersen* (New York: Broadway Books, 2003), 165–66.

33 Quoted from András Riedlmayer, "Erasing the Past: The Destruction of Libraries and Archives in Bosnia-Herzegovina," *Middle Eastern Studies Association Bulletin*, July 1995, available at http://fp.arizona.edu/mesassoc/Bulletin/bosnia.htm.

34 Stephen C. Puleo, *30,000 Miles from Home: The World War II Journey of Tony Puleo* (Boston: privately printed, 1997), i–ii.

35 One of the most dramatic examples of this is the trial, initiated by Holocaust-denier David Irving, of Deborah Lipstadt for her book about these deniers. The trial put on the stand the veracity of historical evidence, the appropriateness of historical methodologies, and the importance of archival records. See Deborah Lipstadt, *Denying the Holocaust: The Growing Assault on Truth and Memory* (New York: The Free Press, 1993) and Richard Evans, *Lying About Hitler: History, Holocaust, and the David Irving Trial* (New York: Basic Books, 2001).

36 "Columbia University Rescinds Bancroft Prize," Organization of American Historians *Newsletter*, February 2003, available at http://www.oah.org/pubs/nl/2003feb/bellesiles.html.

37 For a full treatment of these subjects, see Dard Hunter, *Papermaking* (New York: Dover, 1978).

38 Abigail J. Sellen and Richard H. R. Harper, *The Myth of the Paperless Office* (Cambridge, Mass.: MIT, 2001) is an interesting study about the persistence of paper.

39 Maygene Daniels, "The Ingenious Pen: American Writing Implements from the Eighteenth Century to the Twentieth," *American Archivist* 43 (1980): 312–24.

40 Henry Petroski, *The Pencil: A History of Design and Circumstance* (New York: Alfred A. Knopf, 1990).

41 Margaret Shepherd, *The Art of the Handwritten Note: A Guide to Reclaiming Civilized Communication* (New York: Broadway Books, 2002) is a good example of the kind of advice being offered about when to write such a note.

42 For an overview of the historical impact of printing, see Elizabeth L. Eisenstein, *The Printing Press as an Agent of Social Change* (Cambridge: Cambridge University Press, 1979).

43 Fischer, *A History of Reading*, 283–84. If Thomas Jefferson had access to the World Wide Web would he have used it? See Richard J .Cox, "Declarations, Independence, and Text in the Information Age," *First Monday* 6 (1999), available at http://www.firstmonday.dk/issues/issue4_6/rjcox/index.html.

44 Concerning the typewriter, see Michael H. Adler, *The Writing Machine* (London: Allen and Unwyn, 1973); see also Daniels, "Ingenious Pen," 320–22.

45 Lisa Gitelman, *Scripts, Grooves, and Writing Machines: Representing Technology in the Edison Era* (Stanford, Calif.: Stanford University Press, 1999), 208.

46 Margery W. Davies, *Woman's Place Is at the Typewriter: Office Work and Office Workers 1870–1930* (Philadelphia: Temple University Press, 1982) and Sharon Hartman Strom, *Beyond the Typewriter: Gender, Class, and the Origins of Modern American Office Work, 1900–1930* (Urbana: University of Illinois Press, 1992).

47 Silvio A. Bedini, *Thomas Jefferson and His Copying Machines* (Charlottesville: University Press of Virginia, 1984).

48 For a brief history of copying technology, see Daniel J. Boorstin, *The Americans: The Democratic Experience* (New York: Random House, 1973), 397–402.

49 Peter Lyman and Hal Varian, *How Much Information? 2003*, available at http://www.sims.berkeley.edu/research/projects/how-much-info-2003/. The bigger problem has been society's becoming accustomed to copies to the degree that the distinction between copy or replica has become, for many, a nonessential matter; see Hillel Schwartz, *The Culture of the Copy: Striking Likenesses, Unreasonable Facsimiles* (New York: Zone Books, 1996).

50 Jon Butler, *Becoming America: The Revolution before 1776* (Cambridge, Mass.: Harvard University Press, 2000), 130, 133 and Richard J. Cox, "Records in the Hands of an Angry God: Jonathan Edwards and Eighteenth Century Records Management," *Records & Information Management Report* 19 (November 2003): 7–11.

51 For a history of filing systems in the nineteenth century, see JoAnne Yates, *Control Through Communication: The Rise of System in American Management* (Baltimore: Johns Hopkins University Press, 1989), especially chapter 2.

52 See Donald Albrecht and Chrysanthe B. Broikos, eds., *On the Job: Design and the American Office* (New York: Princeton Architectural Press and the National Building Museum, 2000) for a good introduction to the evolving design of offices and their furnishings (with lots of illustrations).

53 There is a good summary of the history of photography in Mary Lynn Ritzenthaler et al., *Archives and Manuscripts: Administration of Photographic Collections* (Chicago: Society of American Archivists, 1984). Some interesting

questions about the use of photographs as historical evidence are raised in Carl Fleischauer and Beverly W. Brannan, eds., *Documenting America, 1935–1943* (Berkeley: University of California Press, 1988).

54 See Elisabeth Kaplan and Jeffrey Mifflin, "'Mind and Sight': Visual Literacy and the Archivist," *Archival Issues* 21 (1996): 107–27. Alberto Manguel suggests "that if looking at pictures is equivalent to reading, then it is a vastly creative form of reading," in *Reading Pictures: What We Think About When We Look at Art* (New York: Random House, 2002), 149. Despite the pervasiveness and power of images such as photographs, they have remained underutilized by researchers such as historians, partly because of the more complex challenges they present. Peter Burke provides a guide to the use of visual images, expressing surprise about how historians' training in the use of source materials seems to have ignored the visual ones: "The 'source criticism' of written documents has long formed an essential part of the training of historians. By comparison, the criticism of visual evidence remains undeveloped, although the testimony of images, like that of texts, raises problems of context, function, rhetoric, recollection (whether soon or long after the event), secondhand witnessing and so on"; Peter Burke, *Eyewitnessing: The Uses of Images as Historical Evidence* (Ithaca, N.Y.: Cornell University Press, 2001), 15.

55 Frederic Luther, *Microfilm: A History* (Annapolis, Md.: National Microfilm Association, 1959).

56 See, for example, William J. Mitchell, *The Reconfigured Eye: Visual Truth in the Post-photographic Era* (Cambridge, Mass.: MIT Press, 1992) and *It's About Time: Research Challenges in Digital Archiving and Long-term Preservation*, published in August 2003 and available at http://www.digitalpreservation.gov/repor/ NSF_LC_Final_Report.pdf.

57 The origins of sound recording came laden with inflated promises of permanence, partly generated by the agility of the technologies in capturing sound, thoroughly documented by Jonathan Sterne, *The Audible Past: Cultural Origins of Sound Reproduction* (Durham, N.C.: Duke University Press, 2003).

58 Barry M. Leiner, "A Brief History of the Internet," available at http://www.isoc.org/ internet/history/brief.shtml. The Internet Society's website, http://www.isoc.org, provides considerable information about the Internet/World Wide Web.

59 On the growth of computerized storage of government information, see James Gregory Bradsher, "An Administrative History of the Disposal of Federal Records, 1950–1985," *Provenance* 4 (Fall 1986): 57–60. On the impact of computers generally, see J. David Bolter, *Turing's Man: Western Culture in the Computer Age* (Chapel Hill: University of North Carolina Press, 1982), and James R. Beniger, *The Control Revolution: Technological and Economic Origins of the Information Society* (Cambridge, Mass.: Harvard University Press, 1986).

60 See, for example, Mary Rawlings-Milton, "Electronic Records and the Law: Causing the Federal Records Program to Implode?" (PhD diss., Virginia Polytechnic Institute and State University, April 2000); Robert F. Sproull and Jon Eisenberg, eds., *Building an Electronic Records Archive at the National Archives and Records Administration: Recommendations for Initial Development* (Washington, D.C.: The National Academies Press, 2003), available at http://www.nap.edu/books/0309089476/html.

61 For a breezy account of the positive benefits of these devices, see, as just one example, Howard Rheingold, *Smart Mobs: The Next Social Revolution* (New York: Perseus Books, 2002).

62 The famous silent hound provides Holmes a key clue in Arthur Conan Doyle's story "Silver Blaze." On the history of the telephone, see John Brooks, *Telephone: The First Hundred Years* (New York: Harper and Row, 1976), and Ithiel de Sola Pool, ed., *The Social Impact of the Telephone* (Cambridge, Mass.: MIT Press, 1981).

63 For a sense of the nineteenth century, see Thomas Augst, *The Clerk's Tale: Young Men and Moral Life in Nineteenth-Century America* (Chicago: University of Chicago Press, 2003).

64 One commentator on the promises and challenges of digital technologies uses as his inspiration Leonardo da Vinci's penchant for personal recordkeeping: "Inspired by Leonardo's penchant for portable notebooks, and larger sketchbooks, and by his frescoes, we as users and technology developers might imagine the need for a comprehensive line of computers from small but elegant wearable devices to ornate desktop machines and impressive wall-sized models." The potential power of computing is compared to the ability of the elite to establish archives and museums being rivaled by the new potential of computing sensitive to human needs: "Royalty and presidents have libraries of their archives with photos of their accomplishments but in the future more people will create museums on the Web and slide shows about their lives and ancestors." Ben Shneiderman, *Leonardo's Laptop: Human Needs and the New Computing Technologies* (Cambridge, Mass.: MIT, 2002), 8, 9, 98.

65 Fischer, *A History of Writing*, 319.

66 F. Gerald Ham, "Archival Choices: Managing the Historical Record in an Age of Abundance," *American Archivist* 47 (1984): 11–22.

67 See, for example, E. Wayne Carp, *Family Matters: Secrecy and Disclosure in the History of Adoption* (Cambridge, Mass.: Harvard University Press, 1998).

68 Ellen Fitzpatrick, *History's Memory: Writing America's Past, 1880–1980* (Cambridge, Mass.: Harvard University Press, 2002), 63.

69 The example of electronic mail is quite dramatic and challenging as a preservation problem, with archivists and records managers alike torn about whether to save them as paper printouts or as part of digital systems or even how to evaluate all the traffic in these ubiquitous systems. Three scientists wrote a letter to the prestigious journal *Nature* commenting on the growth of e-mail to 225 million corporate mailboxes and more than 35 billion messages annually, worrying "Little of this staggering volume is translated to hard copy. Even formal documents are frequently discarded by simply erasing them to avoid the tedium and expense of printing and archiving, on the erroneous assumption that previous iterations are of no value. The threat to the existence of hard-copy records of e-mail will become more acute as younger generations become less culturally and educationally attuned to their importance for the preservation of historical records." Eroll C. Friedberg, Herbert K. Hagler, and Kevin J. Land, "How E-mail Raises the Spectre of a Digital Dark Age," *Nature* 801 (19 June 2003), available at http://www.nature.com/cgi-taf/DynaPage.taf?file=/nature/journal/, vol. 42.

70 John Seely Brown and Paul Duguid, *The Social Life of Information,* and David M. Levy, *Scrolling Forward: Making Sense of Documents in the Digital Age* (New York: Arcade Publishing, 2001) both provide this sense.

71 Benedict Anderson, *Imagined Communities: Reflections on the Origin and Spread of Nationalism,* rev. ed. (New York: Verso, 1991) is the classic text on this idea. See also Thomas Richards, *The Imperial Archive: Knowledge and the Fantasy of Empire* (London: Verso, 1993) with more of an archival notion of this, although not archives in a traditional sense.

72 T. R. Schellenberg, *Modern Archives: Principles and Techniques* (Chicago: University of Chicago Press, 1956), 13–14.

73 See, for example, James H. Cassedy, *Demography in Early America: Beginnings of the Statistical Mind 1600–1800* (Cambridge, Mass.: Harvard University Press, 1969).

74 David Weinberger, in his description of the World Wide Web, notes that it is, among other things, a "loose federation of documents—many small pieces loosely joined. But in what has turned out to be simply the first cultural artifact and institution the Web has subtly subverted, the interior structure of documents has changed, not just the way they are connected to one another. The Web has blown documents apart. . . . What the Web has done to documents it is doing to just about every institution it touches." David Weinberger, *Small Pieces Loosely Joined (A Unified Theory of the Web)* (Cambridge, Mass.: Perseus Publishing, 2002), ix.

75 See Richard J. Cox and David Wallace, eds., *Archives and the Public Good: Accountability and Records in Modern Society* (Westport, Conn.: Quorum Books, 2002), and Althan G. Theoharis, ed., *A Culture of Secrecy: The Government Versus the People's Right to Know* (Lawrence: University Press of Kansas, 1998).

76 James M. O'Toole, ed., *The Records of American Business* (Chicago: Society of American Archivists, 1997) provides a good sense of the issues faced in administering the archival records of these institutions.

77 See Mike Brewster, *Unaccountable: How the Accounting Profession Forfeited a Public Trust* (New York: John Wiley & Sons, Inc., 2003) for a popular account of the demise of this discipline and the immense void left in its wake. For an insider's view, with lots of references to the general handling of records, see Toffler, with Reingold, *Final Accounting.*

78 See, for example, Robert Brent Toplin, ed., *Ken Burns's The Civil War: Historians Respond* (New York: Oxford University Press, 1996) and Gary R. Edgerton, *Ken Burns's America* (New York: Palgrave, 2001).

79 Robert Brent Toplin, ed., *Oliver Stone's USA: Film, History, and Controversy* (Lawrence: University Press of Kansas, 2000) and David R. Wrone, *The Zapruder Film: Reframing JFK's Assassination* (Lawrence: University Press of Kansas, 2003) are interesting insights into the film of the Kennedy murder.

80 While there are many gaps in how generally archives and archivists have been perceived (there is, for example, no adequate perception in children's literature), it is also true that the popular perception of archives is becoming the

topic of scholarly scrutiny, perhaps a backhanded acknowledgement of the importance of such records to society. See Richard J. Cox, "A Sense of the Future: A Child's View of Archives," *Archivists: The Image and Future of the Profession; 1995 Conference Proceedings*, eds. Michael Piggott and Colleen McEwen (Canberra: Australian Society of Archivists Inc., 1996), 189–209.

Chapter 2. The History of Archives and the Archives Profession

1 Paul Conway, "Perspectives on Archival Resources: The 1985 Census of Archival Institutions," *American Archivist* 50 (Spring 1987): 174–91 provides the last detailed analysis of archival programs.

2 Nearly half of all advertisements for entry-level archivists are posted by colleges and universities; see, for example, Richard J. Cox, "Employing Records Professionals in the Information Age: An Analysis of Entry-Level Archives Advertisements, 1976–1997, in the United States," *Information Management Journal* 34 (January 2000): 18–33.

3 Roy Rosenzweig and David Thelen, *The Presence of the Past: Popular Uses of History in American Life* (New York: Columbia University Press, 1998) provides a detailed glimpse of such interest.

4 The list is the "Repositories of Primary Sources," maintained by the University of Idaho Libraries; it can be found at http://www.uidaho.edu/special-collections/Other.Repositories.html. For a sense of the growth in the number of archives and archivists, see Philip M. Hamer, ed., *Guide to Archives and Manuscripts in the United States* (New Haven: Yale University Press, 1961); National Historical Publications and Records Commission, *Directory of Archives and Manuscript Repositories in the United States* (Washington, D.C.: NHPRC, 1978); National Historical Publications and Records Commission, *Directory of Archives and Manuscript Repositories in the United States,* 2nd ed. (Phoenix: Oryx Press, 1988). Membership information for the society is in J. Frank Cook, "The Blessings of Providence on an Association of Archivists," *American Archivist* 46 (1983): 376, 389. Because many archivists are not members of the SAA, the current figure seriously undercounts the profession. The most recent effort, dubbed A*Census and supported with funding by the Institute for Museum and Library Services, has as a goal to get a count of every archivist working in the United States; the first, preliminary results of the census were being released as this volume was being completed. The Society of American Archivists maintains an active list of archival associations at its website at http://www.archivists.org/assoc-orgs/directory/index.asp and maintains a list of many of the archival listservs at http://www.archivists.org/listservs/index.asp.

5 One might also wonder why the history of the archival profession and its repositories, a field heavily populated by individuals educated as historians or possessing one or more history degrees, remains understudied as well. See, for example, Richard J. Cox, "American Archival History: Its Development, Needs, and Opportunities," *American Archivist* 46 (Winter 1983): 31–41; "On the Value of Archival History in the United States," *Libraries and Culture* 23 (Spring 1988): 135–51; and "The Failure or Future of American Archival History: A Somewhat Unorthodox View," *Libraries and Culture* 35 (Winter 2000): 141–54.

6 The standard work in English on the origins of archives in Western civilization is Ernst Posner, *Archives in the Ancient World* (Cambridge, Mass.: Harvard University Press, 1972). See also Maria Brosius, ed., *Ancient Archives and Archival Traditions: Concepts of Record-Keeping in the Ancient World* (Oxford: Oxford University Press, 2003) and Denise Schumandt-Beserat, "The Earliest Precursor of Writing," *Scientific American* 238 (June 1978): 50–59. As early as the ninth millennium BCE, she finds, the Sumerians were keeping track of accounts and other important information with clay tokens of various shapes, each with its own meaning. The shapes later evolved into written ideographs. Thus, some archives may have predated writing by thousands of years.

7 For debate about the nature and meaning of archives in the ancient world, see, in addition to Posner's book, now reprinted by the Society of American Archivists, Rosalind Thomas, *Literacy and Orality in Ancient Greece* (Cambridge: Cambridge University Press, 1992); James P. Sickinger, *Public Records and Archives in Classical Athens* (Chapel Hill: University of North Carolina Press, 1999); and Brosius, ed., *Ancient Archives and Archival Traditions*.

8 Hugh Taylor, "'My Very Act and Deed': Some Reflections on the Role of Textual Records in the Conduct of Affairs," *American Archivist* 51 (1988): 456–69. The emergence of the study as a separate room in the home by the Renaissance, a place where collections might be displayed as well as an office and repository for family archives, reveals the steadily growing importance of documents in society. Dora Thornton, *The Scholar in His Study: Ownership and Experience in Renaissance Italy* (New Haven and London: Yale University Press, 1997).

9 Some commentators have suggested that during the medieval era, near-modern archives and records management principles and practices were formulated, developing partly because of the growth of government and the resulting pro-liferation of records. Lawrence J. McCrank, "Documenting Reconquest and Reform: The Growth of Archives in the Medieval Crown of Aragon," *American Archivist* 56 (Spring 1993): 256–318.

10 For a scholarly, informative, and delightful history of this record, as well as an excellent guide through the substantial historical literature about it, see Elizabeth M. Hallam, *Domesday Book Through Nine Centuries* (London: Thames and Hudson, 1986); see especially chapters 2 ("The Reputation and Uses of Domesday Book, 1087–1272") and 3 ("Domesday Book as a Working Record, 1272–1700").

11 "Digital Domesday Book Unlocked," BBC *News*, 2 December 2002, available at http://news.bbc.co.uk/1/hi/technology/2534391.stm.

12 Patrick J. Geary, *Phantoms of Remembrance: Memory and Oblivion at the End of the First Millennium* (Princeton, N.J.: Princeton University Press, 1994), 114. See also M. T. Clanchy, *From Memory to Written Record: England 1066–1307* (Oxford: Blackwell, 1993) and Anthony Grafton, *Forgers and Critics: Creativity and Duplicity in Western Scholarship* (Princeton, N.J.: Princeton University Press, 1990).

13 Quoted in Michael Camille, *Mirror in Parchment: The Luttrell Psalter and the Making of Medieval England* (Chicago: University of Chicago Press, 1998), 178.

14 See Ernst Posner's seminal essay, "Some Aspects of Archival Development since the French Revolution," *American Archivist* 3 (1940): 159–72. Judith M. Panitch,

"Liberty, Equality, Posterity?: Some Archival Lessons from the Case of the French Revolution," *American Archivist* 59 (Winter 1996): 45, significantly revises some of Posner's conclusions, chronicling how records of the old regime were destroyed as well as saved, a hated symbol of those who controlled France and were now out of power. In subsequent centuries, the governments of nations, some new and some old and established, would be concerned with issues of access, privacy, security, and control, but the archival principles, at least in democratic regimes, would be definitely drawn in opposition to any efforts to fabricate, revise, or subvert the content and meaning of their records. For a less constructive episode in European archival history—Napoleon's attempts to consolidate in Paris the archives of all the countries he conquered—see Owen Chadwick, *Catholicism and History: The Opening of the Vatican Archives* (Cambridge: Cambridge University Press, 1978), esp. 14–19.

15 Margaret Wickens Pearce, "Native Mapping in Southern New England Indian Deeds," in *Cartographic Encounters: Perspectives on Native American Mapmaking and Map Use,* ed. G. Malcolm Lewis (Chicago: University of Chicago Press, 1998), 161. For one of the best descriptions of such matters, see Jill Lepore, *The Name of War: King Philip's War and the Origins of American Identity* (New York: Vintage Books, 1999).

16 David Cressy, *Coming Over: Migration and Communication between England and New England in the Seventeenth Century* (New York: Cambridge University Press, 1987), chapter 9.

17 See James G. Moseley, *John Winthrop's World: History as a Story, The Story as History* (Madison: University of Wisconsin Press, 1992).

18 Kenneth A. Lockridge, *The Diary and Life of William Byrd II of Virginia, 1674–1744* (New York: W. W. Norton and Co., 1987), 66. This was not, of course, unique to America. Byrd's near contemporary, James Boswell, viewed his journal as a "vast hoard of memory," compulsively taking down as much as he could, with self-conscious references to his journal and other notes as his "archive" in an era when there was no real public sense of archives. A recent biographer of Boswell speculates that he was driven by a terror of oblivion, noting that he day-dreamed about his papers being discovered some two thousand years in the future (it only took a little less than a century for the discovery to be made). Boswell's sense of the archival record as a memory device was, perhaps, ahead of his time, a concept drawn on in the late twentieth century by scholars and others trying to understand evidence and collective memory; Adam Sisman, *Boswell's Presumptuous Task: The Making of the Life of Dr. Johnson* (New York: Farrar, Straus, and Giroux, 2000), 34.

19 Lepore, *The Name of War* provides some interesting insights about this. Another invaluable historical assessment is Karen Ordahl Kupperman, *Indians and English: Facing Off in Early America* (Ithaca, N.Y.: Cornell University Press, 2000).

20 For a survey of the origins of colonial recordkeeping practices (one that discusses all the colonies, despite its restrictive title), see George L. Haskins, "The Beginnings of the Recording System in Massachusetts," *Boston University Law Review* 21 (1941): 281–304. See also Joseph H. Beale, Jr., "The Origin of the System of Recording Deeds in America," *The Green Bag* 19 (1907): 335–39.

21 In all parts of the New World, the colonizing nations jump-started massive (for the time) recordkeeping systems in order to have as much detailed information as possible to exploit the Americas' resources and to administer them well. The Spanish, through their Relaciones Geograficus, sent out in 1577 to all their agents a comprehensive fifty-question survey, compiling vast amounts of information; the questionnaire can be seen on pp. 227–30 in Barbara E. Mundy, *The Mapping of New Spain: Indigenous Cartography and the Maps of the Relaciones Geograficus* (Chicago: University of Chicago Press, 1996). A few centuries later, as the British Empire reached its height, cartography and its accompanying recordkeeping was being used to govern the empire; Matthew H. Edney, *Mapping an Empire: The Geographical Construction of British India, 1765–1843* (Chicago: University of Chicago Press, 1997).

22 Quoted in Roger J. P. Kain and Elizabeth Baigent, *The Cadastral Map in the Service of the State: A History of Property Mapping* (Chicago: University of Chicago Press, 1992), xvii, 335.

23 See James H. Cassedy, *Demography in Early America: Beginnings of the Statistical Mind 1600–1800* (Cambridge, Mass.: Harvard University Press, 1969) and Patricia Cline Cohen, *A Calculating People: The Spread of Numeracy in Early America* (Chicago: University of Chicago Press, 1982) for accounts of this development and some interesting descriptions of the role of records.

24 See, for example, Richard D. Brown, *The Strength of a People: The Idea of an Informed Citizenry in America 1650–1870* (Chapel Hill: University of North Carolina Press, 1996).

25 For a general introduction to the origins of these organizations, see Leslie W. Dunlap, *American Historical Societies, 1790–1860* (Madison: Privately printed, 1944), and Walter Muir Whitehill, *Independent Historical Societies: An Enquiry into their Research and Publication Functions and Their Financial Future* (Boston: Boston Athenaeum, 1962). An interesting interpretation of the collecting impulse in these societies is given in Henry D. Shapiro, "Putting the Past under Glass: Preservation and the Idea of History in the Mid-Nineteenth Century," *Prospects: An Annual of American Cultural Studies* 10 (1985): 243–78.

26 These repositories have continued to be founded, usually at times of heightened historical awareness (such as the Centennial and the Bicentennial of the American Revolution), playing a variety of roles regarding the preservation of the nation's documentary heritage. These local repositories often helped to maintain a sense of the past close to the neighboring populations, but often creating immense problems as well, as so many often lacked adequate financial and professional resources to ensure that their holdings would be preserved. The great diversity of repositories and their holdings is referred to by Walter Muir Whitehill in his important analysis of American historical societies as being a "cloud of witnesses," but as subsequent studies have pointed out these witnesses are often housed in impoverished circumstances; Whitehill, *Independent Historical Societies*, chapter 18. For a dramatic accounting of the financial issues, see Charles Phillips and Patricia Hogan, *A Culture at Risk: Who Cares for America's Heritage?* (Nashville: American Association for State and Local History, 1984).

27 Ronald J. Zboray, *A Fictive People: Antebellum Economic Development and the American Reading Public* (New York: Oxford University Press, 1993), chapter 8. See also William Merrill Decker, *Epistolary Practices: Letter Writing in America before Telecommunications* (Chapel Hill: University of North Carolina Press, 1998).

28 J. E. Fields, "Israel K. Telft: Pioneer Collector," *Manuscripts* 6 (Spring 1954): 131–35; Richard Maass, "William Buell Sprague, Super Collector," *Manuscripts* 27 (Fall 1975): 247–55; Francis C. Haber, "Robert Gilmor, Jr.: Pioneer American Autograph Collector," *Manuscripts* 7 (Fall 1954): 13–17; F. B. Adams, Jr., "The Morgans as Autograph Collectors," *Autograph Collectors Journal* 2 (July 1950): 2–7, all provide brief descriptions of some of the pioneer autograph collectors. Autograph collecting was even wrapped up in the guise of teaching individuals how to write, as described in Tamara Plakins Thornton, *Handwriting in America: A Cultural History* (New Haven: Yale University Press, 1996).

29 The plight of these kinds of institutions as collectors can be seen in Sally F. Griffith, *Serving History in a Changing World: The Historical Society of Pennsylvania in the Twentieth Century* (Philadelphia: Historical Society of Pennsylvania, 2001); Kevin M. Guthrie, *The New-York Historical Society: Lessons from One Nonprofit's Long Struggle for Survival* (San Francisco: Jossey-Bass Publishers, 1996); and H. G. Jones, ed., *Historical Consciousness in the Early Republic: The Origins of State Historical Societies, Museums, and Collections, 1791–1861* (Chapel Hill: North Caroliniana Society, Inc. and North Carolina Collection, 1995).

30 American Antiquarian Society, *Archaeologia Americana: Transactions and Collections of the American Antiquarian Society* (Worcester, 1820), 1:18; Logan Historical Society statement, quoted in Dunlap, *American Historical Societies,* 142. On the origins of American historical writing and the use of sources, see Peter Novick, *That Noble Dream: The "Objectivity Question" and the American Historical Profession* (Cambridge: Cambridge University Press, 1988), chapters 1–2, and Richard Hofstadter, *The Progressive Historians: Turner, Beard, Parrington* (New York: Random House, 1968), chapter 1.

31 Massachusetts Historical Society, *Collections* 1 (Boston, 1803): 3. A useful summary of the origins of historical editing and publication is provided in Daniel J. Boorstin, *The Americans: The National Experience* (New York: Random House, 1965), 345–49 and 368–69. For an idea of how publishing played a dominant role in the preservation of records in the early American venture, see H. G. Jones, *For History's Sake: The Preservation and Publication of North Carolina History 1663–1903* (Chapel Hill: University of North Carolina Press, 1966). Careful scholarship in documentary editing has continued to be a critical need, especially as published forgeries regularly appear, such as that perpetuated by the widow of General George E. Pickett in 1913 and reissued in 1928. Pickett's widow may have carried out the hoax for money, to confirm her own image as the archetypical Southern belle, or to add to the Lost Cause mystique; see Gary W. Gallagher, *Lee and His Generals in War and Memory* (Baton Rouge: Louisiana State University Press, 1998). Yet, even to this day, documentary editors have continued to function separately from archivists and manuscripts curators, possessing their own professional association, journal, and confer-

ences. This can be seen in Lester J. Cappon's career, spanning the late 1920s until his death in 1981, in which he worked as historian, archivist, publications editor, and documentary editor, coming by the end of his career to see documentary editing closest to what he thought archivists should be doing and how they should be trained; see Richard J. Cox, *Lester J. Cappon and the Relationship of History, Archives, and Scholarship in the Golden Age of Archival Theory* (Chicago: Society of American Archivists, 2004).

32 See, for example, Richard J. Cox, "A Century of Frustration: The Movement for the Founding of the State Archives in Maryland, 1811–1935," *Maryland Historical Magazine* 78 (Summer 1983): 106–17.

33 Even today, similar barriers between archivists and records managers remain, with many of the latter achieving their positions because of reasons (such as length of service or experience) other than formal education; it is still the rare event where university and other archivists mingle with local and other govern-ment records administrators. The addition of new players with greatly different professional loyalties in the late twentieth century, such as database administra-tors or information resource and policy managers, has only accentuated the challenges of developing effective mechanisms and policies for managing records systems.

34 Historian William Gilmore, studying the nature of reading on the New England frontier, notes, "Most rural New Englanders did not make a connection between the messages they received and the particular media involved, whether these were books, periodicals, almanacs, oral discourse, visual objects, dance, instrumental music, singing, writing, or reading"; William J. Gilmore, *Reading Becomes a Necessity of Life: Material and Cultural Life in Rural New England, 1780–1835* (Knoxville: University of Tennessee Press, 1989), 35, 37. The same is true for how they viewed objects of the past.

35 As a result, nearly everything and anything could be swept up as being a valu-able source of evidence, and in the twentieth century, many of these older repositories delved into the painful and often controversial process of fine-tun-ing their missions and divesting themselves of their eclectic holdings. The establishment of manuscripts and archival repositories can be fit neatly into the two archival traditions model proposed by Richard Berner thirty years ago; see Richard C. Berner, *Archival Theory and Practice in the United States: A Historical Analysis* (Seattle: University of Washington Press, 1983) for a convenient sum-mary of his writings. Yet, we also know that the archival landscape is a bit more complicated than this model suggests (especially as new digital records systems suggest postcustodial or distributed custody models), with many archives, pub-lic or private, having roles cutting across what these traditions represent. A Dutch notary laboring in New Amsterdam (later New York) in the seventeenth century creates what becomes the de facto local archives by accumulating records related to a myriad of legal and personal transactions; Donna Merwick, *Death of a Notary: Conquest and Change in Colonial New York* (Ithaca, N.Y.: Cornell University Press, 1999). A century later, a New England midwife main-tains a journal likewise becoming a kind of local archives, capturing much more detail about life in her town and region than most of the official records

could ever hope to do; as her biographer suggests, "in the very act of recording her work, she [Martha Ballard] became a keeper of vital records, a chronicler of the medical history of her town"; Laurel Thatcher Ulrich, *A Midwife's Tale: The Life of Martha Ballard, Based on Her Diary, 1785–1812* (New York: Vintage Books, 1990), 40.

36 In a recent effort to characterize the drift of historical inquiry away from the centrality of archival sources as evidence, one study describes the emergence of professional history during the last century as follows: "The development of new techniques of teaching and research guaranteed the mastery of facts. The master historian would teach students how to distinguish fact from legend by the rigorous examination of documents. History would henceforth depend on research in archives and original sources as tests of the facts. University training would teach an attitude of impartiality toward those facts"; Joyce Appleby, Lynn Hunt, and Margaret Jacob, *Telling the Truth about History* (New York: W. W. Norton, 1994), 56.

37 On the early work of the Historical Manuscripts Commission, see the AHA published annual reports for the years 1896 and following; the quotations are from the reports of 1900 (1:589) and 1896 (1:471). A good summary of this and subsequent work of the AHA may be found in Berner, *Archival Theory and Practice in the United States*, especially 11–23.

38 JoAnne Yates, *Control through Communication: The Rise of System in American Management* (Baltimore: Johns Hopkins University Press, 1989) provides an analysis of the influences of these ideas on records and communication systems. For an introduction to Taylor and Taylorism, see Robert Kanigel, *The One Best Way: Frederick Winslow Taylor and the Enigma of Efficiency* (New York: Viking, 1997).

39 The work of the Public Archives Commission is chronicled in the AHA annual reports from 1900 onward. For a summary, see Victor H. Palsits, "An Historical Resume of the Public Archives Commission from 1899 to 1921," AHA, *Annual Report, 1922* (Washington, D.C.: Government Printing Office, 1926), 1:152–60. On the work of one records efficiency study, see Bess Glenn, "The Taft Commission and the Government's Record Practices," *American Archivist* 21 (1958): 277–303. Portions of the manual were published; see Robert F. Reynolds, "The Incunabula of Archival Theory and Practice in the United States: J. C. Fitzpatrick's *Notes on the Care, Cataloguing, Calendaring and Arranging of Manuscripts* and the Public Archives Commission's Uncompleted 'Primer of Archival Economy,'" *American Archivist* 54 (Fall 1991): 466–82.

40 See Larry J. Hackman, "From Assessment to Action: Toward a Usable Past in the Empire State," *Public Historian* 7 (Summer 1985): 23–34. The 1970s and 1980s was a period when state government archives and records management programs seemed to strengthen, bolstered by funding support from various federal and other agencies. This can be seen partially as the last quarter of the twentieth century became a period of renewed focus on county, municipal, and other local government records programs, leading to many new kinds of manuals, model programs, and the greatest sustained interest in local records in the profession's history; see H. G. Jones, *Local Government Records: An Introduction to*

Their Management, Preservation, and Use (Nashville: American Association for State and Local History, 1980) and Bruce Dearstyne, *The Management of Local Government Records: A Guide for Local Officials* (Nashville: American Association for State and Local History, 1988).

41 The most comprehensive study of the origins and programs of public archives in the United States remains Ernst Posner, *American State Archives* (Chicago: University of Chicago Press, 1964). See also Berner, *Archival Theory and Practice,* 13–16.

42 Victor Gondos, Jr., *J. Franklin Jameson and the Birth of the National Archives, 1906–1926* (Philadelphia: University of Pennsylvania Press, 1981).

43 William F. Birdsall, "The American Archivist's Search for Professional Identity, 1909–1936," (PhD diss., University of Wisconsin, Madison, 1973), is the best assessment of these years and archival development.

44 The establishment and early years of the agency are described in detail in Donald R. McCoy, *The National Archives: America's Ministry of Documents, 1934–1968* (Chapel Hill: University of North Carolina Press, 1978), especially 3–91.

45 Cook, "Blessings of Providence," 374–99, provides a fine overview of SAA's history from its origins to the 1970s.

46 A general history of the HRS is provided in William F. McDonald, *Federal Relief Administration and the Arts* (Columbus: Ohio State University Press, 1969), 751–828. For the not-always-happy story of what happened to the original survey records, see Leonard Rapport, "Dumped from a Wharf into Casco Bay: The Historical Records Survey Revisited," *American Archivist* 37 (1974): 201–10. See also Loretta L. Hefner, comp., *The WPA Historical Records Survey: A Guide to the Unpublished Inventories, Indexes, and Transcripts* (Chicago: Society of American Archivists, 1980). For an analysis of the HRS with an emphasis on its jobs relief, see Burl Noggle, *Working with History: The Historical Records Survey in Louisiana and the Nation, 1936–1942* (Baton Rouge: Louisiana State University Press, 1981).

47 Many of these early publications are available on the National Archives website, http://www.archives.gov/.

48 The Society of American Archivists issued reprints of these critical volumes, with new introductions, in 2002 and 2003.

49 Norton's essays, collected into a single volume only in 1975, reflect a much stronger affinity to modern records management principles and practices, and her ideas have had a stronger influence on the profession since the publication of the collected essays. The Norton volume, published in 1975 with an introduction by Thornton W. Mitchell, was reissued by the Society of American Archivists in 2003 with a new essay by Randall Jimerson.

50 Although there were alternatives, such as Australian Peter Scott's emphasis on series and Jenkinson's concerns about the moral defense of archives, by and large it was Schellenberg's terminology that took hold. Even among records managers, Schellenberg's ideas seemed to resonate, although many seem unable to identify the source of these ideas.

51 For a biographical sketch of Norton and a collection of her most important

writings, see Mitchell's edition of *Norton on Archives: The Writings of Margaret Cross Norton on Archival and Records Management* (Carbondale: Southern Illinois University Press, 1975), which was reissued by the Society of American Archivists in 2003. On the early theoretical work at the National Archives, see Ernst Posner, "The National Archives and the Archival Theorist," *American Archivist* 18 (1955): 207–16; McCoy, *National Archives,* 105–89; and Jane F. Smith, "Theodore R. Schellenberg: Americanizer and Popularizer," *American Archivist* 44 (1981): 313–26. Schellenberg's "European Archival Principles in Arranging Records," was Staff Information Circular No. 5 (Washington: National Archives, 1939); it was also incorporated into his *Modern Archives: Principles and Techniques* (Chicago: University of Chicago Press, 1956), especially 133–60. Holmes's influential work was not codified in print until somewhat later; see his "Archival Arrangement: Five Different Operations at Five Different Levels," *American Archivist* 27 (1964): 21–41. The American edition of the Muller, Feith, and Fruin manual, translated by Arthur W. Leavitt, was published by H. W. Wilson Company in 1940.

52 Even when challenged, their views elicit spirited defenses; see, for example, Linda Henry, "Schellenberg in Cyberspace," *American Archivist* 61 (Fall 1998): 309–27.

53 There is no complete history of the emergence of records management as a distinct professional identity (budding archival scholars take note!), but see McCoy, *National Archives,* 146–67 and 274–90. See also Frank B. Evans, "Archivists and Records Managers: Variations on a Theme," *American Archivist* 30 (1967): 45–58, and Richard J. Cox, *Closing an Era: Historical Perspectives on Modern Archives and Records Management* (Westport, Conn.: Greenwood Press, 2000).

54 Many people entering the archival profession in the 1960s and 1970s, at least those with a history background, had been sensitized to look at the past from a variety of perspectives challenging the long-established predominant focus on politics, intellectual history, and economics. It was natural that these new archivists would examine their repository's holdings and notice the gaps in documentation. See for example, Tom Nesmith, "Archives from the Bottom Up: Social History and Archival Scholarship," *Archivaria* 14 (Summer 1982): 5–26.

55 The literature on each type of archives is substantial. The best sense of development may be obtained by comparing the varieties and kinds of repositories reporting to the standard archival reference guides. See also the reports of two surveys of the archival profession: David Bearman, "1982 Survey of the Archival Profession," *American Archivist* 46 (1983): 233–41, and Paul Conway, "Perspectives on Archival Resources: The 1985 Census of Archival Institutions," cited above. The former is a survey of archivists, the latter a survey of archives.

56 See the two articles by Jesse Lemisch, "The American Revolution and the Papers of Great White Men," *AHA Newsletter* 9 (November 1971): 7–21, and "The Papers of a Few Great Black Men and a Few Great White Women," *Maryland Historian* 6 (1975): 60–66. On the response of archives to these challenges, see Dale C. Miller, "The New Social History: Implications for Archivists," *American Archivist* 48 (1985): 388–99, and Fredric Miller, "Use, Appraisal, and Research: A Case Study of Social History," *American Archivist* 49 (1986): 371–92.

57 The documentary universe had expanded, both because the technologies gird-
ing records generation had become more complex and because the perspective
of archivists and their repositories had grown in scope as well. Ideas such as
documentation strategies and "total archives" addressed these concerns, and
they morphed into ideas such as functional analysis and macro-appraisal.
Richard J. Cox, "The Archival Documentation Strategy: A Brief Intellectual
History, 1984–1994 and Practical Description," *Janus* no. 2 (1995): 76–93 provides some sense of what was happening with archival appraisal.

58 For an overview of these programs, see Ronald Berman, *Culture and Politics*
(Lanham, Md.: University Press of America, 1984), and Stephen Miller,
Excellence and Equity: The National Endowment for the Humanities (Lexington:
University of Kentucky Press, 1984). See also Andrea Hinding et al., eds.,
*Women's History Sources: A Guide to Archives and Manuscript Collections in the
United States* (New York: Bowker, 1979). While such federal funding agencies
have come under attack for a variety of political and fiscal reasons, it remains
surprising that archival and documentary editing projects have generally not
received much scrutiny; this might reflect deeper problems in the public visibil-
ity of archives and archivists, a matter that is, at best, a two-edged sword.

59 Local government development projects did not always lead to the establishment or rejuvenation of these operations. The same can be said for its efforts in
electronic records management. Other problems, such as the dividing of funds
between archival and documentary editing projects, have not been fully
addressed. On the other hand, its support of SAA's fledgling publications program seems to have been critical to what has become a self-sustaining and energetic program; the archival community never has had a more varied lot of
publications, ranging from theory to the most practical matters. For early
assessments of this program's impact, see Larry J. Hackman, "The Historical
Records Program: The States and the Nation," *American Archivist* 43 (1980):
17–32, and F. Gerald Ham, "NHPRC's Records Program and the Development of
Statewide Archival Planning," *American Archivist* 43 (1980): 33–42. The narrower
concerns of the earlier publication programs of the commission are described
in Mary A. Giunta, "The NHPRC: Its Influence on Documentary Editing,
1964–1984," *American Archivist* 49 (1986): 134–41. Volume 63, Spring 2000, of the
American Archivist includes a variety of essays considering the NHPRC over a
longer period of time, although the essays are written by individuals associated
with the commission and lack a balanced assessment.

60 A current list of these professional associations can be found at the SAA website.

61 James M. O'Toole, "On the Idea of Uniqueness," *American Archivist* 57 (Fall
1994): 632–58.

62 The state of graduate archival education reflected, in many ways, the continuing emphasis of uniqueness in the profession during this period. Fredric M.
Miller, "The SAA as Sisyphus: Education since the 1960s," *American Archivist* 63
(Fall/Winter 2000): 224–36, originally given in 1983, suggests how during this
time education standards (what there were) were developed from the foundation of the few programs existing. Those programs operated more like apprenticeship experiences than graduate education programs.

63 On the origins and early history of NUCMC, see Lester K. Born, "The National Union Catalog of Manuscript Collections: Progress," *American Archivist* 23 (1960): 311–14, and Richard C. Berner, "Archivists, Librarians, and the National Union Catalog of Manuscript Collections," *American Archivist* 27 (1964): 401–9. Berner correctly identified NUCMC as "a major step in the direction of standardization."

64 The basic texts in this area are Nancy Sahli, MARC *for Archives and Manuscripts: The* AMC *Format* (Chicago: Society of American Archivists, 1985) and Max J. Evans and Lisa B. Weber, MARC *for Archives and Manuscripts: A Compendium of Practice* (Madison: State Historical Society of Wisconsin, 1985). See also David Bearman, ed., *Toward National Information Systems for Archives and Manuscript Repositories: The National Information Systems Task Force Papers, 1981–1984* (Chicago: Society of American Archivists, 1987); Richard H. Lytle, "An Analysis of the Work of the National Information Systems Task Force," *American Archivist* 47 (1984): 357–65; Nancy Sahli, "Interpretation and Application of the AMC Format," *American Archivist* 49 (1986): 9–20; and Katherine D. Morton, "The MARC Formats: An Overview," *American Archivist* 49 (1986): 21–30.

65 The summer and fall 1997 issues of the *American Archivist* (volume 60) are devoted to the history, theory, and case studies of EAD. The SAA EAD Roundtable also provides considerable information and links to additional information at its website at http://www.iath.virginia.edu/ead/. Another useful resource is Daniel V. Pitti and Wendy M. Duff, eds., *Encoded Archival Description on the Internet* (New York: Haworth Press, 2001).

66 See Society of American Archivists, *Inventories and Registers: A Handbook of Techniques and Examples* (Chicago: SAA, 1976). This slim volume had a tremendous significance for the merger of the two traditions by demonstrating graphically how much alike the supposedly different approaches were.

67 These concerns probably reflected more deep-seated differences in the perception of the mission of archivists and archival repositories held by different segments of the field, but these differences continued to play a critical role in the field despite the firmer encroachment of standardization in nearly every aspect of archival work. As Australian archivist Adrian Cunningham stated in 1995, capturing some of the same feelings of archivists in the United States, "A number of archivists, in their rush to find new allies and to deploy the powerful argument of 'organizational accountability,' appear to be willing to jettison, or at the very least down play, our historical/cultural role. In the process they may wittingly or unwittingly marginalize and stigmatize those archivists, most particularly collecting archivists, for whom historical/cultural considerations provide their *raison d'etre*." Adrian Cunningham, "Beyond the Pale?—The 'flinty' relationship between archivists who collect the private records of individuals and the rest of the archival profession in Australia," *Provenance* 1 (March 1996), available at http://www.netpac.com/provenance/vol1/no2/features/paleconf.htm. For a similar view, see Mark Greene, "The Power of Meaning: The Archival Mission in the Postmodern Age," *American Archivist* 65 (Spring/Summer 2002): 42–55.

68 Posner's career is described in Paul Lewinson, "Introduction: The Two Careers of Ernst Posner," *Archives and the Public Interest: Selected Essays of Ernst Posner,*

ed. Ken Munden (Washington, D.C.: Public Affairs Press, 1967), 7–19. For a list of some of the important articles on the education of archivists, see the appendix to Paul Conway, "Archival Education and the Need for Full-Time Faculty," *American Archivist* 51 (1988): 254–65.

69 The literature on archival education is vast and still growing. For a useful summary of current conditions, see Timothy L. Ericson, "Professional Associations and Archival Education: A Different Role or a Different Theater?" *American Archivist* 51 (1988): 298–311. On archival education in Canada, see Terry Eastwood, "The Origins and Aims of the Master of Archival Studies Programme at the University of British Columbia," *Archivaria* 16 (1983): 35–52, and "Nurturing Archival Education in the University," *American Archivist* 51 (1988): 228–52.

70 A useful list of definitions of public history can be found at the Public History Resource Center, compiled by Jennifer Evans, http://www.publichistory.org/what_is/definition.html. For a discussion of the problems in the relationship between public history and archival education, see Richard J. Cox, "Archivists and Public Historians in the United States, *Public Historian* 8 (Summer 1986): 25–41.

71 The current guidelines are available on the SAA website, http://www.archivists.org/prof-education/ed_guidelines.asp.

72 The earlier education guidelines can be seen as benchmarks for tracking changes and are available in Society of American Archivists, "Guidelines for a Graduate Minor or Concentration in Archival Education," *American Archivist* 41 (1978): 105–6, and "Society of American Archivists Guidelines for Graduate Archival Education Programs," *American Archivist* 51 (1988): 380–89. The importance of full-time archival educators was first voiced in Frank G. Burke, "The Future Course of Archival Theory in the United States," *American Archivist* 44 (1981): 40–46. For a general guide through the issues of professional advancement, see Richard J. Cox, "Professionalism and Archivists in the United States," *American Archivist* 49 (1986): 229–47.

73 For general historical background, refer to Richard C. Berner, "Archival Education and Training in the United States, 1937 to Present," *Journal of Education for Librarianship* 22 (Summer/Fall 1981): 3–19; Jacqueline Goggin, "'That We Shall Truly Deserve the Title of Profession': The Training and Education of Archivists, 1930–1960," *American Archivist* 47 (Summer 1984): 243–54; Robert Sidney Martin, "The Development of Professional Education for Librarians and Archivists in the United States: A Comparative Essay," *American Archivist* 57 (Summer 1994): 544–58.

74 For an idea of the debates and continuing discussions about graduate archival education during this period, see Edwin Bridges, Gregory S. Hunter, Page Putnam Miller, David Thelen, and Gerhard Weinberg, "Toward Better Documenting and Interpreting of the Past: What History Graduate Programs in the Twenty-First Century Should Teach About Archival Practices," *American Archivist* 56 (Fall 1993): 730–49; F. Gerald Ham, Frank Boles, Gregory S. Hunter, and James M. O'Toole, "Is the Past Still Prologue? History and Archival Education," *American Archivist* 56 (Fall 1993): 718–29; Frank G. Burke, "The Future Course of Archival Theory in the United States," *American Archivist* 44 (Winter 1981): 40–46; Conway, "Archival Education and the Need for Full-Time

Faculty," *American Archivist* 51 (Summer 1988): 254–65; Richard J. Cox, "The Masters of Archival Studies and American Education Standards: An Argument for the Continued Development of Graduate Archival Education in the United States," *Archivaria* 36 (Autumn 1993): 221–31; Luciana Duranti, "The Archival Body of Knowledge: Archival Theory, Method, and Practice," *Journal of Education for Library and Information Science* 34 (Winter 1993): 8–24; Terry Eastwood, "Nurturing Archival Education in the University," *American Archivist* 51 (Summer 1988): 228–51; Timothy L. Ericson, "Professional Associations and Archival Education: A Different Role, or a Different Theater?" *American Archivist* 51 (Summer 1988): 298–311; Vernon R. Smith, "Pedagogy and Professionalism: An Evaluation of Trends and Choices Confronting Educators in the Archival Community," *Public Historian* 16 (Summer 1994): 23–43.

75 Mary Jo Pugh and William Joyce, eds., *Evaluation of Archival Institutions: Services, Principles, and Guide to Self-Study* (Chicago: Society of American Archivists, 1982); Paul H. McCarthy, Jr., ed., *Archives Assessment and Planning Workbook* (Chicago: Society of American Archivists, 1989). The plans for certification of archivists have been reported regularly since 1985 in the SAA *Newsletter.* For a general discussion, see William J. Maher, "Contexts for Understanding Professional Certification: Opening Pandora's Box?" *American Archivist* 51 (1988): 408–27.

76 Richard J. Cox has discussed these problems in his "Who Are We? Who Knows What We Are? Some Thoughts on the Continuing Debate About Credentials and Professional Identity," *Records & Information Management Report* 18 (December 2002): 1–14.

77 The phrase "age of archival analysis" was coined by Bruce W. Dearstyne in his "Archives and Public History: Issues, Problems, and Prospects," *Public Historian* 8 (1986): 6–9. Important essays challenging received archival wisdom include Leonard Rapport, "No Grandfather Clause: Reappraising Accessioned Records," *American Archivist* 44 (1981): 143–50; Max J. Evans, "Authority Control: An Alternative to the Record Group Concept," *American Archivist* 49 (1986): 249–61; and David Bearman and Richard Lytle, "The Power of the Principle of Provenance," *Archivaria* 21 (1985/6): 14–27. For an idea of the nature of the writings about electronic records management, see Richard J. Cox, "Readings in Archives and Electronic Records: Annotated Bibliography and Analysis of the Literature," in *Electronic Records Management Program Strategies,* ed. Margaret Hedstrom (Pittsburgh: Archives and Museum Informatics, 1993), 99–156. One of the most provocative products emanating from the Bentley fellowships was David Bearman's *Archival Methods,* critiquing the basic functions of archival work. In his preface, Bearman mused, "Of each of these activities I ask whether our present methods are adequate and if not, how they can be adjusted within the practical limitations which cultural repositories face." Bearman's work summarized the debates of the 1980s and set the stage with issues and questions for the next generation; David Bearman, *Archival Methods,* Archives and Museum Informatics Technical Report #9 (Pittsburgh: Archives and Museum Informatics, 1989), available at http://www.archimuse.com/publishing/archival_methods/.

78 Joint Committee on the Archives of Science and Technology, *Understanding Progress as Process: Documentation of the History of Post-War Science and Technology in the United States* (Chicago: Society of American Archivists, 1983); Joan K. Haas, et al., *Appraising the Records of Modern Science and Technology: A Guide* (Cambridge, Mass.: Massachusetts Institute of Technology, 1985); Bureau of Canadian Archivists, *Toward Descriptive Standards* (Ottawa: Bureau of Canadian Archivists, 1985); Society of American Archivists Task Force on Goals and Priorities, *Planning for the Archival Profession* (Chicago: Society of American Archivists, 1986); Society of American Archivists Committee on Goals and Priorities, *An Action Agenda for the Archival Profession: Institutionalizing the Planning Process* (Chicago: Society of American Archivists, 1988). The literature on documentation strategies is still growing. The critical essays that defined this approach are Helen W. Samuels, "Who Controls the Past?" *American Archivist* 49 (1986): 109–24, and Larry J. Hackman and Joan Warnow-Blewett, "The Documentation Strategy Process: A Model and a Case Study," *American Archivist* 50 (1987): 12–47.

79 See, for example, Richard M. Kesner, "Automated Information Management: Is There a Role for the Archivist in the Office of the Future?" *Archivaria* 19 (Winter 1984–85): 162–72.

80 David Crystal, *Language Death* (Cambridge: Cambridge University Press, 2000), 78–79.

81 See, for example, Thomas A. Stewart, *Intellectual Capital: The New Wealth of Organizations* (New York: Currency Books, 1999).

82 The most sophisticated analysis of archival records in the training of historians, Walter Rundell, Jr., *In Pursuit of American History: Research and Training in the United States* (Norman: University of Oklahoma Press, 1970), is now more than thirty years old.

83 Richard J. Cox, "Archives, Records, and Knowledge Management in the Twenty-first Century: What Is the Future of the Records Professional?" *Records and Information Management Report* 19 (April 2004): 1–13.

84 Mary Sue Stephenson, "Deciding not to Build the Wall: Research and the Archival Profession," *Archivaria* 32 (1991): 145–51.

85 For a series of case studies demonstrating this point, see Richard J. Cox and David A. Wallace, eds., *Archives and the Public Good: Accountability and Records in Modern Society* (Westport, Conn.: Quorum Books, 2002).

Chapter 3. The Archivist's Perspective: Knowledge and Values

1 Since records managers have more often than not been tied closely to records creators' interests, this explains one major reason why the chasm between archivists and records managers seems so wide.

2 This perspective may explain why even the best-informed researchers often seem to hold such quaint views of archival records and records systems more generally. Archivists are sometimes dismayed at researchers' lack of knowledge about the records they are examining. Archivists are even more perturbed to see researchers hold naïve views about the nature of their holdings; historians often express the

view that the role of an archives is to preserve everything and some researchers (even accomplished scholars) approach archival repositories as if all the older records have been gathered there without any selection process (except, unfortunate accidental loss or deliberate destruction in times of civil strife or warfare).

3 For an idea about the increasing richness of archival knowledge, see Terry Cook, "What Is Past Is Prologue: A History of Archival Ideas Since 1898, and the Future Paradigm Shift," *Archivaria* 43 (Spring 1997): 17–63, and Richard J. Cox, "Forming the Records Professional's Knowledge: North American Archival Publishing in the 20th Century," *Records & Information Management Report* 20 (March 2004): 1–13.

4 As Giovanni Levi suggests, "microhistory as a practice is essentially based on the reduction of the scale of observation, on a microscopic analysis and an intensive study of the documentary material"; Giovanni Levi, "On Microhistory," in *New Perspectives on Historical Writing,* ed. Peter Burke (University Park: Pennsylvania State University Press, 1991), 95. While archivists certainly did not always see the full potential of the records they were preserving, they often had developed enough of a feel for the important records documenting society that they made decisions paying off decades later in new varieties of research.

5 David Klaassen, "The Provenance of Social Work Case Records: Implications for Archival Appraisal and Access," *Provenance* 1 (Spring 1983): 5–26 provides a sense of this relationship between regulation, the social work profession, and the records. See, for example, E. Wayne Carp, *Family Matters: Secrecy and Disclosure in the History of Adoption* (Cambridge, Mass.: Harvard University Press, 1998). One case regarding a scandalous rape in an Australian public home for children has continued to have serious implications about the records of these organizations; see Chris Hurley, "Records and the Public Interest: The 'Heiner Affair' in Queensland, Australia," in *Archives and the Public Good: Accountability and Records in Modern Society,* ed. Richard J. Cox and David A. Wallace (Westport, Conn.: Quorum Books, 2002), 293–317.

6 The records manager may come close, but the archivist's progeny is more likely to focus on matters concerning the efficiency and economy of administering records; while there should be a closer connection between the process of appraising (archivists) and scheduling (records managers) records, in general there has not been because of the different orientations and missions of these records professionals. For one effort at relating appraisal and retention scheduling, see Richard J. Cox, *No Innocent Deposits: Forming Archives by Rethinking Appraisal* (Metuchen, N.J.: Scarecrow Press, 2004), chapter six.

7 This is one reason why the recent emergence of graduate archival education programs can only provide a foundation for archival work and careers; archival knowledge is built and refined through the research about and experience of working with records. It is also why archivists are primarily *records* not *information* professionals, despite the negative connotations that records seem to have accumulated. The problem of defining information can be seen in any number of books and articles about this matter. Hans Christian von Baeyer, *Information: The New Language of Science* (Cambridge, Mass.: Harvard University Press,

2004) is a recent example by a physicist considering the scientific notion of information and the problems with this (and other kinds of definitions).

8 While paleography is only taught to and used by archivists with the most specialized types of collections and responsibilities, diplomatics has made a resurgence in North America as a means for comprehending the nature of a record and, most specifically, for supporting work to ensure the reliability and authenticity of records in digital environments. See Luciana Duranti, *Diplomatics: New Uses for an Old Science* (Metuchen, N.J.: Scarecrow Press for the Society of American Archivists and the Association of Canadian Archivists, 1998). An understanding of paleography can be gleaned from Bernard Bischoff, *Latin Palaeography: Antiquity and the Middle Ages,* trans. Dáibhí Ó Cróinín and David Ganz (Cambridge: Cambridge University Press, 1990).

9 Sue McKemmish, "Yesterday, Today and Tomorrow: A Continuum of Responsibility," *Proceedings of the Records Management Association of Australia 14th National Convention, 15–17, September 1997,* http://www.sims.monash.edu.au/ research/rcrg/publications/recordscontinuum/smckp2.html. In the best volume integrating archives and records management concepts and practices, Elizabeth Shepherd and Geoffrey Yeo write that the "life-cycle concept has been subject to much adverse criticism," criticism stemming from the fact that records do not "die," the stages in the cycle are "artificial," and that the concept is "too focused on records as physical entities and on operational tasks, especially those associated with the custody of paper records"; Elizabeth Shepherd and Geoffrey Yeo, *Managing Records: A Handbook of Principles and Practice* (London: Facet Publishing, 2003), 7.

10 See Richard J. Cox and Margaret Pett, "Records Life Cycle and Records Continuum," *Records & Information Management Report* 19 (May 2003): 1–14.

11 For discussion about the physical custody issue, see Luciana Duranti, "Archives as a Place," *Archives and Manuscripts* 24, (November 1996): 242–55; Terry Eastwood, "Should Creating Agencies Keep Electronic Records Indefinitely?" *Archives and Manuscripts* 24 (November 1996): 256–67; and David Bearman, "An Indefensible Bastion: Archives as a Repository in the Electronic Age," in *Archival Management of Electronic Records,* ed. David Bearman (Pittsburgh: Archives and Museum Informatics, 1991), 14–24. For some discussion about the migration/emulation matter, see Margaret Hedstrom and Clifford Lampe, "Emulation vs. Migration: Do Users Care?" *RLG DigiNews* 5 (December 2001), available at http://www.rlg.org/preserv/diginews/diginews5-6.html#feature1.

12 The computer and information scientist's co-opting of the term "archiving" to distinguish the backing up of magnetic tapes has additionally confused the clarity of this disposition function, especially since so many following the information side of the equation are looking at the same technologies as a means to preserve (in a usable format) everything.

13 The problem with digital forgery has most often been pointed in the realm of digital photography, such as by William J. Mitchell, *The Reconfigured Eye: Visual Truth in the Post-Photographic Eye* (Cambridge, Mass.: MIT Press, 1992). This has prompted some scholars to argue for a kind of diplomatics for photography, as historian Peter Burke does in his *Eyewitnessing: The Uses of Images as*

Historical Evidence (Ithaca, N.Y.: Cornell University Press, 2001). Archivists also have devoted a considerable amount of time trying to define what authenticity or reliability means in the digital realm, most recently characterized by the work of InterPARES members Luciana Duranti, Terry Eastwood, and Heather MacNeil, *Preservation of the Integrity of Electronic Records* (Dordrecht, Netherlands: Kluwer Academic Publishers Group, 2002) and *The Long-term Preservation of Authentic Electronic Records: Findings of the InterPARES Project* (San Miniato, Italy: Archilab, 2004).

14 Martin Lloyd, *The Passport: The History of Man's Most Travelled Document* (Thrupp-Stroud-Glouchestershire, U.K.: Sutton Publishing Limited, 2003), 258.

15 The writings are extensive on these and related topics. Archivists ought to consider Stanton A. Glantz, John Slade, Lisa A. Bero, Peter Hanauer, and Deborah E. Barnes, *The Cigarette Papers* (Berkeley: University of California Press, 1996) with Robin Chandler and Susan Storch, "Lighting Up the Internet: The Brown and Williamson Collection," *Archives and the Public Good: Accountability and Records in Modern Society*, eds. Richard J. Cox and David A. Wallace (Westport, Conn.: Quorum Books, 2002), 135-62.

16 Laurel Thatcher Ulrich, *A Midwife's Tale: The Life of Martha Ballard, Based on Her Diary, 1785–1812* (New York: Vintage Books, 1990).

17 Terry Cook, "Mind Over Matter: Towards a New Theory of Archival Appraisal," in *The Archival Imagination: Essays in Honour of Hugh Taylor,* ed. Barbara Craig (Ottawa: Association of Canadian Archivists, 1992), 60–69.

18 Certain types of records and certain types of organizations share strong, common characteristics in the basic nature of their records; the basic functions of local governments, for example, are very similar across geographical regions and even types (municipal, county, township) of governments. The study of records and recordkeeping systems will reveal both such commonalities as well as unique aspects of organizations and people creating records, but these similarities are minor when compared to what librarians discover when working with books and other print materials.

19 These questions plague archivists not only in describing their records, but in other functions such as appraisal. It is why many archivists have turned from issues of content management to explore the viability of functions, activities, business processes, and other aspects of organizational and societal life as means for evaluating and describing records. Archivists believe that the content of a record is only understandable as part of its overall system, while at the same time recognizing that content is very important for researchers.

20 Museum curators use the term to focus on the chain of ownership, and archaeologists use the idea to connect recovered artifacts from particular strata.

21 The common sense behind this is not unlike how chains of ownership of an artwork or physical location of a pottery shard can be used for dating and authenticity. The basic aspects of provenance are close to a universal principle for classifying or organizing information or evidence.

22 The pioneering Dutch archivists stated, "an archival collection is an organic whole, a living organism, which grows, takes shape, and undergoes changes in

accordance with fixed rules." S. Muller, J. A. Feith, and R. Fruin, *Manual for the Arrangement and Description of Archives*, trans. Arthur H. Leavitt (Chicago: Society of American Archivists, 2003), 19. The *Manual* was originally published in 1898.

23 The technical and cultural aspects of recordkeeping sometimes help archivists to see a broader dimension to their work. John McDonald, discoursing on the growing interest in accountability in the records disciplines, indicated that one of the factors was the growing importance of "collective societal memory... also raising the issue of accountability and record keeping but at the very broad level of society itself. Society depends upon records to understand its past and to provide the context it requires to set direction for the future. The information in government records forms one component of a rich landscape of information and information holdings which, collectively, serve as the basis for enhancing social consciousness and a sense of identity and context. In an era of rapid social and economic change, however, especially at the global level, where politically sensitive issues concerning national identity are coming to the fore, concerns are being raised about the depth, quality, and survivability of the recorded memory of society; . . ." John McDonald, "Archives at Risk: Accountability, Vulnerability and Credibility," Australian Society of Archivists Conference, 1999, available at http://www.archivists.org.au/events/conf99/keynote.html. In a sense, the notion of public memory extends the concept of provenance, whereby records cannot be considered apart from social and other concerns critical to a group's self-awareness and identity.

24 Richard J. Cox, "The Mythology of the Basic Archives Textbook," *Archival Outlook* (March/April 2004): 12–13.

25 Peter Lyman and Hal Varian, "How Much Information 2003?" available at http://www.sims.berkeley.edu/research/projects/how-much-info-2003/.

26 *Content management* is the focus on the efforts to store and locate data when needed, and the concept of *archive* is sometimes used to represent such stores. Gerry McGovern argues, "Content is a key resource of the information economy; . . ." Gerry McGovern, "Reestablishing the Value of Content," *Ubiquity* (2001) available at http://www.acm.org/ubiquity/views/g_mcgovern_1.html. Clearly, archivists are in more than the content business, even though they might employ such systems from time to time to convey information about their records.

27 Despite such principles, archivists have generally used processing backlogs as the reason why so many other activities and responsibilities cannot be tackled. Terry Abraham, while critiquing the concept of the archival documentation strategy, kept relating it to all the other burdens (processing backlogs especially) archivists already faced, suggesting that another one was not necessary or wise. While he made some important points about the changing concepts of appraisal, it is also hard not to sense that any new approach was going to be given short shrift because of concerns about matters such as processing backlogs. In fact, new approaches to these old concerns are needed (perhaps approaches enabling archivists to re-evaluate or re-appraise their holdings before declaring them as being an insurmountable burden in human and other resources). Terry Abraham, "Collection Policy or Documentation Strategy:

Theory and Practice," *American Archivist* 54 (Winter 1991): 44–52 and "Documentation Strategies: A Decade (or More) Later," April 1995, available at http://www.uidaho.edu/special-collections/papers/docstr10.htm.

28 Despite the importance of cooperation, it is not a topic that has received sustained analysis. The best introduction to the nature of archival cooperation remains Richard A. Cameron, Timothy Ericson, and Anne R. Kenney, "Archival Cooperation: A Critical Look at Statewide Archival Networks," *American Archivist* 46 (Fall 1983): 414–32 and Frank G. Burke, "Archival Cooperation," *American Archivist* 46 (Summer 1983): 293–305.

Chapter 4. The Archivist's Task: Responsibilities and Duties

1 For an example of the kinds of concerns being expressed, see Adrian Cunningham, "Beyond the Pale? The 'Flinty' Relationship between Archivists Who Collect the Private Records of Individuals and the Rest of the Archival Profession," *Archives and Manuscripts* 24 (May 1996): 20–26.

2 The generally accepted archival mission emerged in the spate of planning characterizing the profession in the 1970s and the 1980s. The epitome of these efforts came in the work of the Society of American Archivists Goals and Priorities Task Force, issuing a report in 1986 and merging into the Committee on Goals and Priorities. Essentially, the articulation of the archival mission in this process captured what archivists had been doing and debating for at least the previous generation; the published report, *Planning for the Archival Profession*, was a kind of consensus of that earlier work.

3 Models for such collecting policies abound. Faye Phillips, "Developing Collecting Policies for Manuscript Collections," *American Archivist* 47 (Winter 1984): 30–42 remains the classic and most cited description of such policies.

4 Abigail J. Sellen and Richard H. R. Harper, *The Myth of the Paperless Office* (Cambridge, Mass.: MIT, 2001).

5 It was no fluke that the dust cover of the Martha Cooley novel, *The Archivist*, featured a stack of books and not documents; Martha Cooley, *The Archivist: A Novel* (Boston: Little, Brown and Co., 1998).

6 On user studies, see, for example, Paul Conway, "Facts and Frameworks: An Approach to Studying the Users of Archives," *American Archivist* 49 (Fall 1986): 393–407; Fredric M. Miller, "Use, Appraisal, and Research: A Case Study of Social History," *American Archivist* 49 (Fall 1986): 371–92; and Dianne L. Beattie, "An Archival User Study: Researchers in the Field of Women's History," *Archivaria* 29 (Winter 1989–1990): 33–50. On analyzing processing costs, see Paul Ericksen and Robert Shuster, "Beneficial Shocks: The Place of Processing-Cost Analysis in Archival Administration," *American Archivist* 58 (Winter 1995): 32–52. On collection analysis, see Judith E. Endelman, "Looking Backward to Plan for the Future: Collection Analysis for Manuscript Repositories," *American Archivist* 50 (Summer 1987): 340–55.

7 For a description of such matters, refer to Richard J. Cox, *No Innocent Deposits: Forming Archives by Rethinking Appraisal* (Metuchen, N.J.: Scarecrow Press, 2004).

8 Terry Cook, "Mind Over Matter: Towards a New Theory of Archival Appraisal,"

in *The Archival Imagination: Essays in Honour of Hugh Taylor*, ed. Barbara Craig (Ottawa: Association of Canadian Archivists, 1992), 38–70 is the breakthrough essay in these new approaches. Nancy E. Peace, "Deciding What to Save: Fifty Years of Theory and Practice," in *Archival Choices: Managing the Historical Record in an Age of Abundance*, ed. Nancy E. Peace (Lexington, Mass.: D.C. Heath, 1984), 1–18, provides a good introduction to these varying views of appraisal. For fuller treatment, see Frank Boles, *Selecting and Appraising Archives and Manuscripts* (Chicago: Society of American Archivists, 2005).

9 David Wallace has commented on the existence of three views about archival custody, including that embracing actual physical custody, its opposite extreme where records are maintained in the offices of creation, and a middle ground offering adaptive methods suitable to particular circumstances of the records creator and the technologies of records creation and maintenance. This commentator offered generally sage advice, continuing, "So, if you are an advocate of custody, please forge ahead and report back to the profession. Likewise, if you are an advocate of distributed custody. Especially if you are exploring hybrid options. Only through invigorated information sharing will we develop reproducible methodologies that hopefully will make a difference in preserving humanity's electronic record." David Wallace, "Custodial Theory and Practice in the Electronic Environment," paper presented in Pretoria, South Africa, 21 February 2002, available at http://www.archives.org.za/wallace.htm.

10 Preservation has had to be expanded because of the digital environment and other concerns, such as financial and intellectual property. The demise of the quality of documentation, because of the increased fragility of recording media, is evident everywhere we look. If nothing else, the archivist now must admit that the long-term maintenance of any particular document may have to include business or fiscal decisions that put the archivist in the position of not merely being the recipient of records but an advocate and lobbyist concerning the production of records.

11 Many archivists consider their work on finding aids to be their primary intellectual contribution to scholarship, although the number of studies revealing that researchers (historians especially) do not use finding aids ought to have called this assumption into question long ago. Margaret F. Steig, "The Information of [*sic*] Needs of Historians," *College & Research Libraries* 42 (November 1981): 549–60 demonstrated this problem long before archivists had developed descriptive standards or before the advent of the World Wide Web.

12 See, for example, Helen Tibbo, "Interviewing Techniques for Remote Reference: Electronic Versus Traditional Environments," *American Archivist* 58 (Summer 1995): 294–310.

13 Paul Conway, "Facts and Frameworks: An Approach to Studying the Users of Archives," *American Archivist* 49 (Fall 1986): 393–407 is the clearest description of the possibilities of thinking this way.

14 See, for example, Linda J. Long, "Question Negotiation in the Archival Setting: The Use of Interpersonal Communication Techniques in the Reference Interview," *American Archivist* 52 (1989): 40–50.

15 Mary Jo Pugh, "The Illusion of Omniscience: Subject Access and the Reference

Archivist," *American Archivist* 45 (Winter 1982): 33–44 and David Bearman and Richard Lytle, "The Power of the Principle of Provenance," *Archivaria* 21 (1985): 14–27 provide a sense of such matters.

16 Elizabeth Yakel and Laura L. Bost, "Understanding Administrative Use and Users in University Archives," *American Archivist* 57 (1994): 596–615.

17 Miles Harvey, *The Island of Lost Maps: A True Story of Cartographic Crime* (New York: Random House, 2000) is an extremely important case study about security, collecting, and access to rare and valuable materials. See Richard J. Cox, "Map Thefts, Library Security, Collecting, and Me: A Review of Harvey's *The Island of Lost Maps,*" *Library and Archival Security* 34 (October 2002): 31–42.

18 Heather MacNeil, *Without Consent: The Ethics of Disclosing Personal Information in Public Archives* (Metuchen, N.J.: Scarecrow Press, 1992) remains the most complete assessment of such procedures.

19 For a revealing assessment about this from a family member's perspective, see Janna Malamud Smith, *Private Matters: In Defense of the Personal Life* (Reading, Mass.: Addison-Wesley Publishing Co., 1997). Smith is the daughter and executor of the estate of the famed writer Bernard Malamud. See also Sara S. Hodson, "In Secret Kept, In Silence Sealed: Privacy in the Papers of Authors and Celebrities," *American Archivist* 67 (Fall/Winter 2004): 194–211.

20 See, for example, Janet Malcolm, *In the Freud Archives* (New York: Alfred A. Knopf, 1984), describing the controversy over the access to the papers of Sigmund Freud at the Library of Congress. See also Richard J. Cox, "America's Pyramids: Presidents and Their Libraries," *Government Information Quarterly* 19 (2002): 45–75.

21 Karen Benedict, *Ethics and the Archival Profession: Introduction and Case Studies* (Chicago: Society of American Archivists, 2003).

22 Anthropologist Michael F. Brown seeks a middle ground in such conflicts, with the somewhat startling idea that we are now witnessing the restriction of access to archives and artifacts, not because of some wishes of powerful governments seeking closure in the name of national defense and security but because of new sensibilities of cultural groups. "Those who traffic in cultural information—historians, folklorists, anthropologists, museum curators, archivists," writes Brown, "are learning to live with restrictions on access to cultural records formerly available for public use." Michael F. Brown, *Who Owns Native Culture?* (Cambridge, Mass.: Harvard University Press, 2003), 7.

23 Stanton A. Glantz, John Slade, Lisa A. Bero, Peter Hanauer, and Deborah E. Barnes, *The Cigarette Papers* (Berkeley: University of California Press, 1996) provides an example of proprietary records removed from a corporation and the decision by the archives and researcher getting access to these records to go public with them.

24 The Repositories of Primary Sources site, administered by Terry Abraham, now features over 5,300 repositories maintaining a Web presence, and the number is regularly expanding. The site is located at http://www.uidaho.edu/special-collections/Other.Repositories.html.

25 Some of the potential and challenges were recognized very early, in such essays

as William Landis, "Archival Outreach on the World Wide Web," *Archival Issues* 20, no. 2 (1995): 129–47, Jenni Davidson and Donna McRostie, "Webbed Feet: Navigating the Net," *Archives and Manuscripts* 24 (November 1996): 330–51; and David Wallace, "Archival Repositories on the World Wide Web: A Preliminary Survey and Analysis," *Archives and Museum Informatics* 9, no. 2 (1995): 150–68.

26 For example, the New York State Archives created in 1992 the Archives Partnership Trust "to build an endowment and provide project support to enhance humanities programs, increase access to these outstanding treasures, and continue the preservation needs." The trust has been used to support a "Research Residency Program, the Student Research Awards Program, history conferences, special exhibitions, public education programs, book signings and lectures, publications, teacher training institutes, preservation projects, an Internet marketing and web-site redesign, a Membership Program and a Corporate Partners Program." Information about the trust can be found at http://www.nysarchivestrust.org/apt/aboutapt/. Such ventures can only be successful if the archives program has built a sustained public presence, and the New York State Archives has proved to be one of the most effective in such activities. Larry J. Hackman, "State Government and Statewide Archival Affairs: New York as a Case Study," *American Archivist* 55 (Fall 1992): 578–99.

27 Elsie Freeman Finch, ed., *Advocating Archives: An Introduction to Public Relations for Archivists* (Metuchen, N.J.: Society of American Archivists and Scarecrow Press, 1994).

28 David B. Gracy, "Archivists, You Are What People Think You Keep," *American Archivist* 52 (1989): 72–78.

Chapter 5. Archivists and the Challenges of New Worlds

1 This definition comes from *The Concise Oxford Dictionary of Literary Terms* (New York: Oxford University Press, 2001).

2 The debate about the postmodernist approach to archives (and all sources of evidence) continues. Some scholars have argued that postmodernism has already run its course as an original or influential intellectual trend. One historian argues that "postmodernism has proved to be neither a fad. . . nor a product of an overheated intellectual fashion industry," while at the same time contending that postmodernism has not been the "ultimate answer to life in general and historical understanding in particular." Ernst Breisach, *On the Future of History: The Postmodernist Challenge and Its Aftermath* (Chicago: University of Chicago Press, 2003), 193.

3 Terry Cook and Joan Schwartz, "Archives, Records, and Power: The Making of Modern Memory," *Archival Studies* 2 (2002): 5, 8. Cook and Schwartz argue in another essay in the collection, "very little notice is still paid by non-archivists to how the record is chosen and shaped, privileged or marginalized, by archivists' interventions." Terry Cook and Joan Schwartz, "Archives, Records, and Power: From (Postmodern) Theory to (Archival) Performance," *Archival Studies* 2 (2002): 174.

4 Francis X. Blouin, "History and Memory: The Vatican Archives and Constructs

of the Past," in *Essays in Honour of Michael Cook,* ed. Margaret Procter and Caroline Williams (Liverpool, U.K.: University of Liverpool, Liverpool University Center for Archive Studies, 2004), 5.

5 Cook and Schwartz, "Archives, Records, and Power," 17.

6 Andrew Odlyzko, "The Myth of 'Internet Time,'" *Technology Review* 104 (April 2001): 92–93.

7 The director of the Center for Communication Policy at the University of California at Los Angeles tries to enumerate some of the "facts" of the Internet, namely, that the "Internet is an important part of most Americans' lives," that "for users, the Internet is now the most important source of information," and that "use of the Internet increases productivity" (among other things). Coupled with some predictions, such as "more Americans will go online" and "it will become hard to do some tasks offline," it is clear that archivists need to adjust to this Internet era. Jeffrey Cole, "Now Is the Time to Start Studying the Internet Age," *Chronicle of Higher Education,* 2 April 2004, B18.

8 The statement was issued in February 2004 and is available at http://www.coshrc.org/issues/publ-rec-auctions.htm.

9 See Ken Silverstein's *The Radioactive Boy Scout: The True Story of a Boy and His Backyard Nuclear Reactor* (New York: Random House, 2004).

10 Gregory Sanford, "An Empty Toolbox? Archives and the Future of Research," *Vermont History* 71 (Winter/Spring 2003): 98–102 (quotation p. 99).

11 Copies of these and other SAA statements can be found on the society's website at www.archivists.org. A good example is when SAA president Steve Hensen called on members of the profession to contact their legislators and work against Executive Order 13233, entitled "Further Implementation of the Presidential Records Act." According to Hensen, "The archival and public information implications aspects of this order are profound, being contrary to established archival principles and standards, being inconsistent with existing statutory law, and, most important, being at odds with the principles of open access to information upon which our country is founded."

12 Richard J. Evans, *Lying About Hitler: History, Holocaust, and the David Irving Trial* (New York: Basic Books, 2001), xi, 265.

13 A good example of strange allies in a public controversy, one that had archivists on opposite sides of the issue, is the Iran-Contra PROFS case. The Iran-Contra Affair led to a controversy and protracted legal suit over electronic mail and became known as the PROFS case. Writings on the PROFS case from a legal perspective include Catherine F. Sheehan, "Opening the Government's Electronic Mail: Public Access to National Security Council Records," *Boston College Law Review* 35 (September 1994): 1145–1201; James D. Lewis, "White House Electronic Mail and Federal Recordkeeping Law: Press 'D' to Delete History," *Michigan Law Review* 93 (February 1995): 794–849; and Philip G. Schrag, "Working Papers as Federal Records: The Need for New Legislation to Preserve the History of National Policy," *Administrative Law Review* 46 (Spring 1994): 95–140. The most complete assessment of this case was David A. Wallace, "The Public's Use of Federal Recordkeeping Statutes to Shape Federal

Information Policy: A Study of the Profs Case," PhD diss., University of Pittsburgh, 1997.

14 Archivists have worked through fundamental recordkeeping changes generated by the telephone, the electrostatic photocopier, and the fax machine. And while the transition to dealing with these new recordkeeping systems has often been bumpy, archivists have adjusted and developed workable solutions for managing the resulting records. The rise of the personal computer has posed different problems because of the less centralized control of the documents they generate and the rate of change of both hard- and software, but there is no reason to assume that archivists aren't learning valuable new lessons that will assist both the organizations needing to administer their records and succeeding generations of researchers who will want access to those documents with continuing value.

15 Robert K. Logan, *The Fifth Language: Learning a Living in the Computer Age* (Toronto: Stoddart, 1995), 215.

16 Roy Rosenzweig, "Scarcity or Abundance? Preserving the Past in a Digital Era," *American Historical Review* 108 (June 2003), 738.

17 However, by the 1990s, graduate archival education was most strongly planted in library and information science schools; see Richard J. Cox, Elizabeth Yakel, David Wallace, Jeannette Bastian, and Jennifer Marshall, "Archival Education in North American Library and Information Science Schools: A Status Report," *Library Quarterly* 71 (April 2001): 141–94.

18 See, for example, Richard J. Cox, *Managing Records as Evidence and Information* (Westport, Conn.: Quorum Books, 2001); Luciana Duranti, *Diplomatics: New Uses for an Old Science* (Metuchen, N.J.: Scarecrow Press for the Society of American Archivists and the Association of Canadian Archivists, 1998); and Luciana Duranti, Terence Eastwood, and Heather MacNeil, *Preservation of the Integrity of Electronic Records* (Dordecht, Netherlands: Kluwer, 2002).

19 Eldon Frost, "A Weak Link in the Chain: Record Scheduling as a Source of Archival Acquisition," *Archivaria* 33 (Winter 1991–92): 34–56; James Gregory Bradsher, "The FBI Records Appraisal Project," *Midwestern Archivist* 13, no. 2 (1988): 51–66; and David A. Wallace, "The Public's Use of Federal Recordkeeping Statutes to Shape Federal Information Policy: A Study of the PROFS Case," PhD diss., University of Pittsburgh, 1997, all provide examples of this problem.

Biographic Essay

1 The last effort to produce a comprehensive bibliography was Frank B. Evans, *Modern Archives and Manuscripts: A Select Bibliography* (Chicago: Society of American Archivists, 1975). Additions to Evans's work appeared somewhat fitfully in the *American Archivist* in the 1970s into the early 1990s. The Society of American Archivists is working to transform its publication catalog into something like a professional clearinghouse, but the ever-expanding professional and scholarly literature makes this nearly an impossible task.

2 Works such as Michael E. Hobart and Zachary S. Schiffman, *Information Ages: Literacy, Numeracy, and the Computer Revolution* (Baltimore: Johns Hopkins University Press, 1998), this study suggesting how each era has been an informa-

tion age, provide a valuable context for archivists to reflect on when working with documents from different periods.

3 Even if these volumes are referred to less frequently as time goes on, they remain benchmarks for professional identity. They cease to be the critical texts that students and practitioners refer to for the answers to specific questions, but despite their age they continue to set the terms of discussion and debate. They also become legitimate objects of study in themselves, providing evidence for the history of the profession and how it has evolved.

4 Individuals interested in Jenkinson's ideas and career also should consult the Robert Ellis and Peter Walne edited *Selected Writings of Sir Hilary Jenkinson*, originally published in 1980 and reissued with a new introduction by Terry Eastwood by the Society of American Archivists in 2003.

5 For a sense of the influence of Taylor on succeeding generations of archivists, see Barbara L. Craig, ed., *The Archival Imagination: Essays in Honour of Hugh A. Taylor* (Ottawa: Association of Canadian Archivists, 1992).

6 Bruce W. Dearstyne, "Archives and Public History: Issues, Problems, and Prospects," *Public Historian* 8 (1986): 6–9.

7 Volume 63, Spring 2000, of the *American Archivist* includes a variety of essays considering the NHPRC's impact.

8 At its 1987 annual meeting, three commissioned papers were presented describing needs for research in the identified major sections of the archival mission, subsequently published as Richard J. Cox and Helen W. Samuels, "The Archivist's First Responsibility: A Research Agenda for the Identification and Retention of Records of Enduring Value," *American Archivist* 51 (Winter/Spring 1988): 28–42; Lawrence Dowler, "The Role of Use in Defining Archival Practice and Principles: A Research Agenda for the Availability and Use of Records," *American Archivist* 51 (Winter/Spring 1988): 74–86; and Paul H. McCarthy, "The Management of Archives: A Research Agenda," *American Archivist* 51 (Winter/Spring 1988): 52–69.

9 In addition to the many different reports from these and other projects, there have been some comparative assessments of the implications of these projects, such as Margaret Hedstrom, "Building Record-Keeping Systems: Archivists Are Not Alone on the Wild Frontier," *Archivaria* 44 (Fall 1997): 44–71.

10 Examples include Philip C. Brooks, *What Records Shall We Preserve?* Staff Information Paper 9 (Washington, D.C.: National Archives and Records Service, 1975; orginally published 1940) and T. R. Schellenberg, *The Appraisal of Modern Public Records*, Bulletins of the National Archives, no. 8 (Washington, D.C.: National Archives and Records Service, 1956).

11 See Ernst Posner, "The National Archives and the Archival Theorist," *American Archivist* 18 (1955): 207–16.

12 Such as Terry Cook, *The Archival Appraisal of Records Containing Personal Information: A RAMP Study with Guidelines*, PGI-91/WS/3 (Paris: UNESCO, 1991). This Cook writing on appraisal is an example of how some of these publications have played pivotal roles in reformulating archival knowledge, being part of his series of writings on this function in the early 1990s introducing both a reengineering of archival appraisal practice and the conceptual formulation of macro-appraisal.

13 A different perspective on this institution can be seen in Gary Nash's *First City: Philadelphia and the Forging of Historical Memory* (Philadelphia: University of Pennsylvania Press, 2002), reexamining memory making as it revolves around the work of museums, libraries, and historical societies.

14 While archivists ruminate over the meaning and method of appraisal, other scholars and commentators, such as Leah Dilworth, ed., *Acts of Possession: Collecting in America* (New Brunswick, N.J.: Rutgers University Press, 2003) and Philipp Blom, *To Have and to Hold: An Intimate History of Collectors and Collecting* (New York: Penguin Books, 2002), mull over the meaning of collecting.

15 There have been a variety of perspectives on this case, including David Bearman, "The Implications of *Armstrong v. Executive Office of the President* for the Archival Management of Electronic Records," *American Archivist* 56 (Fall 1993): 674–89; Catherine F. Sheehan, "Opening the Government's Electronic Mail: Public Access to National Security Council Records," *Boston College Law Review* 35 (September 1994): 1145–201; James D. Lewis, "White House Electronic Mail and Federal Recordkeeping Law: Press 'D' to Delete History," *Michigan Law Review* 93 (February 1995): 794–849; and Philip G. Schrag, "Working Papers as Federal Records: The Need for New Legislation to Preserve the History of National Policy," *Administrative Law Review* 46 (Spring 1994): 95–140.

Index

Boldface indicates figures.
The letter "n" after page number indicates notes.

James M. O'Toole is Professor of History at Boston College. His archival career has included positions at the New England Historic Genealogical Society, the Massachusetts State Archives, and the Archives of the Roman Catholic Archdiocese of Boston. For 15 years he directed the MA program in history and archives at the University of Massachusetts-Boston. He wrote the first edition of *Understanding Archives and Manuscripts* (1990) and has published on a wide range of archival topics. He also works in the fields of American religious and American Catholic history. Within the Society of American Archivists, he has served on the governing Council and as Publications Editor. He is a Fellow of SAA and a three-time recipient of the Fellows' Ernst Posner Award for an outstanding essay in the *American Archivist* (1991, 1995, and 2004). He has served as president of both New England Archivists and the New England Historical Association.

Richard J. Cox is Professor of Library and Information Science at the University of Pittsburgh, School of Information Sciences, where he is responsible for the archives concentration in the Master's in Library Science degree and the PhD degree. He has served the Society of American Archivists in a variety of leadership roles, including on the governing Council, as editor of the *American Archivist,* and as Publications Editor. Dr. Cox is a Fellow of SAA. He has written extensively on archival and records management topics and has published thirteen books in this area, winning SAA's Waldo Gifford Leland Award for superior writing in 1991, 2002, and 2005. He is presently working on new books on professional education and personal recordkeeping, and is the editor of the *Records and Information Management Report.*

·